Mammy

Mammy

A CENTURY OF RACE, GENDER, AND SOUTHERN MEMORY

Kimberly Wallace-Sanders

UNIVERSITY OF MICHIGAN PRESS • ANN ARBOR

Copyright © by the University of Michigan 2008
All rights reserved
Published in the United States of America by
The University of Michigan Press
Manufactured in the United States of America
⊗ Printed on acid-free paper

2011   2010   2009   2008   4   3   2   1

A CIP catalog record for this book is available from the British Library.

Library of Congress Cataloging-in-Publication Data

Wallace-Sanders, Kimberly, 1962–
     Mammy : a century of race, gender, and southern memory /
Kimberly Wallace-Sanders.
          p.   cm.
     Includes bibliographical references and index.
     ISBN-13: 978-0-472-11614-0 (cloth : acid-free paper)
     ISBN-10: 0-472-11614-2 (cloth : acid-free paper)
     1. American literature—20th century—History and criticism.
2. Women domestics in literature.   3. African American women
in literature.   4. Southern States—In literature.   5. Stereotypes
(Social psychology) in literature.   6. African American women in
popular culture—History—20th century.   7. Racism in popular
culture—United States—History—20th century.   8. Jemima, Aunt.
I. Title.
PS173.D65W35   2008
810.9'352208996073—dc22   2007052486

This book is dedicated to my mother, who taught me to love books, and to my father, who taught me to love the pictures in books;

to Mark,

"Te amo en un lugar donde no hay espacio ni tiempo / Te amaré toda mi vida porque tu eres mi amigo";

and

to Isaiah Anthony and Joshua Allen, who gave me the best possible reason to leave my office and come home.

ACKNOWLEDGMENTS

The support and encouragement of friends, family members, colleagues, and students helped me to navigate my way through terrain that was far more challenging than I ever expected.

A Five College Dissertation Fellowship at Smith College and a Senior Fellowship at the Smithsonian made much of the research and writing for this book possible. Elizabeth Spellman at Smith and Fath Ruffin at the Smithsonian were especially helpful to me.

Chapter 1 was based on a presentation made at the Narrative Conference for the Study of Literature in 1999. An earlier version of chapter 3 appears in *Burning down the House: Recycling Domesticity,* edited by Rosemary Marangoly George (HarperCollins, 1998).

My dissertation advisers at Boston University, William Vance, Nancy Bentley, Susan Mizruchi, and Shirley Wadja, assisted me with very early stages of this work and helped me to believe this project was worthwhile.

I am grateful to both of my academic departments, the Institute of Liberal Arts and the Department of Women's Studies. My colleagues Rudolph Byrd and Kevin Corrigan were incredibly supportive and encouraging during the final phase of the project. Jean Fagin Yellin first made me aware of the dolls made by Harriet Jacobs, and she continues to inspire me as a scholar and a human being. Thanks to Barbara Whiteman, curator and founder of the Philadelphia Doll Museum, for spending hours with me talking about mammy dolls.

I am also grateful for the financial support offered by Emory College and Emory University Graduate School of Arts and Letters.

The enthusiasm of my editor, LeAnn Fields, for this book has completely renewed my faith in editor-author relationships. Senior copy editor Marcia LaBrenz also provided invaluable assistance to me throughout the final stages of the book.

I extend my deep gratitude to graduate students who took time away from their own work to proofread the manuscript: Sheri Davis, Brittney Cooper, and Danica Tisdale.

I'd like to paraphrase Toni Morrison and thank the following women who took up the role of being a "friend to my mind, for gathering me, the pieces that I am and giving them back to me in the right order": Beverly Guy Sheftall, Kathryn Naylor, Adrienne Norcia, Robyn Thurston, Norma Kate Brandon, Leslie Harris, and my sisters-in-law Claire Sanders and Kim Hall Wallace. Thanks to Yejide St. Fort for her translation of lyrics from "A Song for You" in my dedication to Mark.

My parents, Rose and Raymond Wallace, and my brothers, Christopher and Greg Wallace, have listened to me talk about this book for many years. I appreciate their patience and support. My mother and my mother-in-law, Arthrell Sanders, provided endless hours of child care when it was needed most.

Extended family members Earl Sanders, Burton Balfour, and Jeffrey Weiser deserve thanks for kind words and general affection.

As always, my most affectionate gratitude goes to my partner in life, Mark A. Sanders, and our sons, Isaiah Anthony Wallace Sanders and Joshua Allen Wallace Sanders: you bring me joy and keep me sane.

There were so many African and African American women whose names and identities were lost when they became "Mammy." We honor their spirits when we acknowledge their existence.

The author is grateful to the following people and institutions for permission to use artwork.

The Andy Warhol Foundation for the Visual Arts/ARS, New York
The Boston Athenaeum, Boston, Massachusetts
Georgia Archives
Mortimer Rare Book Room, Smith College, Northampton, Massachusetts
Ronald Feldman Fine Arts, New York
San Francisco Museum of Modern Art
Strong Museum, Rochester, New York
University Museum, University of California at Berkeley
Jessie B. Harris
Kathleen Miler

Andrew Tabbat
Elaine Brenenbaum
Michael Ray Charles
Charles Nelson
Joyce Scott
Tina Dunkley
Betye Saar
Rose Hardman Wallace (cover)

CONTENTS

PREFACE

Gathering the Stories

Behind This Book

I teach at Emory University, a large, predominately white, southern research institution. Many of my African American colleagues have relatives who worked for white families, and many of my white southern colleagues grew up in families that hired African American women as domestic servants or to do "day work." We do not talk about this past that both binds us together and drives a wedge between us. Yet the reality of this history is palpable when the subject of the southern "mammy" is raised. Language seems to fail us at these moments—shadows fall across faces, eyes become moist, bodies shift nervously. The moment I say the words "black mammy," a disruptive presence enters the room; we all know it, we all feel it, but even with our advanced degrees and our penchant for academic discourse, we cannot speak about it.

My colleagues and friends who hire African American or Afro Caribbean women as caregivers for their children worry that they are replicating a troubled and troubling relationship for yet another generation. They are caught in a conundrum that is not unusual for thoughtful and well-intentioned parents: they want to provide financial opportunities for black women, but they don't want to be insensitive to the stereotype.

Whenever I appear at conferences and invited lectures to present material from this book, there are always several people in the audience who want to share a secret with me about the black women in their lives called "Mammy," "Auntie," or known only by a first name. Sometimes white people confess to me that they loved this woman more than their own mother.

Sometimes black people confess that they hated the white children associated with their mother's job, hated the hand-me-down clothes and leftover food, hated losing their mothers to children who already had so much.

While researching this book I learned that my subject matter was much more controversial than I had originally imagined. It seems that everyone has an opinion about the mammy, about who she was, what she meant, opinions sometimes based upon real and personal experiences, and at other times based upon a written history that remains incomplete and one-sided. In writing the book, I focused on the cultural representations of the stereotypic mammy, instead of collecting the biographies and personal narratives of African American women working as housekeepers and childcare workers. I made that choice because I wanted to better understand the curious power behind the image of a large black mother with a small white child.

I have been researching cultural representations of the mammy figure for the past fifteen years. In December 1991, while I was still working on my dissertation on the subject, Howell Raines's essay "Grady's Gift" appeared in the *New York Times Magazine*. The essay was an account of the author's childhood relationship and adult reunion with Grady Williams Hutchinson, who worked as a housekeeper for his family in Birmingham, Alabama, during the George Wallace years. Grady's picture appeared on the cover; it was the first time I had ever seen an African American woman on the cover of that venerable publication. Comparing her to other women in his family, Raines describes Grady's appearance this way:

> Most of the women in my family ran from slender to boxy. Grady was buxom. She wore a blue uniform and walked around our house on stout brown calves. Her skin was smooth. She had a gap between her front teeth, and so did I. One of the first things I remember Grady telling me was that as soon as she had enough money she was going to get a diamond set in her gap and it would drive the men wild.[1]

As seen through the eyes of a young boy, Grady is more like himself than like the other women in his family. In that one sentence about her teeth Grady establishes herself as a woman with self-awareness, with plans for the future, and with an appreciation for her own romantic and sexual possibilities. These are not qualities typically assigned to the mammy figure. Raines tries to confront the sticky issue of how relations between black and white may have distorted his memories and therefore the history told through memory:

> There is no trickier subject for a writer from the South than that of affection between a black person and a white one in the unequal world of segregation. For the dishonesty upon which such a society is founded makes every emotion suspect, makes it impossible to know whether what flowed between two people was honest feeling or pity or pragmatism. Indeed, for the black person, the feigning of an expected emotion could be the very coinage of survival. (90)

Raines admits, "I can only tell you how it seemed to me at the time. I was 7 and Grady was 16 and I adored her and I believed she was crazy about me. She became the weather in which my childhood was lived." This is a beautifully evocative phrase—she was "the weather in which my childhood was lived." The idea is wonderful to me: a young black woman working in segregated Alabama who is allowed to express herself as cloudy, stormy, or sunny, and perhaps even allowed to rain on her employers occasionally.

Raines tells us that although Grady attended nursing school at Dillard University, she had to drop out after one semester and return to work cleaning his family's home. During the family reunion he arranged some thirty-seven years later, his sister and his mother have a conversation about whether or not the family could have helped her complete her education. His mother says wistfully, "If only we had known . . ." To which his sister wisely adds, "How could we not know?"

"Grady's Gift," the most eloquent and moving piece I have ever read about a white family's relationship with the African American woman who worked for them, is built upon Raines's memories of the long talks about race and segregation in Alabama that he and Grady had. Yet it is oddly silent on one topic. Grady and her husband had three children; in 1991 their ages were thirty-seven, thirty-three, and twenty-nine. Since Grady worked for his family from the time she was sixteen until she was twenty-three, she would have given birth to two children during that time (unless they were adopted or brought into the marriage by her husband), but Raines does not mention these events. At a question-and-answer session at a book signing in Atlanta, I asked him about these births, and he said that he could not remember. When he thought ahead to the implications of his answer, Raines became embarrassed and moved quickly to take another question. He had suddenly realized that although the essay regales us with his appreciation for her "gift to him" and says that his well-known oral history of the Civil Rights movement, *My Soul is Rested: Movement Days In The Deep South Remembered* (1977), is really "her book," he did not know whether or not Grady's children were biological or adopted, and that Grady, a woman who worked in his family's home nearly every day for seven years might have been pregnant without his remembering it.

I wasn't trying to embarrass Raines. I was impressed with his essay (which went on to win a Pulitzer Prize) and I wanted to learn something about Grady's children and about Raines's relationship to them. I found myself hoping with all my heart that his sister's question, "How could we not know?" rang like a chime in his ears when he left that book signing. I hope that he cared enough to call his beloved Grady (who was still alive) and ask her questions about her own children until they became real to him, real children that Grady might have left at home in order to go to work and tell him the stories about segregated racism that changed his life and helped him to win a Pulitzer Prize.

The unnamed tension surrounding this account of Raines, Grady, and Grady's children is not unique to their story; it has come to the forefront whenever I have talked with people about my work on this book. I want to recount some of these conversations here.

After I delivered a lecture to a women's studies class, a young African American man, a colleague of mine, told me that he worried that people would think of his grandmother as a mammy because she is a large woman who takes care of white children for a living. He said, "It's what she *does* and she gets paid for it. But I don't want people to think that this stereotype that you've described, where they prefer white children to black children— I don't want people to think that's who she *is*."

After the same lecture, a fifty-something white woman told me that she was raised by a mammy and that she's always been embarrassed about it even though this woman was the most important person in her childhood. She recounted several incidents from her childhood, some in great detail. "What was her name?" I asked her gently. Relief flooded her voice as she said, "Katie. We called her Katie." I told her, "You should try to refer to her by name, that's what we do for people who are important to us."

On another occasion a student told me that she had never forgiven her parents for making their black housekeeper, Alice, eat in the kitchen, even though they often told people that Alice was a like member of the family.

"I thought this was terrible," she admitted. "We're Jewish and we know what it meant to be mistreated for stupid reasons."

Recently an African American graduate student told me that her grandmother worked for four different white families in rural Georgia before being disabled by a stroke that left her with physical and mental impairments. The families had rallied around her, paying for her hospital bills and bringing her food and bags of used clothing. Despite this kindness, the student was shocked one day to see her disoriented grandmother wearing an old "I love the KKK" T-shirt. The student was furious about this disrespectful treatment, but she did not know how to approach her grandmother's neighbors for an explanation.

During a university-sponsored program on race and gender, a white colleague introduced herself by describing the African American woman who raised her and left her a large inheritance. This money financed her graduate school education and allowed her to become a well-established professor of theology. She said that she felt guilty that *she* was given this money when this woman, "Aunt Mary," had other relatives who needed it.

In the 1990s I visited the president of a small liberal arts college in New England who displayed a picture of an African American woman on his desk along with pictures of his family. In the picture she wears a light blue uniform and small white cap. When I asked him about the photograph, he seemed delighted to talk about her, saying that it was a picture of "Sadie," who helped raise him and his brothers. His father had left them, and his mother was often drunk and abusive. "Sadie," he said reverently, "saved my life. I will never forget her." "Where does she live now?" I asked. He looked surprised and shrugged, admitting that he had no idea.

Not long after this, a dean from an Ivy League school and I attended the same formal dinner party. After hearing the subject of my research, he suddenly began to sing a haunting lullaby he said he learned from his "Mammy." The attendees seemed startled to see this playful side of their dean and even more surprised when he ended the song and then abruptly changed the subject. (He actually said: "I know a song my Mammy taught me," before he started to sing.)

Over the years I have kept these tales, these secrets, and these confessions in my pocket like worry stones. They are significant simply because they provide vivid evidence of how provocative and inexhaustible the subject of the mammy continues to be for us Americans, as we struggle to reconcile our realities with our histories, our truths with our memories.

INTRODUCTION

The "Mammification" of the Nation:

Mammy and the American Imagination

Nostalgia is best defined as a yearning for that
which we know we have destroyed.
— DAVID BLIGHT

The various incarnations of the mammy figure have had a profound influence on American culture. There is virtually no medium that has not paid homage to the mammy in some form or another. In his series "American Myths," for example, artist Andy Warhol included both the mammy *and* Aunt Jemima, along with Howdy Doody, Uncle Sam, Dracula, and the Wicked Witch of the West (figs. 1 and 2).[1] In the late 1980s, Italian photographer Olivero Toscani created an advertisement for Benetton featuring a close-up of a white infant nursing at the breast of a headless, dark-skinned black woman wearing a red Shetland sweater (fig. 3). The advertisement was met with unbridled criticism from African Americans, yet it won more advertising awards than any other image in Benetton's advertising history.[2] Today, tourists visiting Lancaster, Kentucky, can tour the former slave plantation of Governor William Owsley, ironically called Pleasant Retreat. The restored home features many remnants of the Old South, including a "charming mammy bench," a combination rocking chair and cradle designed to allow mammies to nurse an infant and rock an additional baby at the same time.[3] Diminutive mammy "nipple dolls" made in the 1920s from rubber bottle nipples with tiny white baby dolls cradled in their arms are both a "well-kept secret" and an excellent investment by collectors of southern Americana (fig. 4).[4]

This book probes these images and themes as they proliferated between the 1820s and 1935.

The most recognizable mammy, the one immortalized in 1930s films by African American actresses Hattie McDaniel, Ethel Waters, Louise Beavers, and Butterfly McQueen, marks a pivotal moment in the history of the stereotype, but the success of their portrayals was predicated upon its being deeply embedded within the popular imagination long before *Gone with the Wind* opened in Atlanta in 1936.[5]

"Mammy" is part of the lexicon of antebellum mythology that continues to have a provocative and tenacious hold on the American psyche. Her large dark body and her round smiling face tower over our imaginations, causing more accurate representations of African American women to wither in her shadow. The mammy's stereotypical attributes—her deeply sonorous and effortlessly soothing voice, her infinite patience, her raucous laugh, her self-deprecating wit, her implicit understanding and acceptance of her inferiority and her devotion to whites—all point to a long-lasting and troubled marriage of racial and gender essentialism, mythology, and southern nostalgia.

This wedding took place between the 1820s and the mid–twentieth century as the mammy became the most widely recognized representation of an African American woman, putting her at the center of a dynamic interracial debate over constructions of loyalty, maternal devotion, and southern memory. There is a rich and unmined history of responses by African American artists to the mammy stereotype. They range from Frederick Douglass's revised portrait of his mother in his autobiography, *My Bondage and My Freedom* (1855), to an early-twentieth-century tale of a mammy who kills a white baby. The range of responses and appropriations reflects the contradictions inherent in the original image.

Who created this mammy-mother, and what does she reveal about race and American culture? Why do so many portraits of her insist that she preferred white children to her own? How did her size and shape, her color, and her wardrobe contribute to this representation of her as the other mother, as über-nanny, as the ultimate symbol of maternal devotion? How did she become so crucial to our understanding of slavery, gender, motherhood, and memory in the American South?

This book treats the mammy figure as one example of how myth, biography, fiction, history, and material culture merge in a dispute about race, about motherhood, and about southern nostalgia in American culture. In addition to famous literary representations of mammy characters, this study highlights visual images and cultural artifacts as integral to the mammy figure. As we broaden our ability to interpret cultural forces by reading relevant material culture, we can better understand how objects function in tandem with words. This is crucial because both the historic and the contemporary interpretations of the mammy too often isolate the image within narrow categories: as a literary stereotype, or as a historic reality, or as an advertising trademark, or as a visual subject. These approaches reduce the complexity of the mammy's powerful presence in American consciousness. This book examines the mammy figure as a signpost pointing to concepts and ideals extending far beyond the stereotype; the wide-ranging representations of the mammy figure reflect the various ways in which this image has shaped and continues to influence American concepts of race and gender. My work is informed by Foucault's theory of the body as a site of struggle; with that lens in place, the representation of the mammy's body is the site where fiction, history, autobiography, memoir, and popular culture meet in battle over the dominant representation of African American womanhood, and African American motherhood more specifically.

For example, when we reimagine the antebellum plantation as the body politic, we see how the mammy's body serves as a tendon between the races, connecting the muscle of African American slave labor with the skeletal power structure of white southern aristocracy. Her body nurtured both African American slave children and their future owners—sometimes simultaneously. Focusing on the mammy's body, and by extension her maternity, means seeing the body in a metonymic relationship to personhood, an essential component of recasting the mammy as more than a turban and a smile—as a transitional object for a nation moving from one developmental stage to another. This emphasis pushes us to better understand why sentimental southern representations of black corporeality, like the mammy, continue to be both provocative and evocative.

One significant point to establish is the difference between the literary character and stereotype of the mammy, or the famous advertising trademark of Aunt Jemima, and the actual African American women whose names were lost when they became "Mammy."

Where No One Knows Your Name

Every border in that big house knows mammy, but I doubt if one of them knows her name; I do not.

—ELIZA M. RIPLEY

The words *mammy, Auntie,* and *Negro nurse* or *colored nurse* are all used in antebellum fiction to describe both a person and a role within the antebellum plantation home; she serves as baby nurse, cook, and all-around domestic help. Many historians have argued that she was "invented" after the Civil War as part of the Lost Cause mythology, an excellent point of departure for this study, which is strictly speaking neither historical nor sociological but interdisciplinary.

The earliest use of the word *mammy* in reference to slave women caring for white children occurs in 1810 in a travel narrative about the American South. The *American Dictionary of Regional English* traces the etymological roots of the word to a blending of *ma'am* and *mamma*.[6] There is evidence that the term was first used as a more common southern term for mother. The term *mammy* is not consistently linked to specific patterns of behavior before 1850, but by 1820 the word was almost exclusively associated with African American women serving as wet nurses and caretakers of white children.

Mammy and *Aunt Jemima* are often used interchangeably today, but it is significant that the former predates the latter by almost a century. Aunt Jemima was introduced to the world at the 1893 Chicago World's Fair as a Reconstructionist alter ego to the mammy; the mammy's domain is the nursery, while Aunt Jemima's is the kitchen. Aunt Jemima offered northerners the southern antebellum experience of having a mammy, without actually participating in slavery. In this way, her popularity bolstered the romantic mythology of the southern plantation.

As I discuss in chapter 3, in the texts of Aunt Jemima advertisements the terms *Old South, old time,* and *plantation home* appear as incantations invoking the spirit of the antebellum South.[7] Aunt Jemima was created as a trademark that tapped into the national longing for an established and mythological Old South. This romanticized mythology of the plantation as a utopia was transferred into the commercial and marketing arena as an effort to reunite the country after the Civil War. The comprehensive history of Aunt Jemima as an advertising trademark is well documented in M. M. Manning's

Slave in a Box: The Strange Career of Aunt Jemima.[8] This book evaluates her role as a healing balm intended to reconcile a shattered nation.

In another excellent analysis of the mammy's role in visual culture, "Mammy the Huckster," JoAnn Morgan explains, "Not only did Mammy and scores like her promote consumer goods but more importantly, they sold the public a bill of goods about the old south."[9] In addition to serving as a symbol of reconciliation and redemption, the mammy became a "requisite fantasy for any southerner seeking to establish his or her pedigree" (96). By extension, one of the ways to interpret the body of the mammy figure is to consider how it has been used to *reify* racial purity for white southerners. Like the one drop of "black dope"—the chemical that makes Liberty white paint "whiter than white" (the company motto is "Keep America Pure with Liberty Paints") in Ralph Ellison's *Invisible Man*—the mammy body produced the milk that made white southerners more *purely white* and therefore more genteel than their less affluent counterparts.[10] The existing analyses of the mammy, however, don't focus explicitly on her maternity.

The image of a large, dark, powerful body with a small, white vulnerable one was enormously appealing, first in the South, and later on a national level. Figure 5 is a reproduction of an imprint that appeared on decorative envelopes during the Civil War. An African American woman's exposed breast served as a "return address" for the U.S. Postal Service. Her body is arranged to hold an enormous white baby as a sarcastic reminder that the South has grown fat on slave labor and owes its wealth to African Americans.

Consider as well a quotation from Isabel Drysdale's popular book *Scenes in Georgia* (1827): "Perhaps a more interesting picture is seldom seen, than that which was often exhibited by Aunt Chloe and her little nursling, its fair face pillowed in her faithful bosom, contrasting the sable but loving countenance bent above it."[11] By placing an aesthetic value on the image of a dark-skinned woman holding a white child, the author makes Aunt Chloe's slave status more innocuous and benign. She hardly seems to be describing a slave at all but rather a dark-skinned Madonna, holding a Sacred Child to her breast. Aunt Chloe offers a classic image of the mammy stereotype, but the standard type reflects specific characteristics.

Drawing Boundaries: Mapping Mammy

I define the standard, most recognizable mammy character as a creative combination of extreme behavior and exaggerated features. Mammy's body is grotesquely marked by excess: she is usually extremely overweight, very tall, broad-shouldered; her skin is nearly black. She manages to be a jolly presence—she often sings or tells stories while she works—and a strict disciplinarian at the same time. First as slave, then as a free woman, the mammy is largely associated with the care of white children or depicted with noticeable attachment to white children. Her unprecedented devotion to her white family reflects her racial inferiority. *Mammy* is often both her title and the only name she has ever been given. She may also be a cook or personal maid to her mistress—a classic southern belle—whom she infantilizes. Her clothes are typical of a domestic: headscarf and apron, but she is especially attracted to brightly colored, elaborately tied scarves. Mammy speaks the ungrammatical "plantation dialect" made famous in the 1890s by popular white southern authors like Joel Chandler Harris and by subsequent minstrel shows.[12] Her own children are usually dirty and ill mannered, yet they serve as suitable playmates for her white charges. She is typically depicted as impatient or brusque (sometimes even violent or abusive) with her own children, in contrast to her lavish, affectionate patience for her white charges. Mammy wields considerable authority within the plantation household and consequently retains a measure of dubious, unreliable respect in the slave quarters; many slaves consider her untrustworthy because she allegedly identifies so completely with the culture that oppresses them.

The fundamental elements of the standard mammy fall into two categories: appearance and behavior. Because her identity as a mother supplies rich nuances that have not been adequately addressed by scholars, her maternal status constitutes a third category here. Mammy's relationship to her biological children is crucial to my study. I base my analysis upon the character's relationship with both black and white children, isolating those provocative indications that the mammy character prefers the latter. The constants and variables in the patterns of her appearance are also examined.

Some scholars speculate that the term *black mammy* was developed to draw boundaries between the various maternal figures on the plantation. One scholar writes, "She is referred to as the 'Black Mammy,' a name probably given to distinguish her from the real mother and also from the elderly slave woman, 'Mammy,' who took care of slave children while their mothers worked in the fields or in master's home."[13] The term *black mammy* appears in both historic and fictional accounts of plantation life, often as a uniquely southern term of endearment. More often it served as a generic name for all slave women who served as a wet nurse or baby nurse for white children. Historian Deborah Gray White writes that the mammy was the "perfect slave for the antebellum south."[14] She became the center of white southern perception of the perfectly organized society. The word *Mammy* eventually replaced the woman's own name; it is not unusual for white southerners to describe her as the most influential force in their childhood, and yet not know her real name. This is true of little Eva's Mammy and Scarlett's Mammy, well-known literary characters in *Uncle Tom's Cabin* and *Gone with the Wind,* respectively.

In her description of the mammy prototype, the late feminist literary critic Barbara Christian equates the earliest mammy characters with the stereotype established later. Christian sees the mammy as "a normal part of the Southern fabric. Enduring, strong and calm, her physical characteristics remain the same."[15]

This study corrects the assumption that the mammy we now recognize has always been such, a static figure over the decades. It is not the case that her form, speech, and behavior remained unchanged from the figure's original incarnation. Chapter 1 traces the inconsistency in the physicality of the earliest mammy characters; there is more heterogeneity in the mammy characters in antebellum plantation fiction than in those that appear after *Uncle Tom's Cabin*. My method of literary archaeology begins with close readings of both abolitionist and proslavery fiction and plantation memoirs that reflect genuine efforts to convey individual differences in African American women's appearances. In fact, not one of the mammy characters is described as large or overweight before the publication of *Uncle Tom's Cabin* in 1852.

The complexity of the mammy image goes unappreciated by scholars who for the past two decades have focused on uncovering more obscure representations of African American women. As a result, the implications of this stereotype's influence as the most widely recognized symbol of African American maternity have been overlooked. Few scholars separate the mammy from the long list of stereotypical images that developed in the nineteenth century, and as a result, much of the criticism is as reductive as the type itself. Most previous attempts to deconstruct the contented mammy have focused on her role as loyal servant, rather than her dual role as surrogate and biological mother, and leading scholars have made exceptional contributions with these examinations of the controlling image of

the faithful, obedient domestic servant. Unlike other plantation characters, the mammy is distinguished by her maternal role for both enslaved and
slave-holding families.[16] In these characterizations her devotion for the
children she cares for is best illustrated by her disregard for her own children. African Americans have historically dismissed such stereotypes as
racist propaganda; the mammy figure was so painful that it warranted a
continuum of fierce opposition. Counterefforts to return this mother to
her *own* family are sporadic but have not died out in African American literature, art, and material culture. My aim here is to redefine the mammy's
significance by exploring her maternity more fully through several kinds of
creative expression, and by detailing the insights to which this innovative
emphasis on maternity lends itself.

This study engages questions that demand a reconceptualization of the
mammy as a quintessential interdisciplinary topic. How do we begin to develop new theories about this pervasive image that will push us toward a
greater understanding of the intersectionality of race and gender?

Rethinking slavery and motherhood as institutions deeply influenced
by patriarchy, we shift our understanding of how the mammy's role was
both experienced and imagined in nineteenth-century American culture.
For example, because of widespread theories of nineteenth-century racial
essentialism, African American women were thought to be innately superior in their abilities as caretakers of white children. As late as 1924, a ret-
rospective study of southern plantation life insisted: "There can be no
doubt that with the *peculiar African capacity for devotion,* the old mammy
dearly loved her charges."[17] As a result, the mammy emerges as a mother
who frequently displaces white mothers and has ambiguous relationships
with her own children.

Over the past two decades, the institution of motherhood and the experience of mothering have been investigated with care, urgency, and insight by feminist scholars like Patricia Hill Collins, Julia Kristeva, Hortense
Spillers, Adrienne Rich, Nancy Chodorow, and Deborah Gray White.
These feminist scholars push us toward the complex task of remaking and
re-viewing motherhood as a kind of cultural landscape with complicated
terrain that is constantly shifting and evolving. These theories have
influenced my understanding of the mammy's maternity, as inextricably
linked to and shaped by patriarchy.

To that end, this study examines the mammy's characterization as both
a biological *and* a surrogate mother.[18] I address the literary evolution of the

mammy and material culture as it produces and responds to this evolution during three periods between the nineteenth and twentieth centuries. Each period represents a principal phase in America's racial consciousness. When texts are integrated with visual images and material culture for analysis, each era comes to life and we are able to better understand what the mammy symbolized at different historical moments.

This book both begins and concludes with the premise that the mammy figure looms over the American imagination as a cultural influence so pervasive that only a comprehensive approach will do it justice. This look at the mammy stereotypes uses a wide range of mediums to assess the figure's complex manipulation by both African American and Euro-American audiences. The literary and visual expressions explored here construct a unique layering of texts, visual images, and cultural artifacts. Having insisted on a more critical look at this American icon, I conclude that the mammy type is transformational because it both shapes and is shaped by a consciousness that is uniquely American and uniquely southern. This is necessarily a selective and synthetic approach to a vast topic.

Several new works on the mammy or Aunt Jemima testify to a rising interest in the subject I have been studying for nearly fifteen years. Each work has merit, yet none presents an integrated approach to the mammy figure as a cultural icon of African American maternity. Most often they obscure the most provocative issues: motherhood, sexuality, and the aesthetic value placed on images of dark women cradling white babies.

In chapter 1, I focus on examples of the earliest and the most popular re-creations of the southern plantation in fiction, memoir, and religious propaganda as a way to more accurately contextualize the character's origins. Comparing the complexion, dialect, and size of six mammy characters, I argue that the early mammy character between 1820 and 1852 reflected greater heterogeneity than later models that appear about 1890. For proslavery authors, her appearance is secondary to her unique relationship with white children. Mammy became part of the vocabulary of plantation literature, and as a prop she lends authenticity to the antebellum plantation household. Her behavior was codified well before *Uncle Tom's Cabin* (1852) was published, since nearly all of the mammy characters in this period are commended for their extraordinary ability to put their charges before their own children.

There is increasing evidence that black dolls provide some of the earliest creative expressions of African American slave women. We know from

Jean Fagin Yellin's biography that Harriet Jacobs made black dolls for the children she cared for while hiding as a fugitive.[19] Twenty years ago curator and American folk doll expert Wendy Lavitt made the bold assertion that topsy-turvy dolls (the top halves of two dolls, joined at the waist, with a black face on one end and a white face on the other) "originated in the antebellum South, where they were made by black women who cared for white children."[20] In chapter 2, I use models of topsy-turvy dolls to frame my discussion of enslaved motherhood, as represented by Harriet Beecher Stowe (*Uncle Tom's Cabin,* 1852), Frederick Douglass (*My Bondage and My Freedom,* 1855), and Harriet Jacobs (*Incidents in the Life of a Slave Girl,* 1861). The dolls provide an unusual metaphor for representations of slave motherhood between 1853 and 1861. In *Uncle Tom's Cabin,* Stowe constructs a fictional version of slave life in which surrogacy is the primary motherhood experience for slave women. Douglass responds to her characterization of the mammy in his revised autobiography, with a recovered memory of this mother, whom he depicts as a heroic antimammy figure. Harriet Jacobs positions herself as an authority on enslaved motherhood, since her narrative represents her lived experience as a slave mother and nursemaid. These texts and examples from material culture provide a picture of mid-nineteenth-century America as a society at once racially segregated and racially interactive.

Chapter 3 discusses the Aunt Jemima trademark introduced in the late nineteenth century, when the mammy figure became a prototype of American commercialism and consumerism. The popular visual image of a heavyset black woman serving food to white families became an updated symbol of racial harmony. This chapter examines Aunt Jemima's initial appearance at the World's Fair Columbian Exposition in 1893, in relation to the simultaneous efforts of an elite group of black women to introduce the black female intelligentsia to the World's Congress of Representative Women. In the same year, the novel *Pudd'nhead Wilson* by Mark Twain, and later, the short story "Her Virginia Mammy" (1899) by Charles Chesnutt feature slave mothers who choose to act as mammies in order to allow their children to pass as white. In his novel *The Marrow of Tradition* (1901), Chesnutt uses a more standard mammy image to define and explore emerging political tensions between "Old Negroes" and the "New Negro" ideology. Chesnutt helps us to see how the mammy became a symbol of voluntary peonage and therefore a pariah among African Americans. Cheryl Thurber's careful review of the *Confederate Veteran* magazine (the official publication of the United Confederate Veterans, the Sons of the Confederacy, and the United Daughters of the Confederacy) finds that "the number of references to mammy increased from about 1906 to 1912, which was the peak time for the glorification of mammy."[21] This rise in visibility of the mammy image is also achieved through the Aunt Jemima trademark and Jemima look-alikes. What are we to make of Chesnutt's and Twain's introduction of African American women who recognize and then use the mammy stereotype as a kind of cloak to be worn to achieve their own goals?

In chapter 4 the emphasis shifts to the ways that the mammy's original symbolism is revised as a neo-Confederate effort to honor her historic role with statues or monuments between 1900 and 1935. Simultaneously, as the Harlem Renaissance or "New Negro Movement" gained momentum, the image is appropriated and subverted by artists who celebrate her as a Madonna figure for African Americans.

The New Negroes' struggle to refashion America's perceptions of African Americans, however, could scarcely compete with the phenomenal success of *Gone with the Wind*. Mammy was triumphantly revived, first in the novel, later in the film and accompanying relics. Through textual analysis of *The Sound and the Fury* (1929) and *Gone with the Wind* (1935), in chapter 5 we see how Mitchell and Faulkner affirm and challenge long-standing assumptions about this character's enduring appeal.

The conclusion asks fundamental questions about why African American artists during the black power movement chose Aunt Jemima and mammy over Uncle Tom and Rastus (The Cream of Wheat Man) as the caricature they most wanted to transform. The answer lies both in the ways that this figure has been intrinsically woven in the fabric of American consciousness and in the power of the Aunt Jemima trademark as one of the most well known and immediately recognizable images of an African American woman. The book's conclusion draws on the most contemporary artistic revisions of Aunt Jemima or Mammy, like novelist Alice Randall's parody of *Gone with the Wind* called *The Wind Done Gone;* Michael Ray Charles's *Untitled* (1993), with its thinner, meaner looking Aunt Jemima withholding her piece of "American pie" from an overgrown white child; and Joyce Ann Scott's black leather sculptures depictng the competition of black and white children over the towering Mammy/Nanny persona.

It may be most useful at this time to think of the mammy as a multifaceted prism used to illuminate a continuous spectrum of American views and attitudes about racial hierarchy. Just as Newton's prism demonstrated that white light was composed of rays of different colors, the prism of scholarship exposes the fragments that constitute the mammy as a whole. Newton's theory that prisms could be used to "see beyond the colors to the shape they were assuming"[22] is instructive for new critical approaches to racial and gender stereotypes, when we are determined not to be distracted by flashes of light but to see the mammy from as many angles as possible. Each new angle tells something about how the mammy survives as a cultural force that influences and reflects a national conscience.

CHAPTER ONE

A Love Supreme:

Early Characterizations of the Mammy

In a popular caricature postcard from the 1920s a buxom African American woman is shopping with her three small children. A white saleswoman holds out a pair of white gloves and asks, "Madame, could I interest you in a pair of white kids?"[1] The double entendre of white kid leather gloves and white children is only funny with a black woman because both the image and the reality of black women taking care of white children are ubiquitous in American culture. The word *mammy* does not have to appear on the postcard for her image to be evoked in our minds (fig. 6).

Another postcard from the same era shows a large African American woman vigorously bathing her child and shouting, "Shut yo' mouth and mammy will have you white as snow in a minute" (fig. 7). Of course, neither one of these cards is truly funny anymore. But they are poignant as we delve into the pattern of representatives of African American women taking care of white children and preferring them to their own.

These depictions of African American mothers are consistent with those popularized through literature, travel narratives, and religious propaganda between 1820 and the 1850s. They indicate how black motherhood became defined and shaped as part of the mythology of a benevolent slave system. Before the phenomenal success of *Uncle Tom's Cabin* (1852), proslavery authors use these images of slave women with a white child as a symbol of racial harmony within the slave system. The first section of this chapter engages questions about how her maternity, her body size and shape, and her skin color contribute to our understanding of the mammy as an ultimate representation of maternal devotion. The most formulaic antebellum plantation mammy types reveal a fascinating evolution from a standard plantation character into a one-dimensional caricature. As the introduction explains, the early characters were most often referred to as *negro nurse* or *baby nurse,* instead of as *mammy,* but these slave women function as mammies within the texts. The conclusion of the chapter proposes a contextualizing framework for the way that Frederick Douglass's and Harriet Jacobs's narratives are read against *Uncle Tom's Cabin* in the next chapter.

In this study the fictive plantation and the actual plantation exist in separate yet distinctly related spheres. Nearly every historian writing about plantation slavery is compelled to address the mammy stereotype before he or she can effectively address the lived experiences of those African American women who might have been considered the big-house mammy. Instead of reviewing that vast body of scholarship here, I find it more useful to clarify some key historical questions before isolating the mammy characters found in short stories, novels, travel narratives, and religious chapbooks.

Historians suggest that the term *black mammy* was developed to draw boundaries between the various maternal figures on the plantation. According to Jesse Parkhurst, "[This woman] is referred to as the 'Black Mammy,' a name probably given to distinguish her from the real mother and also from the 'Mammy' of the slave children."[2] Elderly slave women who were responsible for the children while their parents worked in the fields or in the master's house were also known as "Mammy." Twenty-five years ago, Eugene Genovese made this dramatic proclamation about the mammy: "She remains the most elusive and important black presence in the Big House. To understand her is to move towards understanding the tragedy of plantation paternalism."[3]

Deborah Gray White has done exceptional work on the historic mammy in her book on female slaves in the United States, *Aren't I a Woman.*[4] Like other historians looking closely at African American slave life, White acknowledges that little information about the slave women who were called "Mammy" comes from those women themselves: "Most of what we know about Mammy comes from memoirs written after the Civil War. . . . In these and similar sources, Mammy is especially remembered for her love of her young white charges" (46–47). These accounts affirm that there was often an influential slave woman who remained extremely close to the master's family: "All de niggers have to stoop to Aunt Rachel like they curtsy to Missy."[5]

White pointedly confronts this stereotype's haunting power for historians; she concludes that as a cultural force the mammy is "enigmatic." She asks, "If the reality of Mammy and female household service does not square with the Mammy legend, why was the image of this domestic necessary at all and why did the image take the form it did?" (55). The answer to this question is found within the broad spectrum of revisions, renewals, and revivals of the mammy figure over the past century. Additional questions about how the mammy became so crucial to our understanding of slavery, gender, maternity, and memory in the American South lead us to new insights. White aligns the mammy stereotype with that of the Jezebel, noting, "The Mammy image is fully as misleading as that of Jezebel. Both images have just enough grounding in reality to lend credibility to stereotypes that would profoundly affect black women" (55). What does it mean to have "just enough" grounding in reality?

We see one perspective in 1924, about the time of the postcards referred to above, when Frances Gaines wrote an influential comparative study about the southern plantation, juxtaposing fictional plantation types with what he calls "actual types."[6] His effort to establish the difference between the reality of the southern plantation and the romantic mythology concretized by the 1890s plantation genre is admirable. The study is simultaneously well researched and rife with anecdotal assumptions. With regard to the slave women who took care of their master's children, Gaines privileges the recollections of "many mature" white Southerners when he asserts: "The plantation nurse was a fairly constant factor and in some homes was almost an institution. One does not need to go to written records to demonstrate the truth of this statement; many mature Southerners of today recall numerous instances." Gaines explains that the mammy figure is so common, so easily rendered that "a writer of the tradition could come never farther south than Bangor and still draw a mammy wholly acceptable to the popular conception." Asserting that southern roots are unnecessary to construct and present an authentic mammy, Gaines remarks, "It is obvious, nevertheless, that the tradition finding this figure particularly attractive has standardized her. In many cases, tradition has simply put a black mask on a character of romance that was already centuries old, the honored and dependable female retainer" (193–94).

Gaines's remarks remind us that the British handmaid, the Irish nanny, even Juliet's nurse in Shakespeare's *Romeo and Juliet* are well-known versions of feminine servility. This juxtaposition forces us to recall all that makes the mammy different from these loyal retainers; the fundamental differences between servants and slaves are not obscured by burnt cork. By layering racial inferiority on top of class inferiority, adding the possibility that she is both wet-nursing and subsequently raising a child that may actually own her and her family, the mammy moves into another sphere of time-honored loyalty altogether.

In her consummate look at fictional characters in twentieth-century African American literature, Trudier Harris explains that African American women working as domestics had profoundly different meanings for the North and the South.[7] Dividing them into three categories, "transitional" maids, "modern" maids, and "militant" maids, she writes: "Maids who are described as being truly southern are, then, those who generally acquiesce in the paternalist and place-defined relationship between mistress and maid as it has been shaped by the attitudes and traditions of southern society. . . . They are more likely than the others to be 'ideal servants,' the mammy figures traditionally identified with southern plantation households. These women usually compromise everything of themselves and of their connection to the black community in order to exist in the white world" (24–25).

Exhaustive searches of collected slave narratives, former slave autobiographies, diaries, biographies, and memoirs yield a conspicuous silence about this interracial relationship from the perspective of African American women, and specifically about the mammy's preference for white children. Unfortunately, the sentimentalized romance of mammy-charge relationships trumps the reality of lived experience.

The earliest fictional characters displaying characteristics consistent with the mammy type are Granny Mott in *The Valley of Shenandoah*, Aunt Chloe in *Scenes in Georgia*, Aunt Judy in *Linda, or, the Young Pilot of the Belle Creole*, and Nanny from *Mississippi Scenes*. Each is held up as a photograph of normative patterns of the mammy's physicality, speech, behavior, and bearing of children. These proslavery books providing the early formula for the literary plantation tradition established after the Civil War do not provide much fuel for serious literary analysis. What they do supply are regular portraits of slave women who are distinguished by their relationship with their master's children. The texts considered here are united because their portrayals of antebellum plantation life include at least one identifiable mammy character.

The earliest nurse in this study is Granny Mott of *The Valley of Shenandoah* (1824),[8] written by George Tucker, who also wrote both the first complete history of the United States (1856) and the first authorized biography of Thomas Jefferson. Granny Mott bears almost no physical resemblance to the standard mammy type, and she is the first of several mulatto mammy characters. Tucker describes her as being of "a yellowish complexion with delicate and raised features." The novel revolves around general family life in the Shenandoah Valley of Virginia. Granny Mott is a peripheral character who is eighty-four when introduced to the reader, and there is a subtle suggestion that she was once quite attractive. Contrary to the more fully developed and popularized "tragic mulatto" stereotype, these mulatto mammies are biracial and most often light-skinned sisters of the faithful retainer. Their bodies are different from those of black mammies because they are marked by racial impurity, their presence an undeniable announcement of miscegenation. They virtually disappear after 1854, with the notable exceptions of Roxy in *Pudd'nhead Wilson* (1894)[9] and Charles Chesnutt's Mrs. Harper in "Her Virginia Mammy" (1899).[10] (See chapter 4.)

Granny Mott, the narrator explains, is a longtime member of the M'Culloch household, and "has successfully nursed my paternal grandmother, my father, and us, and seems to feel for us in regular succession all the attachment that she could feel for her own children" (68). The word *nurse* here is not synonymous with wet nursing, yet it conveys all of the nurturing associated with taking care of children for three generations. Granny Mott seems to be a family heirloom passed down from one generation to another; she says, "My old master put down my age, and gave me to his eldest daughter, that is, Miss Betsey's mother" (86). (It was not unusual for slaves to be purchased and given to children as "gifts." In the following chapter, we will see that former slave Harriet Jacobs also is unable to speak about herself without mentioning her master's family.) There is almost a level of automation involved; Granny Mott stays in one place as the M'Culloch family pass through her life. Her biological children are evoked solely as a trope for measuring her love for the M'Culloch children. The conditional term "could" ("all the attachment that she could feel for her own children") carries tremendous weight here. Avoiding the declarative language he uses to describe her relationship with her white charges, Tucker skillfully implies that Mott's affection for her own children is limited, magnifying her devotion to her white family. This early characterization lays the troubling foundation for the enigma of the mammy's maternity: her love for her charges becomes more sublime, more extraordinary when it surpasses her love for her own flesh and blood, children who are owned by her master, or at times, by the young charges themselves.

The next fictional example comes from Isabel Drysdale, who writes in glowing terms about the pious Negro nurse Aunt Chloe in *Scenes in Georgia* (1827). Her small book is an unusual blend of children's prayers and travel narratives. Drysdale assumes that the mammy is a well-known type already recognizable to children. Like Granny Mott, Aunt Chloe's biological maternity is seen in competition with her surrogate maternity. As was mentioned in the introduction to this study, the volume replicates the mammy's preference for her white charges with a significant addition: "Those who have never witnessed it, can scarcely conceive of the affecting tenderness displayed by the Negro nurse to her little charge. It seems even to exceed the force of natural affection for her own offspring, combining strong maternal love with the enthusiastic devotedness of loyalty" (37). Drysdale goes a step further than Tucker by placing Chloe's role within the realm of divine service: "She considers her master's child as a superior being, and receives with overflowing gratitude the fond endearments of infantine affection" (37). The assumption here is that Chloe considers her nursling superior both to herself and—since this line follows one referring to her maternity—to her own children, acknowledging and accepting her place in the racial hierarchy that supports slavery. Chloe's natural affection for her own children is surpassed by an emotion that must be considered "supernatural." Drysdale assumes that there is something profoundly unique about the relationship, something that one must "witness" to fully comprehend.

In relaying Chloe's attachment to her charge, Drysdale first separates her readers into two groups, those who are familiar with the nurse-charge relationship and those who are not. Using the Negro nurse as a proslavery weapon is a firmly established technique, as this quotation is directed at increasingly virulent northern attacks on southern slavery.

In *The Southern Plantation* Gaines concedes that a southern heritage is not required to portray the mammy: "A writer of the tradition could come never farther south than Bangor and still draw a mammy wholly acceptable to the popular conception" (193). Yet between the 1820 and 1840s, it is primarily southern authors who use the mammy as an example of a domestic intimacy unique to plantation "families" and completely misunderstood by northerners. What better way to defend the slaveocracy than by using the power of maternal representation?

If the power of the maternal is exploited in this way, why was it not possible for the nurse's love for her children and love for her charges to be equal? Why isn't it enough for her to love her charges as much as her own children? Wouldn't that more effectively characterize the force of her maternal love? The answer is no, for the mammy's preference for white children will become inextricably linked to her ability to embrace and affirm her inferiority. Forty years later, Caroline Hentz writes of Aunt Judy that she "loved her gentle mistress, nay more than loved, adored, and revered her as being of a superior holier race than her own" (15).

As Stephanie Smith's *Conceived by Liberty* demonstrates, during the nineteenth century mothers were used as symbols "to reinforce conventional certitudes about, racial, social, sexual, and political restrictions" (14). Just as motherhood was celebrated as the true fulfillment of woman, slavery was defended as a necessary labor system and social structure based upon racial superiority and inferiority. Slave mothers, then, posed a vexing problem for nineteenth-century mother worship. As a slave, as an African American, as three-fifths of a human being, her ability to comprehend and express herself as mother to her own children is minimal. Her "natural" maternity is constructed as primitive, instinctual, base. Simultaneously, her maternal devotion to whites is constructed as sublime, extraordinary, superhuman. Her behavior and maternal status are inextricably linked when her biological (black) children function only to reaffirm her attachment to her surrogate (white) children.

If, as Smith finds, "maternal iconography was never as untroubled or as static as it was represented to be," then this nascent symbol of African American slave mothers cradling white children is the best example of that iconography's being "rife with moral, social, and politically charged tensions subject to persistent conflict and thus open to dynamic and strategic revisions" (Smith 14). The mammy emerges as a figure exposing the irony of nineteenth-century mother worship: a surrogate mother celebrated for emotionally displacing a biological mother and a caricature of ideal motherhood, as her own children are inconsequential.

When Drysdale writes with complete confidence "that an Old Chloe forms a member of almost every domestic establishment of the South," we see that her strategy is to shift the focus from human bondage to the "domestic establishment," which could be any American home, and of which Chloe is "a member."

In drawing Chloe's physical characterization, Drysdale uses Chloe to play upon racial and cultural differences between white and black southerners: "Her sawed teeth and curiously branded cheek bespeak her a native of Africa" (30). Her sawed teeth and tribal-marked cheeks are typical signs of beauty in West Africa, but Drysdale probably intends for this description to make Chloe seem more exotic, not to convey her beauty. Like the standard mammy, this African Chloe is very dark skinned and energetic: "She was a little, brisk, old woman with the wrinkles and gray hairs of sixty, combined with all the lively alertness of twenty-one." But she is also a small woman, nowhere near the size and weight of the prototype. Unlike light-skinned Granny Mott, Chloe's dark skin serves a specific purpose for Drysdale. "Perhaps a more interesting picture is seldome seen, than that which was often exhibited by Old Chloe and her little nursling, its fair pillowed in her faithful bosom, contrasting the sable but loving countenance bent above it" (31). Here an aesthetic value is introduced with the image of a dark-skinned woman holding a fair-skinned child, Chloe hardly seems to be a slave at all, but rather a dark-skinned Madonna holding her precious Savior to her breast.

Granny Mott and Aunt Chloe exemplify the kind of mammy who "prefers the master's children to her own, for as a member of the lower species, she acknowledges almost instinctively the superiority of the higher race" (Christian 11). Both fulfill the expectation that the mammy, as the human connection between masters and slaves, will and should nurture the system that enslaves them.

Granny Mott is uneducated, yet her grammar is impeccable and her dialogue is completely indistinguishable from that of master and mistresses: "I am eighty-four the tenth day of next October, please God I live so long." Aunt Chloe, on the other hand, often sounds more like an Indian from an old-fashioned Western than a slave on a southern plantation, saying, "Me don't know what ails me—me heart so heavy." Her speech patterns add nothing to her southern authenticity.

As for Granny Mott's demeanor, she is a "rank aristocrat," with a "reverence for everything English" (86). Similarly, in Caroline Hentz's popular novel *Linda, or, the Young Pilot of the Belle Creole* (1852) Aunt Judy is the heroine's mammy, and her physical appearance is tied to a constructed hierarchy of house "servants" and field slaves: "It was evident from Judy's air and style of dress that she belonged to the ancient regime, the class of family servants who are admitted in the confidence of their master's household and are treated with kindness and affection."[11] Hentz calls Judy a member of the "ancient regime" and part of the "class of family servants," as if the hierarchy of slavery is made up in part by willing servants of the dominant culture. Aunt Judy's well-kept "air" connotes privilege, probably meant to offset the important fact that segregation from the field hands might mean being separated from her own family in order to foster this special relationship with the master's family.

Like Old Chloe, Aunt Judy is a "pure African" whose skin is "black as ebony." Caroline Lee Hentz, perhaps best known for her novel *The Planters Northern Bride* (1854), emphasizes Judy's African heritage with a surprising strategy, saying that her "African blood had not been *corrupted* by the *base mingling* of a paler stream" (15; emphases added). Hentz implies that African mammies are preferable to their lighter-skinned sisters, insinuating that the legendary white southern obsession with racial purity extends to slaves. The words "base mingling" carry enough illicit sexual connotation for us to remember that the mulatto mammy and all mulatto slaves are a negative reflection on the sexual mores of slave masters. Mulatto slave characters represent evidence of the "base" and illegal sexual liaison between white men and black women.[12]

In *Linda,* the mean-spirited stepmother Mrs. Walton sells Judy away from the family plantation to punish the heroine, Linda, telling her husband, "I can do nothing with her [Linda] while Judy stays in the house and interferes with my authority." This is an example of the mammy's "power" within the southern home, which does not always show innocuous cooperation, but may instead signal domestic competition between the mammy and the mistress of the house. The most eloquent tribute to the effect of the mammy-charge relationship on white southern mothers is Lillian Smith's reflection, *Killers of the Dream.* Smith writes that the mistress of the house would sometimes joke about her children preferring the mammy, accompanying her remark with a laugh that sounded like "glass bells about to break into splinters."[13] Yet beneath that jovial acceptance, Smith maintains, was genuine jealousy: "Of all the humiliating experiences which southern white woman have endured, the least easy to accept, was that of a mother who had no choice but to take the husk of a love which her son in his earliest years had given to another woman" (138).

Hentz avoids any animosity between the biological mother and the mammy by removing Linda's mother altogether and replacing her with an evil stepmother, legitimizing Aunt Judy as a perfect surrogate. Mrs. Walton, however, is not interested in the "husk of a love" that might be gleaned from her stepdaughter; she wants only blind obedience so that she can rule her new household (Hentz 28).

Ironically, in this novel Linda is the one whipped at Mrs. Walton's command, not the slave Aunt Judy. In the scene where Judy comforts and nurses Linda after the whipping, Judy insists that her body could withstand the punishment much better than Linda: "If it had been poor Judy's back, she no mind it one bit. But this little white, tender creature!" (31). This is the sole moment in the novel where Judy says anything about herself at all; her body appears and then disappears, as the narrative emphasizes Linda's pain.

Linda fantasizes about being old enough to buy Judy herself, so that "they would live together all their lives" (34). Here the mammy-charge relationship anticipates the one in *Gone with the Wind,* in which Scarlett O'Hara has an adult version of that fantasy, admitting at the end of the novel that she wants her mammy to be her lifelong servant-companion.

The relationship between the mammy and her charge is better developed in Hentz's novel than in previous examples; and unlike previous portrayals, there is considerable *mutual* affection between Aunt Judy and Linda. Unlike Linda's stepmother, Judy has no husband or biological children with whom Linda must compete for attention. Aunt Judy's maternity essentially functions as a possession for Linda to obtain, even if she has to buy it for herself.

Shortly after *Linda, or, the Young Pilot of the Belle Creole* was published, Joseph B. Cobb released a collection of "sketches of Southern life" called *Mississippi Scenes* (1851).[14] Cobb includes two mammy characters in these vignettes of plantation life. He writes first of a baby nurse named Nanny who is "an old Negress, of bright mulatto complexion" (84). This is all we learn of her appearance; there is no indication of her size. Her behavior marks her as a mammy character; Cobb introduces her as a slave favored for the "depth of her devotion to her slave master and his children" (85). Nanny's children were all killed by a "relentless fever," and like many of the slave mothers in *Uncle Tom's Cabin,* Nanny is associated largely with grief. Yet this slave mother's grief is also a means by which Cobb may point out the benevolence of slave masters, "for a *master* only *can* know how strongly a Negro mother can love her offspring" (84–85). Nanny's maternity is rendered as primitive; she has "offspring" instead of "children."

Cobb emphasizes the words *master* and *can,* drawing the reader's focus to the master's compassionate ability first to know his slave's grief and then to the slave mother's ability to love her children. The reader's sympathy is deflected from the slave mother to her master, minimizing her grief since it is his burden to witness her sadness; Nanny's devotion to and love for her master's children (who perhaps escaped the relentless fever with better medical treatment) does not have to surpass her attachment to her own children, as with Granny Mott and Old Chloe. Cobb uses a few well-chosen words and sketches a portrait of the mammy without being very specific; Nanny is a slave mother who is devoted to her slave master and his children. Cobb can rely on his readers' imagination to develop her character more fully.

In another vignette, Cobb relays the story of a slave nursemaid who saved the life of her nursling by leaping out of a carriage. This character is nameless and faceless, yet indicates the melodramatic and supernatural powers attributed to truly dedicated mammies. Cobb relays this story as told to him by a "distinguished Southern statesman." The carriage in which both nursemaid and child are traveling is endangered when a driver loses control of the horses while crossing a bridge. The child's nurse jumps out of the carriage with the child, "and then turning so as to make sure of alighting on her back, at the same time holding the infant at arm's length above her so that it might escape the slightest jar, she threw herself out, perfectly regardless of everything but the safety of her master's child" (165).

The slave nurse sustains substantial physical injury in using her body this way, and she is commended for her loyalty—not her courage or quick thinking—but her *loyalty* to her master. Is this mammy's behavior the demonstration of a self-sacrificing slave, or is this a romanticized tribute to a faithful slave? It manages to be both, in the same way that the mammy figure is an artful blending of fiction and selective memory. Her heroism is not linked to maternal instincts, or to the reality that any adult would risk his or her life for the safety of a child; instead it seems that her "fleshy bottom is meant to literally cushion whites from the shocks of life."[15]

This exploration of the earliest mammy characters, the varieties in skin color and body shape and size, even nationality, shows, in a general sense, the individuality of nineteenth-century African American women. Mammy's speech deteriorates into more standardized plantation dialect over the years, but there is still no formulaic way for her to look or sound.

With this careful look at the heterogeneity of the earliest mammy characters, we can see that what was lost with the more standardized mammy was any respectful or insightful distinction made in characterizing black women with white charges. The character became both standardized and stereotyped as *Uncle Tom's Cabin* moved to the stage and the exaggerated caricatures of minstrel actors replaced early representations of the character.[16] In the years before *Uncle Tom* explodes on the literary scene, the mammy is housed in different bodies, but her nature is already set in stone.

John Brown may have been thinking about the power of the mammy stereotype when he requested that a "grey haired old Black grandma" be part of his funeral procession after his execution. When Stephen Vincent Benet wrote his long poetic tribute to Brown, he invoked more than the mammy's appearance or behavior. In the persona "Aunt Bess," Benet evokes the mammy's alleged preferential treatment of white children: "Fat Aunt Bess is older than Time / But her eyes still shine like bright, new dime / Though two generations have gone to rest / On the sleepy mountain of her breast. . . . She has had children of her own / But the white-skinned ones are bone of her bone."[17]

Within the Plantation Cabin:
"She has had children of her own . . ."

A Peek Inside Aunt Phebe's Cabin

By December 1853, more than three hundred thousand copies of *Uncle Tom's Cabin* had been sold, and by 1856 more than thirty "anti-Tom" novels had been written and published in an effort to reverse the nation's negative attitudes toward the South and slaveholding. None of the anti-Tom novels could rival the sales of *Uncle Tom's Cabin,* but they were influential among slavery apologists and read widely by southern and northern women. One anonymous reviewer wrote that it was striking to observe how few of the elements of Stowe's novel needed to be changed in order to "serve the purpose of her detractors."[18]

Two of the most interesting and widely read proslavery responses to *Uncle Tom's Cabin* are *Antifanaticism: A Tale of the South* (1853)[19] by Martha Haines Butt and *Aunt Phillis's Cabin* (1852) by Mary Eastman. Both novels use a mammy character to symbolize slavery's success as a benevolent institution and as evidence of the unique relationships between slaves and slave masters. The female authors seemed to be familiar with one another's writing. Butt heralds Eastman in her "Concluding Remarks" for correcting Mrs. Stowe, "who says that a negro was burned at a certain tree. Mrs. Eastman observes that the tree was struck by lightning, and that is the most probable of the two" (Butt 265).

Antifanaticism is a thinly disguised proslavery rewrite of *Uncle Tom's Cabin;* Phebe mirrors Aunt Chloe from Stowe's work in many ways; one of her sons is even named Moses, similar to Chloe's Mose. The historic mistreatment of slave children is replicated in the way that the mammy's children are portrayed. They are rarely described as children at all: Nanny of *Mississippi Scenes* had "offspring," Aunt Chloe's children in *Uncle Tom's Cabin* are a "pile of woolly heads," and Aunt Phebe's children are "urchins." Originally a baby nurse for her master's child Dora, Aunt Phebe is known now as a cook, and her cabin is the focus of the novel's second chapter. There are no parents being sold away from their families as in Aunt Chloe's cabin: "We will just take a peep into her cabin, while she is preparing supper, and see how nicely all things go on" (Butt 25).

In Aunt Phebe's cabin, we find her complimenting herself on her cooking skills, which she deems above comparison. In this scene she is not making her own family's dinner, but the meal to be sent up to the big house for her master and mistress—an example of how "nicely all things go on." After she makes that meal, she begins to cook for her family (Butt 25). But when Aunt Phebe hears her children becoming impatient while waiting for their meal, her response is an eerie parroting of Aunt Chloe's in *Uncle Tom's Cabin.* Aunt Phebe says: "You Mose, dat you? I'll crack yer head if I comes dar, you audacious villain." As the children continue to annoy her, she continues to threaten them: "Yer Mose, I be de def of yer yit; wait till I gits dis supper in de house, and den yer see if I don't pay yer off!" (Butt 26). Aunt Chloe's lines, for comparison, are, "Here you, Mose and Pete! Get out de way, you niggers! Get away, Polly . . . Get along wid ye! Now. Mas'r George . . . you know your old aunty'd keep the best for you," she tells her children this while "pushing away their woolly heads . . . seconding her exhortations by a slap which resounded very formidably" (Stowe 15–16). There is yet another similar scene in *Sound and the Fury,* where Dilsey threatens her son for touching a cake she has baked for her employer's son Benjy; "Reach it again, and I chop it right off with this here butcher knife" (70).

The scenes of African American slave mothers threatening their children were probably meant to be entertaining. But we have to ask new questions about this literature. Why is the mammy depicted so consistently as being short-tempered and heavy-handed with her own children? Wouldn't it make her more maternally sublime if she were a kind and forgiving mother figure to white children and compassionate with her own children? There are two insults at work in these portrayals. The first is that African American mothers aren't affectionate and loving toward their own children; it is almost as if they exhaust their store of maternal devotion with white children and come home on empty. The second insult is that African American children, particularly slave children, are profoundly different from white children; they were characterized as having fewer, and less refined, needs. We can see evidence of this in fiction and in autobiography. For example, an African American woman named Katie Sutton recalls this from her childhood on the plantation: "Ole Missus and young Missus told the little slave children that the stork brought the white babies to their mothers, but the slaves were all hatched out from buzzard eggs. And we believed it was true."[20] Children who came from such origins would not need be given much to survive.

And consider these two passages from a popular children's book of verses called *Mammy's Baby* (1890) (fig. 8). The verse titled "Care" under the image of a forlorn-looking white baby reads:

> Mamma has gone for a moment,
>   And all the world is awry,
> For it takes so very little
>   To make this baby cry.
>   (Fig. 9)

The verse titled "Don't Care" under the image of a cheerful African American baby reads:

> All alone they have left him,
>   With only tables and chairs,
> And so he laughs and plays to himself,
>   And never a bit he cares.
>   (Fig. 9)[21]

What lingers in these haunting and disturbing portrayals is a strong sense that African American children were both subhuman and dispensable, represented as being more like pets than real children.[22]

After Aunt Phebe's family has eaten, Master Charles comes to visit her and Uncle Dick, just the way that Master George visits Aunt Chloe and Uncle Tom. And just like Aunt Chloe, Aunt Phebe gushes with affection over her master's child: "Ain't dat ar' child one angel? Jist hear how he talks. Ain't he got a kind heart?" (Butt 31).

The kindness of Master Charles's heart is not in question here, because in a conversation that follows, Aunt Phebe, Uncle Dick, and slave neighbor Rufus discuss how much better off they are than free blacks in the North. Uncle Dick is such a happy slave that "his feelings always revolted" at the very thought of abolitionists. Apparently an abolitionist paid a visit to the plantation earlier, and he and Rufus discuss how misguided he was to think that they could be persuaded away from their master. More specifically, they say that they've heard that northerners abuse white servants and that if they were to get one "with a black skin, it would be the death of him" (31). Aunt Phebe joins in to say that she was so disgusted by the sight of this troublemaking abolitionist that she refused to serve him, having another slave bring the abolitionist his breakfast pancakes. This peek into Aunt Phebe's cabin allowed slavery apologists to say exactly what some readers wanted and needed to hear through African American characters.

And a Peek Inside *Aunt Phillis's Cabin*

Mary Eastman's novel was far more successful than *Antifanaticism,* selling between twenty and thirty thousand copies and making it a best-seller among the anti-Tom novels.

There is an early vignette in *Aunt Phillis's Cabin* about a mammy character named Susan, which occurs before Aunt Phillis is introduced in chapter nine. Eastman tells us that Susan is a favorite house servant who only has to tend a baby and take care of her disabled mistress. When the family takes Susan along with them on a trip to Boston, Susan is swayed by the abolitionists lure and abandons the baby in a hotel: "Susan kissed the baby, not without many tears, and then threw herself trembling and dismayed, in the arms and tender mercies of the Abolitionists." Her life with the abolitionists results in a speedy downfall: they are angry with her for not stealing her mistress's purse and eventually she is employed by an abolitionist group paying her four dollars a month to do laundry and housework for ten people.[23]

Aunt Phillis is another mulatto mammy, "a tall, dignified, bright mulatto woman. . . . The blood of the freeman and the slave mingled in her veins" (102). Eastman avoids the discussion about mixed race characters that Caroline Hentz engages in, immediately countering, "It is with the qualities of her heart and mind, rather than her appearance, that we have to do" (102). Phillis is the wife of Uncle Bacchus, an inanely pompous character, obsessed with gaudy clothes and alcohol.

Eastman makes an interesting decision about Aunt Phillis's maternity, describing her as the mother of twelve children whom she turns into apprentices: they "play servants to the white children when she [Phillis] is taking care of them." Phillis maintains the racial boundaries of subordination in her own home; she has a collection of toys that her own children "were not allowed to touch . . . when the owners were not there, but they took a conspicuous part in the play, being the waiters and ladies's [*sic*] maids and coach drivers of the little gentlemen and Alice" (248–49). If she finds it acceptable for her children to play at servitude, it is only to train them as house slaves, since she looks down on "ordinary servants of the plantation and doesn't want her children talking like them." Phillis's daughter Lydia is so deeply steeped in internalized racism that she tells Miss Janet she wishes she was white and asks, "If I was to stay all time in de house, and never go in de sun, would I git white?" (250).

It is obvious that Aunt Phillis would never leave her white family like her sister mammy Aunt Phebe; Phillis is insulted by abolitionists who encourage her to "take" her freedom by escaping with them. Phillis tells them: "I am an honest woman, and am not in the habit of taking any thing. I'll never take my freedom. If my master would give it to me, and the rest of us, I should be thankful. I am not going to begin stealing, and I am fifty years of age." Her mistress, Miss Janet, is "in her eyes, perfection" (Eastman 103). This admiration extends beyond her mistress to the entire family. Eastman does not disappoint her readers who seek reassurance about the mammy's love:

> "It seems but yesterday," said Mr. Weston, "that Phillis sat at her cabin door, with Arthur in her arms, and her own child, almost the same age, in the cradle near them. . . . I never can forget the look of sympathy, which was in her face, when I used to go to her cabin to see my motherless child. She always favored Arthur the preference, putting her own infant aside to attend to his wants." (253)

Even in her own cabin Phillis favors her motherless white charge, linking maternal devotion and sympathy, a familiar narrative strategy in sentimental fiction. Phillis's slighting her own children is not seen as neglectful because the assumption is that her children would not suffer from being put aside, from being always second, even with their own mother. Was the influence and infiltration of white supremacy during slavery so pervasive that even in romanticized fiction, the mammy's cabin fails as a safe domestic space for slave children? Surely not when the cabin is a platform for proslavery propaganda.

The novel also parodies *Uncle Tom's Cabin* by making Aunt Phillis a feminine version of the pious Tom and by giving her a lengthy death scene that reads like an odd reversal of Eva's famous demise. Everyone on the plantation gathers around her bed as Phillis insists that she never needed to be free because she and her family were so well taken care of (103).

An additional example of the mammy's pivotal role in abolitionist discourse occurs in the anonymous 1839 short story "Grace Merry," appearing in *Godey's Lady's Book*.[24] Published in Philadelphia, the *Godey's Lady's Book* was designed to attract the growing audience of educated American women. In addition to fashion plates and sheet music, the periodical published work by Harriet Beecher Stowe, Edgar Allen Poe, Nathaniel Hawthorne, and Henry Wadsworth Longfellow. Feminist Sarah Josepha Hale, author of her own anti-Tom novel *Liberia, or Mr. Peyton's Experiment* (1853), took over as editor in 1836. Hale brought more political substance to the magazine, writing frequently about the notion of the "women's sphere." The magazine flourished under her leadership, reaching a pre–Civil War circulation of 150,000. *Godey's* became a significant female-headed influence in American publishing and is among the most important resources of nineteenth-century American life and culture.

In addition to short stories, the *Godey's Lady's Book* also published a series of fashion plates using dolls to represent "typical" nineteenth-century domestic scenes.[25] In one such scene three dolls are set up: a white lady doll, a black mammy doll, and a white baby doll in a cradle (fig. 10). Implicitly the doll representing the lady of the house has complete autonomy; she is dressed to go out. In contrast, the black doll is dressed to stay home and take care of the child. The description incorrectly reads: "As our southern ladies walk but little, this will be recognized as a carriage costume."

The same scene is replicated in one of the earliest automated toys described thusly: "A very early mechanical toy, it is weight driven to rock the cradle with the white baby while the mammy looks on."[26] In this example toys, targeted to white mothers for their children, assure that the mammy will live on in the hearts and minds of future generations. (In the following chapter I consider more closely the prevalence of dolls replicating the black mammy–white charge relationship because they reflect what adults want to teach children about the world around them.)

Like the anti-Tom novels, the abolitionists in "Grace Merry" are outsiders prone to misunderstanding and misinterpreting southern culture. In this case the abolitionist is Lucy Sexton, who is visiting from England. Sexton is appalled that the heroine, Grace Merry, allows her slaves to use her family's last name. Grace counters with, "It does us no injury, and is a gratification to them." Sexton takes this opportunity to launch into her antislavery rhetoric: "I did not know, that you Americans studied the gratification of your slaves." Grace promptly brings the mammy out as her best example of the misunderstood relationship between masters and slaves. Here the author makes a noteworthy twist by emphasizing the child's love for the mammy rather than the reverse. Grace says, "The affection a child feels for its black nurse, is in many instances as strong, if not stronger, than its love to its natural parent. Indeed, it remains, during its early years, almost constantly with its 'Mammy.'"[27] "Grace Merry" is unusual because the author does not try to articulate the mammy's feelings for the child, but shifts our attention to children's natural attachment to childcare providers instead of emphasizing the gendered and racial essentialism of African American women. Unlike sociological studies about children's relationships with childcare providers, I am not attempting to analyze the relationship between mammy and child; instead, this work is about how this relationship has been represented, revised, renewed, and always linked to an agenda.

Our understanding and our expectations of the mammy stereotype take on a different shape through a comparison with the earliest depictions. Mammy's role as a devoted mother-servant to white children creates friction against her life as slave mother of her own children; in the following chapter her motherhood is magnified until she becomes a site where slavery and motherhood meet in a cloud of struggle, despair, and triumph. The repetitive use of the mammy figure as the solitary or the most prominent representation of slave motherhood sets the stage for well-known authors like Stowe to use slave mothers as a powerful abolitionist trope.

Let me return for a moment to Francis Gaines's comment that readers need no reliable documentation about the mammy because "many mature Southerners of today" remember her. Howell Raines, whose "Grady's Gift" is an eloquently moving tribute to the African American woman who worked for his family, is one of few white southerners to intimate that it is impossible for anyone to truly know how African Americans felt about white southerners during segregation (and by extension during slavery) because of the dishonesty inherent within the social structure itself. Raines writes: "There is no trickier subject for a writer from the South than that of affection between a black person and a white one in the unequal word of segregation." Raines gets to the crux of the matter: "The dishonesty upon which such a society is founded makes every emotion suspect, makes it impossible to know whether what flowed between two people was honest feeling or pity or pragmatism." Indeed, Raines speculates that for African Americans—primarily women—in this instance, "the feigning of an expected emotion could be the very coinage of survival."[28] This candid insight reveals a great deal about what is unsaid and unspeakable in our understanding of maternal affection and intimacy that is purchased. It is almost impossible to take care of a small child day after day without mutual affection emerging. (The contradictory evidence of some horrific "nanny-cams" not withstanding.) The close readings in this chapter have illuminated the way that race-specific caregiver-child affection was exploited to justify an unjustifiable system.

CHAPTER TWO

Bound in Black and White: Bloodlines, Milk Lines, and Competition in the Plantation Nursery

A late-nineteenth-century trade card advertising Clark's Thread uses the image of a black female field-worker holding a basket of cotton bolls spilling over the side and connecting it to the picture below, where a young white woman sits at her sewing machine, threading the cotton through her machine. The bottom of the card bears the postbellum slogan, "The Thread that binds the Union North to South," effectively sewing two women of different races, from different regions together through labor and consumption (fig. 11). This picture is surprisingly reminiscent of the popular nineteenth-century topsy-turvy rag dolls with a black face on one end and a white face on the other. Together the trade card and the dolls indicate how mid-nineteenth-century America was at once racially segregated and racially interactive; the striking metaphor of black and white bodies bound together occurs repeatedly in this chapter. The dolls are used as contextual sidebars revealing nuances of nineteenth-century culture that are missed when we rely solely on books such as Harriet Beecher Stowe (*Uncle Tom's Cabin,* 1852), Frederick Douglass (*My Bondage and My Freedom,* 1855), and Harriet Jacobs (*Incidents in the Life of a Slave Girl,* 1861). These texts are beginning to be read in tandem more frequently in studies emphasizing race and maternity. This chapter foregrounds the hypervisibility of the mammy as slave mother in these texts, a character who becomes the mainstream model of African American motherhood. The

32

Douglass and Jacobs narratives, by former slaves, turn the derogatory concept of black mothers preferring white children on its head through representations of strong, sacrificial black mothers whose lives are defined by their ability to protect their children.

Black Face/White Face: Topsy-Turvy Doll

In her study of nontraditional toys, collector and journalist Mildred Jailer agrees with museum curator and doll collector Wendy Lavitt that topsy-turvy dolls probably "originated in plantation nurseries."[1] The dolls have become more controversial in recent years because some collectors have circulated a troubling narrative about the dolls and how African American slave children might have used them. For example, doll collector Jan Thalberg declared, "During the years before the Civil War, many children of slaves wanted to play with white dolls. Since this was generally disapproved of and not permitted, their mammy's [sic] made them dolls that could quickly convert from White to Black by turning them upside down, thus revealing their approval of the Black side."[2] While her assumptions concerning the desires of black children for a forbidden doll are questionable, I am more alarmed by the speculation that slave mothers would make and give their children a doll that would have to be hidden from whites—this makes slave mothers seem incredibly irresponsible. As well, this implication that African American children preferred white dolls to black dolls gives us an eerie parallel to sentiments expressed in the last chapter about the mammy's preference of white children over her own children.

Yet this assumption that black children prefer white dolls should remind us of the 1940 study by educational psychologists Kenneth Clark and his wife Mamie Phipps Clark on the way segregation caused African American children to prefer white dolls to black ones because of their own feelings of inferiority. Thurgood Marshall, in the landmark case of *Brown v. Board of Education,* cited this study as a way of proving that segregation was detrimental to African American children's self-esteem. Notably, it was the first time the Supreme Court ever admitted a social science study—or dolls for that matter—as hard evidence.

Nationally recognized African American doll collector Jamilla Jones has been collecting dolls for more than forty years. Her current collection features rag, bisque, handmade dolls and some topsy-turvy dolls. Her two-sided dolls feature a black doll with a headscarf on one end and a white doll in an antebellum-style dress on the other. In contrast to Thalberg, Jones speculates that perhaps the dolls were meant for slave children who *had to* display the white face in front of the master for his approval or they might have been given as "maid dolls" to white children.[3] For example, in Figure 12, a 1903 photograph shows a family portrait taken in a professional studio where the girl's dolls have a tea party, with the larger black doll serving tea to the other dolls.

I am encouraged by current scholarship citing evidence that children use toys to imitate adults. Mildred Jailer draws another important connection between these dolls and the ways that young girls imitate their mother's behavior, suggesting that slave children "desired a forbidden white doll (a baby like the ones their mothers cared for)." This explanation not only seems plausible to me, but it also respects the parental relationship between mothers and children by emphasizing a basic need that most children have: to be like their parents. Scholarship has shown that playthings are effective as tools of race and gender socialization.[4] As a sociopolitical gesture, the subversive act of binding together black and white bodies to produce these dolls reflects an attempt to address the reality of racial interconnections during this period. Like other products of material culture, the designs of topsy-turvy dolls and mammy dolls mark significant stages of historical development and accurately reflect the world that adults create and present to children.

Topsy-turvy dolls are among the oldest handmade rag dolls, making the pre–Civil War dolls extremely rare and valuable. Other topsy-turvy dolls from the late nineteenth century have lithographed faces, making them more rare than dolls from the same period with painted faces or hand-stitched features. Later versions of two-sided dolls situate a black mammy at one end and a white infant at the other, like the one in figure 13. These dolls appear at the turn-of-the-century and continue in popularity until the early 1940s.[5] The cloth doll in figure 12 has two lithographed faces; one depicting an adult African American mammy on one end and a blue-eyed blond child on the other. The mammy doll is dressed in a white cotton dress with an apron and cap; the white doll wears a pastel floral print with a lace-edged collar. Like the early topsy-turvy dolls, these dolls speak to the gendered and racialized position of countless African American women who found themselves in a country that was simultaneously segregated and interconnected.

Topsy-turvy dolls again went through a redefinition in purpose and design when the traditional black and white upside-down dolls gave way to storybook character dolls with other features, such as multiple facial expressions painted on different sides of one doll's head. When the topsy-turvy doll changed in design from the prewar years in the South, it retained its essential capacity to emphasize the racial differences between the powerful and the powerless. This doll is unique in its ability to reflect cultural tensions because the dolls evolved along with economic conditions. One anthropologist has said, "A looking glass into the American social order, the two-headed, reversible, upside-down doll is able to turn things . . . topsy-turvy. In this sense, it is more than a doll—it is a symbol of power, of resistance, of secrecy, and of revolution."[6] Any object can be rich with numerous meanings, and dolls, particularly black dolls, have an unrealized potential to reveal essential information about what children learn about race, through doll play.

African American slave women may have given dolls like these to their daughters as a preparation for the possibility of a life devoted to nurturing two babies: one black and one white. Topsy-turvy dolls are designed for children to play with one baby at a time, and this accurately reflects the division of caregiving that African American women encountered, having to care for white children during the day and their own children at night. These handmade dolls are important, creative expressions of those otherwise silent women we know only as "mammy."[7]

By the mid–nineteenth century, doll play was considered to be both more important and more problematic in terms of child socialization. In her study of early American dolls and doll play, Alyssa Zelkowitz writes, "Dolls also became explicit vehicles through which to communicate . . . values, teaching young girls themes of charity, humility and appropriate religious devotion."[8]

One enormously popular mammy doll of the 1920s was Beloved Belindy, created by cartoonist John Gruelle, who also created the most famous rag doll of all time: Raggedy Ann. In 1926, Gruelle developed the Beloved Belindy doll so that Raggedy Ann and her brother, Andy, could have a mammy. In his first Belindy book, *Beloved Belindy,* Gruelle explains that "Beloved Belindy was the mammy of Raggedy Ann and Raggedy Andy and of all the other dolls in the nursery."[9] Gruelle's aesthetic design of these dolls and their relationship to each other reflect the ways in which objects of cultural production do, in fact, serve to interpret our cultural climate and reinscribe race and gender roles (fig. 14). Understood as a didactic, and therefore, an interpretive tool of our culture, it is important to note the way that early mammy dolls, particularly Beloved Belindy, appear, disappear, and reappear in the American marketplace. In 1950, after a twenty-four-year life span, Beloved Belindy was taken off the market as a direct result of protests from civil rights activists. Interestingly, her later appearance as a black version of Raggedy Ann, without her mammy paraphernalia, is an excellent example of revisionist history.

These insights linking dolls with the mammy's role as baby nurse counter the familiar image reviewed in chapter 1, emerging from numerous romanticized narratives of plantation slave life, representing a mammy happily breast-feeding both black and white children, content in her role as milk-laden earth mother. Detailing one mother's experience, the following excerpt from the narrative of former slave William McWhorter disrupts the popular romantic narratives of the late nineteenth and early twentieth centuries. McWhorter recalls a nursery where the competition for a slave mother's body and her role as milk-laden mother was, in fact, devastating:

> My Aunt Mary b'longed to Marse John Craddock and when his wife died and left a little baby—dat was little Miss Lucy—Aunt Mary was nussin' a new baby of her own, so Marse John made her let his baby suck too. If Aunt Mary was feeding her own and Miss Lucy started crying, Marse John would snatch her baby up by the legs and spank him and tell Aunt Mary to go on and nuss his baby fust. Aunt Mary couldn't answer him a word, but my Ma said she offen seed Aunt Mary cry 'til de tears met her chin.[10]

While McWhorter's narrative underscores the emotional strain that slave mothers endured, it also draws attention to the slave mother's vital role as a source of sustenance for both white and black children. This resulted in an intimate interdependency between slaves and slave-owning families. In *Incidents in the Life of a Slave Girl,* for example, Harriet Jacobs connects slave families with slave-owning families in the following way:

> My Mother's mistress was the daughter of my grand-mother's mistress. She was the foster sister of my mother; they were both nourished at my grandmother's breast. In fact, my mother had been weaned at three months old so that the babe of the mistress might obtain sufficient food.[11]

Jacobs describes her grandmother as a slave who fulfilled numerous roles for her owner, "from cook to wet nurse to seamstress." She provides much-needed evidence that slave women had access to sewing materials, and in some very pragmatic ways, her own family is "sewn" together with her master's family. These two narratives detail the way in which slave women serving as wet nurses created an additional or *supplemental* family line in slave-owning families. By honoring this "milk line," we acknowledge the unique relationship between infants of different races nursed and cared for by the same surrogate mother. Jacobs has her own term for this phenomenon; her mother's mistress is simultaneously her mother's "foster sister."[12] Importantly, this reminds us of the numerous accounts of slave women breast-feeding their own child and their owner's simultaneously.

The possibility that the two babies, one black and one white, reflected the way slave nursemaids saw their own world revolutionizes the typical interpretation of these dolls (e.g., the two sides represent good and evil). When we use this approach, the dolls give us crucial insight into the inner lives of those who were both surrogate and biological mothers; one child is "hidden" or absent while they cared for the other child, yet both are somehow "present" in their hearts. In fact, these dolls make a profound and compelling statement about the mutual dependency of slaves and slave-owning families from the perspective of slave women, the very view that is so obviously missing from this discourse. Close readings of slave narratives and letters have not yielded the mammy's words about her own experience. Therefore, any form of material culture made by slave women becomes both more precious and more profound in our look at this intimacy. Unfortunately, the complexity of the relationship between a nursing mother and the child she feeds goes unaddressed by collectors and scholars, who only view these dolls as products of racist propaganda. It is tempting for a twenty-first-century audience to assume that these dolls were made largely by white doll-makers.

A more complete picture of slave motherhood emerges when we consider the dolls in conjunction with the few slave testimonies available. Reading *Uncle Tom's Cabin* against the autobiographies of former slaves Frederick Douglass and Harriet Jacobs further develops that picture. It is my hope that the link between the words and artifacts of slave mother will enhance our understanding of the ways that Stowe, Douglass, and Jacobs construct slave motherhood for an interracial antebellum audience.

Stowe gives us a white woman's imaginative construction of slave motherhood in her two mammy characters, Aunt Chloe and Mammy. Douglass's "reconstructed" memory of his own mother and his portrayal of Aunt Katy challenge those fictional characters. The final text in this chapter deserves our special attention because Jacobs's construction of slave motherhood is based on personal experience.

A Neighborhood of Mammies

In her study of maternal figures in nineteenth-century literature, *Conceived by Liberty*, Stephanie A. Smith comments "To write anything all about sentimentally domestic ideology or maternity in the nineteenth-century American is to invoke Harriet Beecher Stowe" (90).[13] Stowe is automatically invoked whenever the slave mother as a literary character is raised, because *Uncle Tom's Cabin* provides us (as it did nineteenth-century audiences) with so many examples of slave mothers. Indeed, in my emphasis on narratives of antebellum motherhood, *Uncle Tom's Cabin* is fertile ground for uncovering and investigating a wide range of mammy types. There are two black mammies (Aunt Dinah and Aunt Chloe), one mulatto mammy (Mammy), one heroic quadroon slave mother (Eliza), one quadroon slave mother as "mad woman in the attic" (Emmeline), one unnamed suicidal slave mother, and the drunken slave mother, Prue.

Stowe's knowledge of slave motherhood begins with the belief that their motherhood is best understood and articulated by the loss of children. When her infant son died in 1851, Harriet Beecher Stowe wrote, "It was at his dying and at his grave that I learned what a poor slave mother may feel when her child is torn away from her."[14] This kind of sentiment is just one of the many reasons that *Uncle Tom's Cabin* is often called the mother's book. It might be more accurate to call it "the-mothers-without-children-book"; of the six slave mothers in *Uncle Tom,* five of them face the real or threatened danger of separation from their children. As well, the primary white mother of the novel loses her only child to death. Stowe frames her antislavery argument with the powerful concept of slave mothers in absentia. As a result, *surrogate mothering* becomes the primary means for Stowe to simulate mother-child relationships. One of those surrogate relationships is that of the black slave nurse and the white charge.

Little Eva's "Mammy" appears toward the middle of the book and is introduced to the reader as a "middle aged mulatto woman of very respectable appearance." Her relationship with Eva is dramatically juxtaposed with that of Eva's own mother, the fragile, cranky Marie St. Clare. Eva's "rapturous" greeting makes her mother ill. But Mammy "did not tell her that she made her head ache, but on the contrary, she hugged her, and laughed, and cried, till her sanity was a thing to be doubted of" (109). Marie St. Clare's and Mammy's comparative maternity is illustrated through their interaction with one child, the earth angel, little Eva. The reader's criticism of Eva's mother is to be tempered by our relief or gratitude that Eva has a mammy strong enough to withstand her childish enthusiasm.

Although Stowe emphasizes Mammy's role as Eva's nurse, Mammy's primary function in the St. Clare household is as Marie's personal maid. During a discussion between St. Clare, Marie, and Ophelia, both St. Clare and Marie agree that Mammy is "the best creature living" and that Marie could not manage without her. Yet Marie insists that Mammy is selfish because she is difficult to awaken in the middle of the night when Marie needs her. The demands on her time as Marie's maid are therefore more central to her character than her relationship with little Eva. Her relationship with Eva is described only three times—when Eva returns from the boat trip with Uncle Tom, when Eva gives Mammy her locket to take to church, and when Eva is dying.

The scene following Eva's return is the only time Mammy actually speaks at any length. Eva's charity and generosity toward slaves is demonstrated when she offers Mammy a piece of expensive jewelry (120). We learn nothing about Mammy except that her head aches from her fatigue, presumably a result of Marie's incessant demands on her time and energy. Marie dismisses Mammy's familial relations and her complaints of illness with a wave of her hand: "Mammy is just like all the rest of them—makes such a fuss about every little headache or finger-ache; it'll never do to encourage it—never!" (113). Eva gives Mammy a lock of her hair, addressing her as "dear, good, kind Mammy," and Mammy says, "O, Miss Eva, don't see how I can live without ye, no how!" (192). Finally, we hear the last of Mammy when Eva is dying; again, her role as Marie's personal maid is emphasized:

Poor Mammy's heart yearned towards her darling; but she found no opportunity, night or day, as Marie declared that the state of her mind was such it as impossible for her to rest; and, of course, it was against her principle to let anyone else rest. . . . So that stolen interviews and momentary glimpses [of Eva] were all she could obtain. (193)

Mammy's and Eva's affection for one another is established with some subtlety, and Mammy is one of the best examples of mammy characters whose children are made invisible so they don't compete with her nursling. Stowe skillfully suggests that what is important is that Mammy at least has Eva to "mother" since she must be separated from her own children. Marie calls Mammy's children "dirty little things" (112), insisting that Mammy is not capable of true maternal affection because she is black. Of course the irony is that Marie has limited maternal feeling for her own daughter. In this surrogate relationship, we are meant to be relieved that the two have each other—since Eva's mother is so lacking in maternal feeling and since Mammy has so much maternal feeling and is away from her own children. This kind of emotional matchmaking also happens with Topsy and Miss Ophelia; Stowe wants us to believe that these two characters need each other.

In contrast, Mammy's attachment to Eva is much different from Aunt Chloe's relationship with Mas'r George. Aunt Chloe is characterized as more of a plantation family cook than baby nurse, but her preferential treatment of Mas'r George at the expense of her own children links her to the most stereotypical mammy character defined in chapter 1.

What does Chloe reveal about the evolution of the mammy figure at this particular time? I argue that Aunt Chloe is the fly in the ointment for those critics who position *Uncle Tom's Cabin* as a novel about the redeeming qualities of maternal love. In his essay "Mothers, Husbands, and Uncle Tom," Stephen Railton evaluates the idolatry of motherhood in Uncle Tom, and asserts: "Stowe cannot imagine an adversary more potent than mother-love." Stowe also cannot imagine Aunt Chloe as an embodiment of that love.

Within the range of mammy characters Aunt Chloe is, however, a complex and fascinating character often ignored or misinterpreted by critics. She is a rare example of a fictional slave mother who is granted instances of deliberate influential action. The first and perhaps most important action comes when she purposely delays serving a meal so that Eliza can escape with her son, Harry, in chapter 7.

Feminist critics have often interpreted this scene as an example of successful cooperative effort between a white mistress and a black female slave, arguing that Mrs. Shelby and Aunt Chloe conspire together to delay the meal, thus allowing Eliza's escape. Mrs. Shelby doesn't actually take any action to assist Chloe with the "mishaps" in the kitchen or to help Eliza to run away. Mrs. Shelby's role is almost negligent in the scene: "An impression seemed to reign among the servants generally that missis wouldn't be particularly disobliged by delay" (35). If we force an alliance between Aunt Chloe and Mrs. Shelby, we miss the very important point that the *slaves* worked together to assist Eliza, an example of the historical truth that fugitive slaves relied upon the cooperation of other slaves. This example of Aunt Chloe's loyalty to the slave community is completely antithetical to prototypical mammy-behavior and is part of the complexity of Chloe's characterization. We need to rethink feminist interpretations of Aunt Chloe that place her in the position that contemporary African American women are often forced into: an uncomfortable nexus of gender loyalty competing with race loyalty. This interpretation leads readers to overlook the interaction between Aunt Chloe and George. They are bonded, not only in the traditional mammy-charge relationship, but also as the only characters that take decisive measures to save Uncle Tom's life. George declares to Tom, "Aunt Chloe and I have been talking about it. I told her not to fear; I'll see to it" (67). Although Stowe never explicitly states that Aunt Chloe is George's nurse, their interaction in chapter 2 is typical of the nurse-charge relationship. Chloe caters to George's every whim, pushing her own children aside to please him:

> Here you, Mose and Pete! Get out de way, you niggers!
> Get away, Polly, honey, mammy'll give her baby somefin, by and by. Now. Mas'r George, you jest take off dem books, and set down now with my old man, and I'll take up de sausage, and have de first griddle full of cakes on, you know your old aunty'd keep the best for you. (15)

Chloe's impatience with her children seems extreme when compared with her relationship with George. Although he comes to the cabin to teach Uncle Tom to write, George spends more time talking to Aunt Chloe than teaching Uncle Tom. It is most alarming that when Mose and Pete play rambunctiously, Chloe gets irritated, and kicks at them, asking, "Can't ye be decent when white folks comes to see ye?" Is Chloe behaving like a good hostess or a good servant here? There is essentially no difference between the two in a constructed domestic space where race trumps biology and Aunt Chloe is depicted as an agent reinforcing the hierarchy of the slave system within her own home, where George's race assures him special privileges.

Chloe's behavior in this scene is an excellent example of a stereotypical mammy, and this characterization is pivotal. Chloe makes her own children wait while she feeds a young white boy, allowing him to throw food at them and give her orders. She has impressed upon her children that their behavior must be modified because George is "white folks" (even implying that he has come to see them) and finally she loses her patience and gives them a "formidable" slap. In the only scene of the novel where a slave mother who is not mulatto is shown with her own children at length; nearly every word stresses her preference for George. Her children have learned that even in the slave quarters mammy's children are secondary, and most certainly a nuisance compared with this very clever white child. Aunt Chloe's obligation to George extends past the big house and into her own kitchen. Such extended and voluntary obligation translates into an unabated choice of George over her biological children.

Particularly disturbing in this scene is the way both Chloe and George mistreat the three slave children. When George is finished eating, he throws the children his leftovers, the same way his father threw sections of an orange to Harry in the first chapter. "'Here, you Mose, Pete,' he said, breaking off liberal bits, and throwing it at them; 'you want some, don't you?'" (17). Mose and Pete behave exactly the way one would assume little monkeys play, rolling about uncontrollably under the table amid food and dirt. The baby, on the other hand, is described like a piece of crockery, which Chloe "polished, until she shone" (17). We hardly sympathize with them, even as they are about to lose their father, because they do not seem like children at all. We cannot imagine Chloe clutching these children to her breast and risking her life for their safety because we aren't supposed to think of Chloe as *that kind of slave mother*. Chloe's representation as a mammy figure is limited here by her function as foil to Eliza, the *heroic slave mother*.

Although Aunt Chloe gushes over Mas'r George in her cabin, she later has some very harsh words about his father when Tom is sold to Haley. As Tom tries to convince her to be more Christian in her forgiveness, Chloe invokes an incredibly powerful maternal image when describing the horror of slave trading and the inhumanity of men like Haley:

> "Don't dey tear der suckin' baby right off his mother's breast, and sell him, and der little children as is crying and holding on by her clothes,— Don't dey pull 'em off and sells em? Don't dey tear wife and husband

apart?" said Aunt Chloe beginning to cry, "when it's jest takin' the very life on 'em—and all the while does they feel one bit,—don't dey drink and smoke, and take it uncommon easy? Lor', if the devil don't get them, what's he good for?" (36)

In this scene, Chloe's words suggest a philosophy so diametrically opposed to that of her husband that the reader may wonder how they managed to live in the same house. Chloe encourages Tom to run away with Eliza, and then she comes up with a plan to earn money so that she can buy her husband herself. Aunt Chloe's behavior makes her an enigma in the long list of mammy characters, yet this diatribe is also inconsistent with some of her other beliefs.

This speech contradicts most of Chloe's characterization earlier in the novel. When Tom has difficulty with his writing, for example, Chloe points out how much better George is at reading and writing, commenting on "how easy white folks al'us does things!" (14). Similarly when Mrs. Shelby spends too much time in the kitchen, Chloe's body is used to espouse Stowe's racial essentialism:

Now, Missis, do jist look at dem beautiful white hands o'yourn, with long fingers, and all a sparkling with rings, like my white lilies when de dew's on 'em; and look at my great black stumpin hands. Now, don't ye think dat de Lord must have meant me to make de pie-crust, and you to stay in de parlor? (16)

Isolating this passage for a moment, we see that Mrs. Shelby's hands are relative to natural *beauty,* like lilies sparkling with morning dew, fragile, feminine, and delicate. And Chloe's hands are relative to natural *strength,* like tree stumps, large and sturdy. The two examples of corporeal binaries discussed in Bakhtin's *Rabelais and His World* come to mind when we consider the two types of feminine bodies presented in this dichotomy. The examples from Bakhtin are, first, a body that is associated with selfishness and the "discredited bourgeois ego," and second, a body associated with generosity and the "collective ancestral body of popular folklore."[15] The latter has gained considerable standing in theoretical discourse because of its innovative move to foreground the grotesque body. This is slippery terrain. Is Bakhtin's body of popular folklore comparable to Stowe's body? Is a body of folklore the same as a folkloric body of the mammy? It seems almost reductive to peg Mrs. Shelby's body as "egoist and bourgeois" since she is the slave mistress and Aunt's Chloe's body as "generous" given both her body size and her penchant for feeding everyone. Aunt Chloe's emphasis on race and corporeality suggests that white women and white men are obviously and naturally superior to blacks. In keeping with traditional mammy characteristics, Chloe seems to accept her slave status as a divine destiny. Despite her tirade against slave traders, Chloe never comments on her own status as chattel, never relates her life as a slave to the institution of slavery that requires the evil slave dealers. She never articulates any longing for freedom for herself and for her children (as we see in Harriet Jacobs's narrative). Her complaint—or Stowe's complaint through Chloe—is not with the practice of owning slaves, but with selling slaves away from their families.

What are we to make of Chloe's abolitionist rhetoric if she believes that her *own body* is evidence of her inferiority? Additionally, why does Chloe direct her tongue-lashing at Tom, instead of at Mr. Shelby or Haley? In short, Chloe's remarks provide an opportunity for Stowe to impress her readers with Tom's unwavering faith. When Tom reminds Chloe that God's grace will give her the strength to forgive inhuman slave dealers, Tom's Christianity effectively neutralizes Chloe's subversive potential. Stowe characterizes Chloe as a recognizable mammy figure, and then uses her to espouse her own opinions.

What kind of mother is Aunt Chloe? She is utterly unlike any of the other slave mothers in the novel (whose devotion to their children or grief over their loss is quite palpable). Chloe is a mammy-mother, one who falls outside of the cult of true motherhood and well within the cult of true mammyhood.

More significantly, Aunt Chloe serves as a device to further isolate Eliza as the only *tragic slave mother*. A different, more maternal, interaction between Aunt Chloe and her children might undermine this theme in Stowe's book. Despite her good intentions, Aunt Chloe, like several other slave characters, is part of the vocabulary of the proslavery plantation fiction that Stowe might have found offensive. This is an excellent example of what I call the "mammy trap." Although Stowe has given Chloe an intriguing complexity, she is unable to break free from the fact that even in an abolitionist novel, mammy characters behave a certain way. Aunt Chloe is the character that fully exposes Stowe's limitations as a writer. Despite creating an enigmatic character in Aunt Chloe, Stowe is still unable to have her truly transcend typical mammy behavior. As a result, Aunt Chloe's actions toward Mas'r George and her own children are part of the prescriptive mammy that Stowe is unable to *write* around or against.

Reconstructing Slave Motherhood/Rewriting Mammy

Stowe's memorable depiction of Aunt Chloe with her children may have provoked Frederick Douglass to respond to one text that far exceeded his own autobiography as a best-seller. It is precisely the nurturing that Chloe denies her children that Douglass makes a point of writing into the second version of his life story. Chloe's children, Mose and Pete, "the pile of woolly heads and glistening eyes" that hungrily watch George eat, are the very characters to which fugitive slave author Frederick Douglass would be most likely to relate. His own childhood in slavery was filled with both physical and emotional hungers, but it is the denial of adequate food that he remembers most clearly and conveys most convincingly. Food also becomes symbolic of the kinship ties that he craves and is denied repeatedly in the first six chapters of *My Bondage and My Freedom*. The tension between the Douglass and the Stowe texts reveals how this African American intellectual and former slave was driven to contend with depictions of slave motherhood in popular fiction. Douglass responds to the slave mothers in *Uncle Tom's Cabin* by presenting his readers with two slave mothers that were missing from Stowe's mother menagerie.

In Douglass's *Narrative,* he made his own maternal loss a powerful metaphor for familial loss among African Americans during slavery. However, in the ten years between his first *Narrative* and *My Bondage and My Freedom* (1855), Frederick Douglass's mother is miraculously transformed from the solemn, hard-working slave who makes a few nocturnal visits to her son into a heroic slave mother who saves him from near starvation. Douglass expands his mother's character from two short paragraphs to five pages; this could be seen as a strategy establishing a sentimental emblem of home that was not written into his original *Narrative*.[16] While his more detailed account of his mother has been key in the attempts to understand Douglass's attitude about his biracial heritage, it is never interpreted for the powerful message he transmits about motherhood under slavery, or for its subtle rebuttals to the two mammy-type characters in *Uncle Tom's Cabin*.

In her study of nineteenth-century maternal figures, Stephanie Smith points out that in his revision Douglass uses the same paradigms of sentimental fiction about his mother's role in his life that Stowe uses. But "his revisions accomplish something other than a simple transposition of white sentimental motherhood to black slave women . . . his revision of African American motherhood shows how he used the sentimental maternal icon to create an ideal American homeland."[17]

In addition to creating this ideal, Douglass is speaking directly to Stowe through his revision of black maternity. Let me recount the revision briefly here: Douglass's mother appears out of the night at the moment when he is being punished by his master's cook, Aunt Katy. Denied his dinner, young Frederick is so hungry he cannot sleep and resorts to stealing a few kernels of Indian corn to roast in the fire. Harriet Bailey sweeps into the room, chastises Aunt Katy, and gives her son a large, heart-shaped, glazed ginger cake. The attention to minute detail here is important. The cake is not just specifically *ginger,* but glazed and *heart-shaped,* features that embellish the whole scene conspicuously. Douglass's effort to include particulars like this was undoubtedly made to lend validity to the memory. Ironically, these are the very details that aroused my initial suspicion, and led me to consider that this revision could be a response to *Uncle Tom's Cabin* with Aunt Katy as a rewriting of Aunt Dinah and Harriet Bailey a revised Eliza.

Aunt Katy is the slave mother who bears the greatest similarity to both Aunt Dinah and Aunt Chloe; she, too, is a valued cook and "the only mother who was permitted to retain her children around her" (Douglass, *My Bondage and My Freedom* 51).[18] Douglass tells us she is "ill tempered and cruel," but insists that she was "not destitute of maternal feelings" (52). Douglass gives his readers a nightmarish version of plantation domesticity to counter Stowe's. Instead of a jolly mammy serving hotcakes we find an almost demonic Aunt Katy starving Douglass and injuring one of her own sons with a butcher knife. Embedded in this portrait of a "fiendishly brutal" slave mother are clues about how some slave women contended with the duality of their positions as enslaved mothers. Aunt Katy's behavior strikes us as not only unusual but unnatural. Perhaps Douglass poses the question, What happens to the natural properties of motherhood within the unnatural institution of slavery? With a brilliant nod to Stowe's penchant for absent slave mothers, Douglass shows us that present slave mothers also suffer from their oppression. Aunt Katy's psychic turmoil reveals an aspect of emotional desperation that tells us much more about the realities of slave motherhood than Stowe's portraits of Aunt Dinah or Aunt Chloe.

Similarly, Douglass uses Harriet Bailey to help establish an alternative heroic slave mother—one very different from Stowe's ice-jumping Eliza because her maternal courage is not linked to her white ancestry.

Douglass's specific concern with the image of the slave mother is seen relatively early in *My Bondage and My Freedom*. In a passage that precedes the updated description of his mother, he, like Stowe, bemoans the absence of parental rights for slave mothers: "The slave mother can be spared long enough from the field . . . when it adds another name to a master's ledger, but not long enough to receive the joyous reward afforded by the intelligent smiles of her child" (39). Douglass's words echo Stowe's theme that the slave master replaces the mother's authority in a slave child's life, making the natural maternal bonds invalid. He also directly addresses an issue that Stowe fails to broach in her novel: the connection between the birth of slave children and an increase in the master's wealth. (Later we will see that Harriet Jacobs also writes quite eloquently about the pernicious monetary aspect of slave motherhood.)

In his *Narrative* Douglass never makes any general statement about slave mothers. The original two pages addressing how infrequently he saw his mother don't confront enslaved motherhood as a broader issue. It is apparent, then, that this section was a significant additional commentary that Douglass felt compelled to include. The strategic placement of this argument directly before the extended recollection of his mother has not been seen as a defensive measure, yet the tone of this passage is *responsive,* not informative. This passage also sets up the entrance of Harriet Bailey as a woman who defeats the odds to see her son and begins to prime the reader for an account of an extraordinary slave mother.

Besides nourishing her child, Harriet Bailey defends him against the crazy Aunt Katy, leading Douglass to realize that he was not just a child, but also a child with a mother. It is implicit that he has a "good mother" who may be powerless to free him from slavery, but can at least protect him from a "bad mother." His introduction to the ginger cake scene is also worth noting:

> And now, dear reader, a scene occurred which was altogether worth beholding, and to me it was instructive as well as interesting. The friendless and hungry boy is in his extremist need—and when he dare not look for succor—found himself in the strong, protecting arms of a mother; a mother who was at the moment (being endowed with high powers of manner as well as matter) more than a match for all his enemies! (41)

The sudden switch to the objective third-person narrator is a stunning example of Douglass's narrative strategy: the use of a more objective voice at key moments in his tale. Douglass places himself in the same position as the "dear reader," and becomes an observer of this scene, instead of a participant. The author has created a space for the reader to participate in the narrative, thus making the reader a partner in the telling of the tale.

Instead of drawing me to identify a recovered memory, I understand that this is a melodramatic scene written into an existing text. Even the formality of the line that follows "I shall never forget the indescribable expression of her countenance" strikes a cold note in an episode intended to be heart-warming. The "friendless and hungry boy" finds himself—not in the arms of his mother—but of "a mother." First he evokes a generic identification (she is generic or like any mother); then he moves to supply his own definition of "mother." The final maternal image is one of supreme heroics.

Douglass's diminution of his father's role in the *Narrative,* from presenting him as his white master to virtual nonpresence in *My Bondage,* is curious; this updated narrative account of his mother is truly remarkable. In the 1845 *Narrative* Douglass writes that he can barely recall his mother: "I never saw my mother, to know her as such, more than four or five times in my life and each of those times was very short in duration and at night." Ten years later Douglass reports that his knowledge of his mother is "very scanty," but it has become "very distinct." Douglass writes: "Her personal appearance and bearing are ineffaceably stamped upon my memory." He concludes, "It has been a life-long, standing grief to me, that I knew so little of my mother; and that I was so early separated from her." Not only has Douglass suddenly recalled his mother's appearance, but he also has come to feel "life-long, standing grief," whereas just ten years earlier her death struck him as would the death of a complete stranger: "Never having enjoyed to any considerable extent her soothing presence, her tender and watchful care, I received the tidings of her death with much the same emotions I should have probably felt at the death of a stranger."

Later, Douglass uses Harriet Bailey as a vehicle to interpret the identity of her famous son. His decision to relate his mother to an Egyptian pharaoh, then, merely embellishes his first characterization of his mother as "sedate." In addition, it befits a distinguished figure to have a distinguished mother, despite the gender difference. In his detailed biography of Douglass, Dickson Preston makes the most innovative analysis of the likeness between Harriet Bailey and Ramses II; his argument is based upon the author's description of the image as being an "ideal Indian" type. Preston goes to great lengths to prove that Douglass identified with Indians, as an explanation for his choice of physical *re*-presentation. Other biographers suggest that this anticipates Douglass's later theory that the Egyptians were black. Douglass made an incredibly daring and calculated move in magnifying his mother to such a grandiose state. He purposely evoked a figure that would have an impact on slave mother representation. An illustration of a male pharaoh is an unusual maternal portrait; but if Douglass risked altering one of the most desperate features of his childhood, it must have been for truly important reasons. When Douglass scholars debate his apparent self-creation, they fail to see the transformed Harriet Bailey as anything more than one piece in the Douglass puzzle.

Most scholars don't read the elaborated passages about his mother as an overt act of defiance. All of Douglass's biographers ignore the fact that the author of the most popular and well-read slave narrative actually changed a recollection, as if his memory had suddenly improved. His motivation is purely political; he uses his mother as a new symbolic slave to reclaim her from the world of sentimental novels and minstrel shows where white people created blacks for white consumption. Douglass "finds" his mother in the pages of a book documenting the history of mankind, proving her a historical figure, not a fictional character (39).

Shifting the focus from interpreting Harriet Bailey as an "enabler" for her son, toward a broader reading that views her as Douglass's chosen image of African American motherhood, we can see that she was a suitably representative slave mother who would combat the stereotypes that appear in plantation fiction. Harriet Bailey is a mother that blacks could be proud of because she is most loyal to *her* children and therefore to the black community, thus countering the depiction of the mammy defined in chapter 1.

In the tradition of Stowe's Eliza Harris, Frederick Douglass's mother comes to represent an "antimammy" figure. Douglass uses her to establish for the American public a heroic slave mother who is different from Eliza and who is not a stereotypical mammy character. The prefix *anti-* connotes an intention that one figure can actually destroy another; the presence of a heroic slave mother in a narrative like Douglass's can correct the damaging image of the mammy. Through the demonic Aunt Katy and the heroic Harriet Bailey, Douglass offers his readers two divergent examples of slave mothers—two renditions of the mammy figure. When Douglass writes that his mother "read Aunt Katy a lecture that she never forgot" (41), he establishes both women as warrior figures in a battle of good mother versus bad mother. These mother-warriors then challenge our assumptions about the jolly cooks of Stowe's imagination.

I have another object in view—it is to come to you just as I am a poor slave
mother—not to tell you what I have heard but what I have seen and what I
have suffered and if there is any sympathy to be given—let it be to the thousands
of slave mothers that are still in bondage.
　—HARRIET JACOBS

Harriet Jacobs adds her voice to this discussion on slave mothers through the persona of Linda Brent in *Incidents in the Life of a Slave Girl* (1861). Like Douglass, Jacobs recognized Stowe's power as a popular author and a key voice in the antislavery movement. Jacobs's interaction with Stowe was fraught with tension, however. Jacobs wanted Stowe's help in writing her story and asked her close friend Amy Post to approach the famous author for her. Stowe arrogantly informed Post that she was sending the manuscript to Jacobs's employer Mrs. Willis for *verification*. If she were then satisfied with the result, she would consider using it herself in her *Key to Uncle Tom's Cabin.* Stowe's insensitivity to Jacobs surfaced again when Jacobs suggested that her daughter Louisa accompany Stowe on her trip to England. Stowe rejected that idea as well, insisting that the British would "spoil" Louisa beyond repair. Jacobs wrote to Stowe that she wanted to send her daughter abroad as "a very good representative of a 'Southern Slave'" (xix). It seems more likely that Jacobs wanted to challenge any stereotypes the British might have about slave children with her nearly white and well-mannered daughter.

It is not surprising that when Jacobs picked up her pen to write her narrative without Stowe's help, she would respond to the novel in some way or another. Since Jacobs was employed as a baby nurse while she wrote *Incidents,* this is not only the autobiography of a slave mother, writing on behalf of other slave mothers, but the story of a slave mother who served as a mammy as well.

Jacobs challenges the assumption that Stowe had some mystical hold on American readers when she insists on making room for her own narrative as an alternative account of enslaved motherhood. Hazel Carby has called Jacobs's book "the most sophisticated sustained narrative dissection of the convention of true womanhood by a black author before emancipation."[19]

In the first chapter of *Incidents,* simply called "Childhood," we see that Jacobs is unable to write about her own family without also writing extensively about the white family that owned her. Her own family is sewn together with her master's family, almost like the topsy-turvy dolls discussed earlier.

Jacobs describes her grandmother as a slave who fulfilled numerous roles for her owner "from cook and wet nurse to seamstress." This account of her grandmother's life supports my argument in the first section of this chapter that mammies had access to sewing materials. When writing about her grandmother, Jacobs strings black and white family members together in one extended family. "My mother's mistress was the daughter of my grandmother's mistress" (7).

The compelling implication here is that slave women who are baby nurses constitute a second blood line, a milk line that connects slave women to the young white children who are quite often their masters. Linda gives a name to the relationship of two babies of different races being nursed by the same woman, calling her mother's mistress her "foster sister." Linda tells us that her grandmother was forced to deprive her own child in order to feed her mistress's child. When Flint threatens to send Linda to work on the plantations if she continues to refuse his sexual advances, her Grandmother makes a desperate attempt to remind him of her sacrifice to his family. "She said she would go to the doctor, and remind him how long and how faithfully she had served in the family and how she had taken her own baby from her breast to nourish his wife" (Jacobs 85). In this same opening chapter, Linda confides to the reader that as a very young child her own mistress was like a mother to her. Linda's life reflects the same tradition of surrogate mothering that we see in *Uncle Tom's Cabin,* where the lives of blacks and whites seem inextricably linked.

The chapter moves quickly from these touching references to closeness between the two families to the cruel reality of slavery:

> She possessed but few slaves; and at her death those were all distributed among her relatives. Five of them were my grandmother's children, and had shared the same milk that nourished her mother's children. Notwithstanding my grandmother's long and faithful service to her owners, not

one of her children escaped the auction block. These God-breathing machines are no more, in the sight of her masters, than the cotton they plant, or the horses they tend. (8)

Jacobs emphasizes the brutality of this sale by reminding the reader that her grandmother's service as a faithful mammy did not protect her children in any way. Jacobs is able to equate slave children with money more effectively than Stowe because of her sense of subtlety and her firsthand experience. When Linda herself gives birth, Flint reminds her that she has only increased his property. "Dr. Flint continued his visits, to look after my health; and he did not fail to remind me that my child was an addition to his stock of slaves" (60).

The death imagery surrounding Jacobs's recollection of her son's birth is striking in many ways. Jacobs's ability to evoke her readers' sympathy and then transcend sentiment is the true genius of this narrative. For example, in this passage, she skillfully invokes similar Christian prayers that comforted Uncle Tom, and challenges their meaning for slave mothers:

> Sometimes I wished that he might die in infancy. God tried me. My darling became very ill. The bright eyes grew dull, and the little feet and hands were so icy cold that I thought death had already touched them. I had prayed for his death, but never so earnestly as I now prayed for his life; and my prayer was heard. Alas, what mockery it is for a slave mother to try to pray back her dying child to life! Death is better than slavery. (62)

I read Jacobs's firsthand account of motherhood as another revision of the mammy figure. Jacobs repeatedly evokes the plight of slave mothers as a trope to a larger point about the inhumanity of the institution. For example, while she is hiding in her grandmother's attic she witnesses a harrowing scene: "I saw a woman rush wildly by, pursued by two men. She was a slave, the wet nurse of her mistress's children. For some trifling offense her mistress ordered her to be stripped and whipped." In a passage reminiscent of Clotel's suicide in William Wells Brown's earlier novel (*Clotel*, 1853),[20] Jacobs tell us that in order "to escape the degradation and the torture, she rushed to the river, jumped in, and ended her wrongs in death" (122). In this passage we can see how well Jacobs knew that her mid-nineteenth-century white readers would immediately be moved by this reference to the beloved mammy figure. Antebellum and post–Civil War narratives by white southerners presented the mammy as the most loved and therefore most protected slave on the plantation; Jacobs's words present a stark contrast to that sentimental myth.

Additionally, describing a scene where several men chase one woman, Jacobs knew that her readers would be affected by the woman's vulnerability. She then quickly links the words "wet nurse," "mistress," "children," and "trifling offense." Thus, her readers would no longer care about the men pursuing the young slave, but about the cruelty of a mistress who would "torture" the slave woman who nurtured her children. Jacobs convinces us of the white mistress's insensitivity without using examples as obvious as Stowe's irritable and insensitive Marie St. Clare.

In the scene from chapter 13 presenting the Methodist meeting she attends, Jacobs echoes Douglass's and Stowe's theme that the role of religious slaveholders is particularly insidious. The teacher of this meeting is a white town constable, a slave trader with a penchant for violence. When a slave mother rises to relay the horror of having one child after another sold from her, this man's laughter resonates with Frederick Douglass's references to his former master's religious hypocrisy. Her own motherhood functions as an opportunity for Jacobs to make a point about the special plight of female slaves. When her daughter is born, she points out that she is only able to associate female slaves with sexual exploitation: "Slavery is terrible for men; but it is far more terrible for women. Superadded to their burden common to all, they have wrongs and sufferings and mortifications, peculiarly their own" (77). Later, when she is sent to the plantation to work, she is separated from her children and, reminiscent of Douglass's mother Harriet Bailey, travels a great distance to steal a few moments with her children. She begins to formulate her plans for escape during these long, arduous trips.

While Douglass was able to exercise a fair amount of independence in planning his escape, Jacobs delineates how children function both as inspiration and hindrance for a fugitive slave mother: "I could have made my escape alone; but it was more for my helpless children than for myself that I longed for freedom. . . . I would not have taken it at the expense of leaving them in slavery" (89). Jacobs's devotion to her children here is clear to the reader, yet it is questioned by her grandmother, who asks her: "Linda, do you want to kill your old grandmother? Do you mean to leave your helpless children? I am old now, and cannot do for your babies as I once did for you" (91). Being a "good" mother became an obsession for Linda Brent. As a result, she is forced to devise a plan that allows her to escape from slavery without leaving her children and becomes a kind of mother-angel who is able to watch over her children from a distance.

Linda often calls her grandmother "the good grandmother," emphasizing her kindness and generosity. What makes her grandmother good is not limited to her kindness but her value system; she holds Linda to standards that are ultimately painful to her, but standards that Linda respects nonetheless. She writes, "I feel that the slave woman ought not to be judged by the same standard as others" (56), and Linda seems to address her white female readers *as well as* her grandmother. Her grandmother is guilty of unrealistic expectations of Linda's purity, but more importantly, she continually insists that Linda be a "good mother." Her grandmother proposes her own hierarchy of maternal flaws: it is terrible to suffer Dr. Flint's abuse, terrible to be a mother without marriage, but nothing is worse than being judged a bad mother.

Once Linda escapes to the North, her first offer of employment is as a baby nurse for the British Mrs. Bruce. In the short chapter "A Home Found," Linda struggles to support her daughter Ellen while caring for the Bruce children. She laments: "I longed to be entirely free to act a mother's part towards my children" (169). With these few words, Jacobs has used Linda to articulate the essence of the mammy's dilemma: how can one mother take care of another woman's children and still be a good mother to her own?

As mentioned in the introduction, Jean Fagan Yellin has unearthed a treasure that is well worth the price of her biography of Jacobs, photographs of three black dolls made by Jacobs while she was hiding in New York and working as a child caretaker. Yellin has dedicated herself tirelessly to discovering and publicizing the evidence of the authenticity of Jacobs's book. The dolls in figure 15 were passed down within that family and remain the property of the family.

To my knowledge this is the first time that these historic dolls have appeared in a color photograph. One wears a long-sleeved, light-colored striped dress with black sash with lace collar; this doll may be unfinished, or may have been made without a nose or mouth, and either was made without hair or a hat or they have disappeared. The middle doll is dressed in beautiful fabric that may have originally been red and has faded to orange, with matching turban knotted in the front. This doll wears a lace-edged slip underneath her dress with bell sleeves, and a black waist sash. She has a complete face with eyes, nose, and mouth and tiny gold hoop earrings sewn to the side of her face and a gold-beaded necklace. The third doll wears a darker-colored dress, with white edging on the sleeves and around the high collar. This doll is decorated with the same kind of gold-beaded necklace (slightly larger); the skirt of her dress has decorative piping about an inch above the hem.

These beautiful dolls reveal Jacobs's exquisite sewing skills; the attention to tiny detail is very impressive. What does it mean that Jacobs chose to make black dolls for the white child for whom she was caretaker? She may have missed her own children so much that the dolls were comforting to her.

Incidents is perhaps the most revealing published narrative written by a slave mother who served as a baby nurse, and her experiences simply do not support or affirm the mammy-charge relations seen in chapter 1. Linda admits that baby Mary's affection for her helped her to feel more at home with the Bruces and that she was a comfort to her later when she was forced to hide from Flint again. But she never alludes to the possibility that she loves Mary more than her own child. Ironically, this fugitive slave mother who resembles Eliza Harris in complexion is fleeing from slave catchers with a white baby, instead of her own.

What Linda does tell us about her short stint as a mammy is that the role *allowed her to "pass" by becoming almost invisible* as a fugitive slave. Black women traveling with white babies was so commonplace in New York at this time that taking Mary Bruce with her made her less conspicuous than she would have been traveling alone. Brent becomes invisible by slipping on the "mammy cloak." Years later the famous lawyer Clarence Darrow made a similar observation about how the presence of a white child makes African American women more tolerable and acceptable to whites who would find her offensive by herself. In a patronizing lecture called "The Problem of the Negro" given on May 19, 1901, to an audience of African Americans at the Chicago Men's Club, Darrow detailed the complaints that a white southerner had made about the "odor" of African Americans on streetcars, and Darrow's reply: "'Well,' I said, 'what is the difference between the odor of the waiter bringing you a dinner and when he rides in a street car?' Well, he said, there was a difference. . . . Then he went on to tell how he loved his old black mammy. There is nothing wrong about the odor of the old black mammy . . . but when the most refined, delicate, clean, colored person in the world meets them upon terms of equality, then there is something wrong about their odor." Darrow draws this conclusion: "A black woman, no matter how black, may sit all day in a Pullman car if she is holding a white child on her lap; nobody objects to that, but if the white child was not there nobody could possibly stand it to be anywhere near that black woman."[21]

Jacobs's writing is admirable in its ability to sustain the tension between poignancy and sentimentality, especially when she describes her intimate connection with baby Mary and Mrs. Bruce's suggestion that Mary offers Linda Brent a unique kind of safety.

> My place as nurse could not be supplied immediately, and this generous, sympathizing lady proposed that I should carry her baby away. It was a comfort to have the child with me; for the heart is reluctant to be torn away from every object it loves. . . . When I spoke of the sacrifice she was making, in depriving herself of her dear baby she replied, "It is better for you to have baby with you, Linda; for if they get on your track, they will be obliged to bring the child to me; and then, if there is a possibility of saving you, you shall be saved." (194)

We should remember that Mrs. Bruce is not Mary's biological mother. It seems very likely that she might have been uncomfortable with the idea of being responsible for Mary since Linda has been her primary caretaker, her mammy.

Unlike Douglass, Jacobs felt no need to be subtle or discreet about the fact that she shared an audience with Harriet Beecher Stowe and hoped to be equally influential. Jacobs gives her readers insights into enslaved motherhood that Stowe was simply incapable of offering. When we read, critique, and teach *Uncle Tom's Cabin,* we hear Harriet Beecher Stowe imploring us to look at the plight of the slave mother; Harriet Jacobs boldly demands that we listen to the slave mother's tale.

The dolls and Harriet Jacobs's narrative enclose this chapter with the handiwork of slave mothers. Whether they used pens or needles, these women were driven to represent their experiences as both blood mothers and surrogate mothers. As a needle sewed one black doll to one white one, Jacobs's grandmother's milk united her own children with the children who owned them. The topsy-turvy dolls also suggest a metaphor for these white-black narratives of slavery and motherhood.

The compelling images from the beginning of this chapter, of black women picking the cotton for white women's sewing, of dolls joined at their very center, and of William McWhorter's aunt breast-feeding her master's child while her own child cried for her attention—all of these images need to be read together so that we may see these slave mothers in a completely new light. Perhaps these mothers swallowed their pain until they could get their hands on a needle, some thread, and a few rags. And perhaps a slave mother could be comforted by sewing a doll with a black baby on one end and a white baby on the other as a gift for her daughter, and as a way of leaving some personal testimony about her own fragmented life.

CHAPTER THREE

Dishing Up Dixie: Recycling the Old South

The story of Aunt Jemima, whom we know as Pancake Queen,
Starts on an Old Plantation, in a charming Southern scene.
There, folks grow sweet magnolias and cotton in the sun,
And life was filled with happiness and old-time Southern fun.
   —QTD. IN MARILYN KERN-FOXWORTH,
    Aunt Jemima, Uncle Ben, and Rastus

In 1994, Grammy-winning singer Gladys Knight appeared in several television commercials advertising Aunt Jemima pancake mix and syrup. Knight was criticized for endorsing a product using a stereotyped African American woman as its trademark. Knight insisted that the Aunt Jemima logo had been appropriately updated—her headscarf had been replaced by a modern curly hairstyle and pearl earrings—and was no longer offensive. *Emerge* magazine responded with a short editorial called "It's the Stereotype, Stupid."[1] The piece included an illustration of Knight dressed, not as the new more modern Aunt Jemima, but as the older stereotype in headscarf, kerchief, and an enormous toothy smile. The caption reads: "Nothing is wrong in the face of it, but a subtext lurks beneath the Aunt Jemima ads." The author, Robert Bates, points out that although Quaker Oats gave Aunt Jemima a "makeover," there were still some disturbing aspects of the product, which continues to use the title *Aunt*. Bates describes her as a "comforting mammy icon" that "beams from the box." Jemima's trademark kerchief was removed, but her trademark smile is very much intact. Bates suggests that her accommodating smile is the problem: "Jemima's pancakes would work just fine, without the whopping smile. . . . Betty Crocker doesn't have to flash her teeth." There has always been a subtext lurking beneath the Aunt Jemima advertisements, one that has been consistent since the early twentieth century.

What does the Aunt Jemima trademark tell us about the significance of the mammy figure after Reconstruction? The advertising campaign that propelled Aunt Jemima from a popular attraction at the 1893 Columbian Exposition is reviewed here as an example of sophisticated, multimedia marketing. Her presence is made so pervasive by commercial media that she seems to block out other representations of African American womanhood.

As we see in the epigraph above, the most romanticized antebellum plantation life has always been the backdrop to the trademark portrait of Aunt Jemima. In these advertisements, the words *Old South, old time,* and *plantation* appear again and again as an incantation invoking the spirit of antebellum America. The early advertisements used the Aunt Jemima rag doll family as an incentive for using the pancake mix. Aunt Jemima is shown with her husband Rastus, whose name was later changed to Uncle Mose to avoid confusion with the Cream of Wheat man. (Uncle Mose was first introduced as the butler on the Higbee's plantation where Jemima lives.) Aunt Jemima and Uncle Mose appear with their four children, who are described as "comical pickaninnies." Their names reflect the fictional slave names of popular plantation literature: Abraham Lincoln, Dilsie, Zeb, and Dinah. The doll family is dressed in tattered clothing and all of them are barefoot.[2] A bizarre twist on the Aunt Jemima dolls is seen in an 1890s advertisement for Aunt Jemima pancake mix that advertises the rag doll family and another unique doll that was short lived: climbing Jemima, a doll modeled on a popular climbing monkey toy (fig. 16).

The later 1920s texts promise "old time plantation flavor" that was once available only to "Aunt Jemima's master and his guests" since it was "a secret from the South before the Civil War," "a famous recipe celebrated in Dixieland." We learn that Aunt Jemima is Colonel Higbee's "old mammy cook" whose incredible "fluffy plantation pancakes," with their "matchless plantation flavor" made the Rosewood household famous "among the plantations along the Mississippi River."[3]

This chapter first explores the role of antebellum romanticism by looking at early Aunt Jemima characterizations and her installment as mammy within the national household. Aunt Jemima is a key element of an early-twentieth-century idealized domesticity projected and promoted as inspired by old southern hospitality.

In 1889 Charles Rutt and Chris Underwood founded the Pearl Milling Company. They created the first ready-mixed pancake flour. Charles Rutt chose Aunt Jemima as advertising's first living trademark. In 1890 Aunt Jemima Manufacturing Company replaced Pearl Milling Company. Chris Underwood's brother Bert was responsible for registering the Aunt Jemima trademark.

In 1893 Aunt Jemima Manufacturing Company was sold to R. T. Davis Milling Company. Nancy Green debuted as Aunt Jemima at the World's Columbian Exhibition, Chicago, 1893. In 1914, the image of Aunt Jemima was so popular that the company was renamed the Aunt Jemima Mills Company. In 1926 Aunt Jemima Mills Company was sold to Quaker Oats Company for over four million dollars. In the 1940s, the pancake mix was redesigned to include a realistic photograph. In 1955 the Aunt Jemima Restaurant opened at Disneyland.[4]

During the 1920s Quaker Oats helped to construct this longing for the Old South, and the company's copywriters effectively transferred a romantic mythology of plantation fiction into the commercial arena. An emerging definition of American domesticity was then enriched and shaped by this fantasy by way of a happy slave narrative.

Second, this chapter examines the origins of the Aunt Jemima trademark, introduced at the 1893 Chicago World's Fair in juxtaposition with nineteenth-century black women's activism. This fair systematically excluded African Americans from most of its venues; one exception was the World's Congress of Representative Women, where several African American feminists spoke eloquently about racial tension and African American progress. Their presence provides a profound contrast to idealized "Old South" accompanying the Aunt Jemima phenomenon.

Awakening a "National Memory"

Elizabeth O'Leary uses the term "national family" provocatively in her look at representations of domestic servants in nineteenth-century American painting.[5] Does the "national family" have a mammy? How does answering this question help us better understand the preoccupation with representations of the mammy as the ubiquitous black domestic servant and childcare provider? Here I propose that Aunt Jemima's success as a trademark was predicated upon a fascinating interweaving of commerce, memory, and racial nostalgia that served as a "vehicle for post–Civil War national consolidation."[6]

At one point the most reliable means for consolidating the country involved inducing a kind of national amnesia about the history of slavery. Aunt Jemima was created to celebrate state-of-the-art technology through a pancake mix; she did not celebrate the promise of post-Emancipation progress for African Americans. Aunt Jemima's "freedom" was negated, or revoked, in this role because of the character's persona as a plantation slave, not a free black woman employed as a domestic. An African American woman, *pretending* to be a slave, was pivotal to the trademark's commercial achievement in 1893. Its success revolved around the fantasy of returning a black woman to a sanitized version of slavery. The Aunt Jemima character involved a regression of race relations, and her character helped usher in a prominent resurgence of the "happy slave" mythology of the antebellum South.

Nancy Green, a former slave from Kentucky, played the first Aunt Jemima. Green was a middle-aged woman living on the South Side of Chicago, working as a cook and housekeeper for a prominent judge. After a series of auditions, she was hired to cook and serve the new pancake recipe at the World's Fair. Part of her act was to tell stories from her own early slave life along with plantation tales written for her by a white southern sales representative. This combination of historic and mythic plantation was designed to perpetuate the "historical amnesia necessary for confidence in the American future." That this amnesia occurred at the expense of African American progress was clearly not an issue for the Pearl Milling Company, the inventor of Aunt Jemima.[7]

For the Pearl Milling Company the myth to be created is not just of black servitude, but servitude associated with slaveocracy. The nostalgia is not simply racial or class specific, but specific to the plantation South. It derived from a romanticized domestic ideal that reproduces and affirms the benign slavery popularized in the late nineteenth century by southern authors Joel Chandler Harris and Thomas Nelson Page in fiction, memoirs, and autobiographies.

"Racial nostalgia" and "national memory" met and merged at the exhibition where Nancy Green entertained a crowd with stories about Aunt Jemima's slave "childhood" in New Orleans.[8] The amalgamated concept that resulted raises questions about whether there was, in 1893, a national nostalgia for a common racial memory. The goal of this kind of advertising is to elicit a comforting memory by using familiar symbols: Aunt Jemima then affirms a remembered sense of a collective or unified American participation in slavery. The plantation kitchen symbolizes slaveocracy as a positive, enriching experience shared by white Americans in the North and in the South.

This unifying nostalgia for slaveocracy supplies a much-needed unification for the 1893 World's Fair. The southern ideal then displaces any historical facts of succession hostilities and the destructive Civil War. This cozy racial nostalgia becomes magnified and extends an invitation for all Americans to remember a time when Aunt Jemima cooked for the national family. This induced or planted recollection fueled Aunt Jemima's popularity; her familiarity was constructed as a universal reality. Aunt Jemima becomes a household product and household name; she is attributed with awakening a national remembrance of southern domesticity.

The Aunt Jemima trademark was constructed as part of the budding concept of an American Dream for the American family. One year after the Fair, the Pearl Milling Company introduced the Aunt Jemima paper doll family: five dolls that could be cut out from the pancake box. The Cream of Wheat chef was introduced in the early 1900s; there are some advertisements depicting Rastus with a small African American boy who dressed in a miniature version of his tall white hat and jacket. But whether this little boy was his son or a protégé is unclear. Aunt Jemima's paper doll family was one of the most popular company premiums; collectors still prize a complete set over the individual dolls.

What is more intriguing is the text accompanying the cutout dolls. The caption below the barefoot dolls reads: "Before the Receipt was sold." (Receipt is an archaism of the word recipe.) There is then an overlay of new elegant clothing to fit over the dolls, and the caption beneath reads: "After the Receipt was sold." By assigning the Aunt Jemima family a rags-to-riches biography, the milling company placed them within the Horatio Alger tradition of American possibility. This step integrated Aunt Jemima into the very fabric of a successful American culture.

This popular re-creation of an African American woman's life stood in direct opposition to the efforts of real African American women struggling to publicly assert their citizenship. As a symbol of racial harmony, Aunt Jemima proved to be the preferred version of African American womanhood—an exaltation of slaveocracy nostalgia. While Nancy Green represented one version of revisionist history, educated activists who would not sing slave songs or serve pancakes to white audiences were at the other end of the spectrum.

Stirring Up Trouble: African American Female Intelligentsia at the Columbian World's Fair

During the summer of 1890, the all-white Board of Lady Managers for the Columbian Fair was besieged by two African American women's organizations. The Woman's Colombian Association and the Women's Columbian Auxiliary Association wanted the women in charge to address the exclusion of African Americans from the fair's exhibitions. Both organizations were comprised of educated, middle-class women who wanted the fair to reflect the success of post-Emancipation African Americans. The latter organization was much clearer about its demands, requesting that the Lady Managers recognize it as a supplemental branch of the original board. The board had its hands full with white southern and northern women attempting to work together on a project "in spirit of national solidarity"; regional differences were proving to be enough of a challenge. Just the notion of interacting intimately with black women was insulting enough for one "Southern Lady" to publicly announce: "We will speak to Negroes and be kind to them as employees but we will not sit with them."[9]

The dispute continued for over a year. Eventually, the two African American women's organizations joined forces with other black women to take their cause all the way to Washington. Together they composed and circulated a petition outlining their charges of racism against the Board of Lady Managers:

> Shall the Negro woman of this country have a creditable display of their labor and skill at the World's Columbian Exposition? The Board of Lady Managers created by an act of congress, says no . . . Shall five million Negro women allow a small number of white women to ignore them in this the greatest opportunity to manifest their talent and ability in this the greatest expression of the age?[10]

The fair commission responded by making several minor concessions. First, Fannie Barrier Williams, an educator and political activist, was appointed to help supervise the exhibitions in the Woman's Building. The board also agreed to her suggestion that two African American clerks be appointed to solicit exhibitions of work by African Americans. Imogene Howard, a schoolteacher dedicated to publicizing the contributions of African American women, was also appointed to the New York contingent of Lady Managers to collect statistics of African American women's work and "provide an example of the progress they had made."[11] Last, Hallie Q. Brown, author of *Homespun Heroines and Other Women of Distinction* (1926) who served as Dean of Women at Tuskegee Institute under Booker T. Washington, was offered an unpaid position in the Department of Publicity and Promotion. Brown, a well-paid university administrator, was hesitant to give up her job and asked to be made board member instead. Mrs. Palmer, head of the Board of Lady Managers, found Brown to be impressive, but worried about antagonizing the southern white women, who were accustomed to hiring black women as maids and nannies rather than working with them as colleagues. Palmer recognized that the board could be a powerful agent in promoting sectional reconciliation and therefore serve as a visible example of northern and southern women united on behalf of the fair.

When the fair finally opened, six African American women addressed the World's Congress of Representative Women. Fannie Barrier Williams and Anna Julia Cooper both used the opportunity to address how young African American women, working as domestics, were being harassed and exploited by white men. Cooper had eloquently attacked the racism of white southern women in her book *A Voice from the South* (1892):

> The Black Woman has tried to understand the Southern woman's difficulties; to put herself in her place, and to be as fair, as charitable, and as free from prejudice in judging her antipathies, as she would have others in regard to her own. She has honestly weighed the apparently sincere excuse, "But you must remember that these people were once our slaves"; and that other, "But civility towards the Negroes will bring us on *social equality* with them."[12]

Cooper also successfully predicts the appeal of Aunt Jemima and the southern domestic ideal when she describes the northern fascination with southern traditions as part of the country's "unwritten history." Cooper wisely proclaims "Southern influence, Southern ideas and Southern ideals, have from the very beginning even up to the present day, dictated to and domineered over the brain and sinew of this nation."[13] Her insight and foresight here is almost a prophetic indication of the Aunt Jemima phenomenon as a metaphor for the competing forces of history and memory.

The fact that Green was a woman of working-class status and Cooper one of an emerging black middle class placed them at opposite ends of a spectrum detailing progress for African American women in the early twentieth century. Nancy Green represented a long-standing tradition of African American women working as domestics around the country, and Cooper represented the growing reality of African American sociopolitical and economic progress.

Since the club women's position on race and gender is clear in this instance, the issue of intraracial class bias becomes troubling. The three black women invited to participate were decidedly middle class and quite accomplished. A mere thirty years after the Civil War, Fannie Barrier Williams was a graduate of the New England Conservatory and the first African American woman appointed to Chicago's Library Board, scholar Anna Julia Cooper was a graduate of Oberlin College and later served as principal of the renowned M Street/Dunbar High School in Washington, D.C., and Hallie Q. Brown was a teacher and administrator at Wilberforce College.

The women representing the nineteenth-century black elite most certainly held elitist attitudes. For example, consider fellow club member Ida B. Wells's concern about yet another instance of strategic racism by the fair's officials. This one was called "Negro Day," and it was scheduled as a large public picnic open to African Americans but held off of the fairgrounds.

Wells was incensed by the exclusion of African Americans from mainstream fair activities. She supported the club women by giving their plight prominent space in the pamphlet she compiled and distributed at the fair: *The Reason Why the Colored American is not Included in the Worlds' Columbian Exposition.* Instead of confronting the fair's authorities, Wells thought it more efficient to address the fairgoers themselves. *The Reason Why* chronicled recent violence against black men and contained several brief biographies of eminent black women including poet Phillis Wheatley and sculptor Edmonia Lewis.

Wells publicly blamed the exposition officials for not making a more appropriate appeal to the black middle class and for enticing the "lower class" with offers of free food.[14] She articulated the feelings of many of the black elite who worried that an appeal to the masses would be embarrassing. Wells worried about a crowd that "will do more to lower the race in the estimation of the world than anything else," because she was so acutely aware of the tenuous nature of interracial solidarity.[15] Did Nancy Green belong to "the class of our race" to whom Wells referred? While women like Anna J. Cooper felt obligated to speak on behalf of domestic workers, we must ask whether or not they would have invited Green to speak on her own behalf.

Returning to the question posed by the petition against the Board of Lady Managers: What was a creditable display of labor and skill for black women in 1893? Was it six highly educated, activist black women—forerunners of the "New Negroes"—giving public speeches about the morality, progress, and worth of African American womanhood? What kind of black woman could have a viable, visible role in the fair's show of regional unity as well as a display of labor and skill? The answer turned out to be the African American woman who, since the early nineteenth century had been the ultimate symbol of racial accord: the mammy, represented at the world's fair as Aunt Jemima.

The elements of classism within nineteenth-century African American women's organizations are presented here solely as a way to encourage a more intricate look at the politics surrounding Aunt Jemima's "birthday." African American women were forced to engage in these polemics because of subtle racial politics surrounding the Fair's re-unification theme and the more overt racism of the Fair officials. Although their motto, "Lifting as we Climb" was no doubt genuine, the clubs represented the growing black elite who struggled for recognition and power at this time. This ideology of intellectual politics existed in direct opposition to whatever impulse lead to Nancy Green being hired to play a happy slave introducing Aunt Jemima products. So while Cooper, Williams, and Brown stressed the morality and intellect of African American women, Nancy Green was playing a part in a post Reconstruction fantasy. Would Nancy Green have been welcome to participate in their program at the Women's Building?

The 1893 World's Fair allowed the Pearl Milling Company to promote an agenda of race relations less threatening than that proposed by Anna Julia Cooper and Hallie Q. Brown. Aunt Jemima and her pancake recipe were reconciliation gifts from the South to the North; reunification meant they could now share her as a southern prize: a mammy for the national household. As the text of one advertisement exclaimed: "Now millions have this famous breakfast." Aunt Jemima's popularity in her role at the Columbian

Exposition illustrates how her race and gender make her an ideal balm to heal Civil War wounds. Her instant acceptance indicates the appealing familiarity of the southern mammy image deeply embedded in the American conscience.

Affirmation of this invented or revised history of Aunt Jemima takes on greater significance when compared with the resistance real black women experienced in their efforts to discuss and celebrate their real histories. Aunt Jemima's popularity directly relates to the belief that slavery cultivated innate qualities in African Americans; the notion that African Americans were natural servants reinforced a racist ideology renouncing the reality of African American intellectualism. This same ideology, transferred into advertising Aunt Jemima products, reveals a deep need to redeem the antebellum South.

A Marketable Past: From Plantation to Pancakes

The owner, Colonel Higbee, a most kind and gracious host,
Served his guests fine dishes, though they liked his pancakes most.
Of course, the cook who made them — or so the legend goes
Was good old Aunt Jemima, as our pretty picture shows.
    —QTD. IN MARILYN KERN-FOXWORTH,
    Aunt Jemima, Uncle Ben, and Rastus

Beyond their primary role of attracting new consumers and selling products, advertisements present value systems framed by the constant reminder that we live in a vibrantly successful capitalist society. The illustrations and texts for Aunt Jemima pancake mix reveal covert and overt messages about the centrality of antebellum idealism in America's developing consumer culture.[16] A close reading of Aunt Jemima pancake advertisements reveals a dramatic shift from the original emphasis of nutritional value to one emphasizing Aunt Jemima as an attractive emblem of revisionist history.

The vignettes describing Aunt Jemima's "life" on the Higbee plantation were written by southern copywriter James Wyatt, whose version of plantation life echoed that of Joel Chandler Harris.[17] Wyatt's imaginative narratives about Aunt Jemima were given credibility by this note appearing in many of the ads: "We are often asked, 'Are these stories of Aunt Jemima and her recipe really true?' They are based on documents found in the files of the earliest owner of the recipe. To what extent they are a mixture of truth, fiction and tradition, we do not know. The Quaker Oats Company, Chicago."[18]

Certainly other food products capitalized on the romance of the Old South: smiling Uncle Ben sold rice, his fraternal twin Rastus the Cream of Wheat chef hawked breakfast cereal, and Maxwell House Coffee is named for a Nashville hotel "famous throughout the old South" as a favorite gathering place for "illustrious visitors to old Dixie."[19] One Cream of Wheat advertisement actually featured Robert E. Lee IV as an example of the cereal's appeal to American children full of "much Southern Charm."[20]

Similar advertisements in domestic magazines encouraged women to believe that certain products would give them access to a special knowledge, a domestic wisdom that transformed ordinary women into exceptional housewives. At the root of promotions of plantation domesticity is a sophisticated plan to confirm the alleged positive aspects of slavery, capitalize on the appeal of "brown hand service," and appeal to the female reader's desire for special traditional hints to improve her own domestic space.

T. J. Jackson Lears addresses this mythmaking in his theory about the commercial appeal of a unified marketable past:

> As the ties to their own past attenuated, the urban bourgeoisie became more susceptible to the commodified version of the past served up in national advertisements. . . . Housewives among this group were more likely to respond to the nostalgia peddled by the Mennen Company (for example) in "Aunt Belle's Comfort Letters," which began in *Good Housekeeping* in 1920. "Aunt Belle is a real person and that is her real name. She really understands babies."[21]

The Mennen Company capitalized on America's fixation with domestic sophistication by making Aunt Belle sound like she might be a professional nanny. In a similar manner, Quaker Oats transformed Aunt Jemima into an expert on the ideal southern breakfast, an image the public accepted because she reminded people of the southern mammy. The Quaker Oats version of the Old South and its benevolent slave system ignored the lives of thousands of historical slave women who cooked and served during their lives as bondswomen.

Innovation that was both modern and old-fashioned was a common strategy between 1900 and 1930, when advertisers still struggled to win

Americans' confidence. Jackson Lears's essay on advertising strategies and the therapeutic ethos is helpful at this point in explaining the move away from nutritional value and quality assurances, "away from sober information and toward the therapeutic promise of a richer fuller life."[22] Among the therapeutic strategies were promises of good health, medicinal properties, and "that the product would contribute to the buyer's physical, psychic, or social well-being; the threat that his well-being would be undermined if he failed to buy it" (Lears 18).

A special blend of flours became the "secret recipe" of Aunt Jemima pancake mix, yet the true uniqueness of the recipe might have been its blend of agrarian and industrialized idealism. Pearl Milling introduced the new mix of flours in the Agricultural Building at the World's Fair to emphasize the wholesome quality of food that was premixed and prepackaged. Early advertisements announced that the pancake flour was a "specially prepared combination of wheat, corn and rice containing all the good qualities of those great food products."[23] Copywriters went to great lengths to convince potential customers that the truly progressive factory was one that could produce homemade flavor in store-bought mixes. For example, "between the mixing machines and the packaging room at the Aunt Jemima Mills, there's a kitchen. As the mixture goes through, our cooks take some out, and every five minutes they make pancakes. This is to make doubly sure that we have retained in Aunt Jemima Pancake Flour the old-time Southern flavor."[24]

Retaining "old-time Southern flavor" is promoted as a science, a tangible value conveyed through both pancake mix and the Aunt Jemima mythology. This example of the southern plantation meeting northern mills in a marriage of progress and tradition repeats the pattern seen in figure 11, where cotton grown and picked in the South becomes thread for sewing machines in the North. It is *women* who represent the rural South and the industrial North in these examples, creating an economic merger between black women and white women.

By the mid-1920s Aunt Jemima advertisements written by James Webb Young became longer and more sophisticated.[25] "How Aunt Jemima saved the Colonel's Mustache and his reputation as a Host" is a coming-of-age story. A young slave girl named Jemima is called upon to save the reputation of the Higbee household when guests arrive unexpectedly for breakfast. Her mother, the "Big House cook" named Eliza (perhaps where Stowe's Eliza might have ended up had she not escaped to Canada), is ill, and this "test" provides Jemima with an opportunity to rise to the occasion and prove herself a skilled cook. Jemima makes flawless pancakes for breakfast and "earns" the title *aunt* usually reserved for much older black women, making Jemima a child prodigy among slave women.

In the advertisements that followed, readers learned about a variety of incidents and adventures involving Aunt Jemima and her pancakes. In all of them, Aunt Jemima is either described or refers to herself as "mammy."

Several narratives cast Aunt Jemima as a heroine in the Civil War. One narrates a tale of two Confederate soldiers separated from their troop and stranded in the woods behind Union lines ("Gray Morn"). They know that they are safe when they hear a voice from a nearby cabin: "Lawzee! You chilluns pestah th' life out o' yo' po' ol' mammy with yo' evahlastin' appetite fo' pancakes!" Of course, it is Aunt Jemima, whose cabin awaits, like a sturdy lap to shelter these men from the enemy; "the mammy, by voice alone, was instantly recognized as an ally by the two white southern men" (Manring 188).

In another tale Aunt Jemima feeds hungry Confederate troops who are camped near her cabin ("The Night the Emily Dunston Burned").[26] By directly associating the Aunt Jemima character with the rebel troops instead of the Union Army, Aunt Jemima is presented as a slave woman who is indisputably loyal to the South and to the slave system: before, during, and after the Civil War. After hiding lost Confederate soldiers in her cabin and feeding Confederate troops, eventually Robert E. Lee himself finds his way to Aunt Jemima's cabin and brings a companion, "who happened to work for a milling company up north" ("When Robert E. Lee Stopped at Aunt Jemima's Cabin"). Robert E. Lee helps to facilitate Aunt Jemima's pancake recipe as a gift from the rural South to the urban North (Manring 119). The pancakes are later nicknamed "Aunt Jemimas," and the mammy herself is given, accepted, and consumed in the name of the Union.

As commercial markets recognized the power to shape a domestic ideal through advertisements, the plantation kitchen validated the South as a region with superior appreciation for good food and for the good life. Consider these lines from an advertisement with the headline: "Why no other pancakes can have that famous Aunt Jemima flavor": "No one can match the Aunt Jemima Flavor. Even in the old time South, in the land of good cooks, that was generally admitted."[27]

In another advertisement the narrative's incremental refrain is almost poetic in extolling the quality of the mix:

A recipe that first won fame when good food meant even more than it does today—down South before the Civil War. A recipe that mammy cooks on many plantations tried in vain to equal. A recipe that has been used and liked by more women than any other in the history of food. While her master lived, so the story goes, Aunt Jemima refused to tell a soul the secret of the wonderful flavor in the tender pancakes she baked for him and his guests.[28]

As I pointed out earlier, this commodified past was served up first at the 1893 World's Fair when Nancy Green was hired to play the Aunt Jemima character. As late as 1953, the company best known as Quaker Oats reminisced about Nancy Green's role as "Pancake Queen" at the 1893 World's Fair. An advertisement featuring Aunt Jemima and "lovely Mrs. Schenk, Mrs. America of 1953," used the headline "Pancake Queen tells Mrs. America about her Newest Pancake Success" (fig. 17). Beneath the headline, two women, one white and slender, one African American and buxom, stand in a red-and-white kitchen decorated to match Aunt Jemima's famous uniform: red-and-white checked dress, white scarf around her neck, white apron around her ample waist, and red, yellow, and white kerchief around her head. Mrs. America actually appears wearing her jeweled crown, so that the reader will not miss the stark difference between the queen of pancakes and the queen of homemaking.[29]

In one photograph the two women stand in a stiff semiembrace, strangely similar to the popular and racially charged Benetton advertisements. In another photograph below, Aunt Jemima stands in the background with an approving smile as Mrs. Schenk serves her husband breakfast. It is unusual that this scene is set in "Aunt Jemima's kitchen," since part of the ready-mix appeal was that buying and cooking these pancakes delivered Aunt Jemima into *your* kitchen with "that famous Old South goodness." This picture of domestic integration still relies on the appeal of the Old South, even on the eve of *Brown v. Board of Education.*

While the logo of Aunt Jemima's face has been altered and updated over the years, the message accompanying that face has been surprisingly consistent. From the 1928 advertising proclaiming, "They awaken childhood memories!" to one 1981 ad inquiring, "Do you remember your first bite of an Aunt Jemima Pancake?" this evocation of a common historic past is manifested through the guise of common childhood memories. All of this provides an incredibly effective connection between consumer and product through a kind of domestic patriotism.[30] Aunt Jemima was even part of the assimilation process of Jewish immigrants. In the 1950s Quaker Oats ran an advertisement in the *Jewish Times* encouraging readers to make Aunt Jemima pancakes instead of potatoes latkes; the subtext indicating that this southern delicacy was what true Americans eat for breakfast.

The story of Aunt Jemima's prominence in American culture is taken up extensively in several excellent studies of the trademark's role in advertising history, and the seemingly endless proliferation of Aunt Jemima collectible items. Aunt Jemima has been associated with everything from Disneyland to a ready-mix bomb, from salt shakers and teakettles to caricatures of Clarence Thomas; she even made an appearance on the popular African American series *A Different World*, where a character is transformed from the stereotype into a regal African queen. And there are more than 44,000 sites related to Aunt Jemima on the World Wide Web.

In the mid-1960s, about the time that many African American artists began to use Aunt Jemima as their target of choice during the Black Arts movement, Caribbean author Paule Marshall wrote an essay about the literary stereotypes of African Americans for the quarterly journal *Freedomways*. In her essay Marshall observed that "the Negro woman as an embodiment of myth and fantasies [has] little to do with her and much to do with the troubled and repressed conscience of the country."[31] As a cultural signpost, Aunt Jemima points beyond the original trademark to broader, more intricate themes that echo those of the mammy figure. Marshall's haunting conclusion, that extensive use of African American women as types rather than fully developed literary characters "has reached so far down in the national psyche that not even the best of the white writers have escaped it," can be applied to authors like Mark Twain, William Faulkner, and Margaret Mitchell, whose novels are considered in the next chapters.

CHAPTER FOUR

Reconstructing Mammy at the Turn of the Century; or, Mark Twain Meets Aunt Jemima

The "recurrent American nightmare of miscegenation"[1] and the subsequent passing of African Americans over the color line proved to be a fear so ripe with possibility that both African American and white authors exploited it extensively. This chapter asks the question, what happens when the American nightmare of miscegenation meets the southern dream of the faithful mammy? The mulatto mammy introduced in 1824 with Granny Mott, seen again with Eastman's Aunt Phillis and Stowe's Mammy, is reshaped in the hands of Mark Twain and Charles Chesnutt as they draw innovative parallels between passing over the color line and passing from mammy to mother. Chesnutt also uses a more stereotypical mammy character to address the rise of a New Negro mentality.

Pudd'nhead Wilson (1893)[2] and the short story "Her Virginia Mammy" by Charles Chesnutt (1899)[3] illustrate the mammy character's versatility at this stage of her evolution, because neither Roxy nor Mrs. Harper is a stereotypical mammy figure. Both texts highlight the experience of black women who *choose* to become mammies to their own children, allowing them to pass as white. Both mammy characters fall into the curious category of a uniquely hybrid stereotype, the mulatto mammy. The mulatto mammy figure is a fascinating mixing of two well-known stereotypes: the mammy and the tragic mulatto.

There is an impressive body of work on the passing narratives of the turn of the century,[4] yet scholars have not yet situated the mammy characters who choose to "pass" as mammies so that their light-skinned black children can pass as white. Almost concurrently, Twain and Chesnutt depict African American maternity, using similar mammy characters to discuss slave motherhood, miscegenation, and African American social progress. Unlike the conventional mammy, Twain's Roxy is a complex character, occupying a major role in the novel. Chesnutt uses Mrs. Harper in much the same way that Twain uses Roxy.

One of the characteristics distinguishing the mulatto mammy from her mammy sisters is that the visual contrast of a large black body with a small white one is replaced by an emphasis on her beauty, because she is "half white." These beautiful and dignified mulatto characters appear in one of the earliest plantation novels, *The Valley of Shenandoah*, in *Uncle Tom's Cabin*, and in the proslavery response *Aunt Phillis's Cabin*.[5]

My approach to the mulatto mammy is informed by the Bakhtinian theory of the grotesque body as one that defies categories. The mulatto mammy's body is marked by racial impurity, and her presence challenges normative forms of representation and behavior. By focusing on the mulatto mammy, we can isolate the ways in which nineteenth-century attitudes about miscegenation, slave loyalties, and motherhood converge upon her body to create this overlooked but fascinating plantation type. The mulatto mammy is usually represented as a more refined mammy character with family connections to the antebellum southern aristocracy or to the Confederacy. In the aftermath of the Civil War, issues of emancipation, miscegenation, and African American social progress were all at the forefront of national discussion. Chesnutt and Twain use the mulatto mammy character as a trope for exploring these engaging themes, and as a vehicle for conducting a profound discussion about passing and motherhood during slavery.

So much has been written about Roxy's role as the catalyst that sets *Pudd'nhead Wilson* (1894) in motion, that it is surprising to find no adequate exploration of her role as both mammy and mother. Roxy embodies opposing characteristics and therefore embodies traits that should negate each other: she looks white, yet she is legally black. As stated earlier, she becomes "mammy" to her own son and "mother" to her white nursling. At times she is so foolish that her monologues descend into farce; at other times she is surely the shrewdest character in the novel.

Carolyn Porter's theory that *Pudd'nhead Wilson* is really the story of a slave mother and her child is surely the best place to begin.[6] By shifting the emphasis away from the mystery element of the novel and toward the relationship Roxy has with both children, we can more fully appreciate the complexity of her characterization. Roxy is a troubled character who is unable to reconcile her dual roles as biological mother and mammy to the same child.

It is instructive to look at the way Twain informs us, with this loaded— or coded—statement, about the birth of the two boys, presumably about Percy Driscoll:

> On the 1st of February 1830, two boys were born in his house; one to him, and the other to one of his slave girls, Roxanna by name. Roxanna was twenty years old. She was up and around the same day, with her hands full, for she was tending both babies. Mrs. Driscoll died within the week. Roxy remained in charge of both children. (23)

The wording here makes Roxy the sole mother, since she actually gives birth, and ends up caring for both children. The result is that both of the children compete for her attention and energy. *They share a birthday and a mother, which, in effect, makes them twins.* There is a literary parallel here to the topsy-turvy dolls from the previous chapter, since Roxy is perhaps the most likely fictional slave mother to represent those double-ended dolls. She certainly treats Tom and Chambers as if they were one topsy-turvy doll, instead of two human beings. When Roxy switches or "flips" the children, she changes their lives and their destinies. Why doesn't Roxy take her inspiration from Stowe's Eliza and try to run away with her son? As she looks at the two children, an echo emerges from the novel's first chapter, when Wilson makes his "fatal remark," saying that if he owned half of an annoying dog, "I would kill my half" (24). She decides to switch the children instead of killing her "half" of the topsy-turvy doll.

The focus on her exchange of Tom and Chambers tends to obscure the scene just preceding the switch. Roxy's state of mind before she decides to make the switch is much more important since it is at that moment we actually see a slave mother's turmoil. Those moments when she considers infanticide and suicide are too often overlooked, because she is so quickly propelled into religious rhapsody. The weight of that scene is also undermined by an absurd display of vanity—the sight of a pretty dress distracts Roxy from her plans to drown herself and her son. Although Twain uses infanticide as a trope of Roxy's dilemma, we should keep in mind that this is the moment when Roxy is most fully a mother to Chambers and that her devotion to him is portrayed in terms of murder.

Those few decisive moments are worth noting in greater detail because the connection between infanticide and slave motherhood is encumbered with mystery and silence. Toni Morrison explores the tenuous relationship between love, sacrifice, and the desire for a child's personal liberty in *Beloved* (1987).[7] Morrison's character Sethe is the best example of the *antithesis* to the mammy type: a slave mother whose love for her children is so extreme that she believes it would be better for them to be dead than to be enslaved. Because Roxy considers this option, briefly but with conviction, she almost becomes an antimammy at the moment directly before she renounces her motherhood to become Chambers's mammy. So Roxy is furthest from the mammy stereotype the very moment before she embraces it as a means to save her life and that of her child. As I pointed out earlier, critics have not properly investigated this notion that Roxy becomes her son's mammy as a lifesaving measure, because there is so much focus on her decision to switch the babies. This flirtation with infanticide is more important than has previously been believed; it adds an important cyclical quality to the narrative structure that I will discuss more fully later.

The moments when Roxy's sensibilities as mother are sharpest occur early in the novel, before the new Tom grows up. Abject helplessness and anguish first characterize her status as a slave mother, because her son is the property of white slaveholders. Once Driscoll terrorizes his slaves by threatening to sell them down the river, Roxy's own status as chattel is secondary when she realizes that she has no control over her son's life:

> A profound terror had taken possession of her. Her child could grow up and be sold down the river! The thought crazed her with horror. If she dozed and lost herself for a moment, the next moment she was on her feet flying to her child's cradle to see if it was still there. Then she would gather it to her heart and pour out her love upon it in a frenzy of kisses, moaning, crying and saying, "Dey sha'n't, oh, dey sha'n't!—yo po' mammy will kill you fust!" (30)

The words "terror," "horror," "frenzy" are not nearly as strong as the image of her checking to see if her son has disappeared within a matter of seconds. Prior to this threat Roxy had enjoyed a certain degree of "privilege" as one of Driscoll's slaves, leading her to feel relatively secure about her future and that of her son.

Roxy is so angry with Driscoll for his betrayal that she can hardly complete a coherent sentence. First she wants to kill Driscoll: "I hates him, en I could kill him!" Then a moment later she realizes that losing her son is unbearable to her: "Oh I got to kill my chile, dye an't no yuther way, killin' *him* wouldn't save de child fume going' down de river. Oh, I got to do it, *yo' po' mammy's got to kill you to save you, honey*" (31; emphasis added). Here lies the slave mother's greatest tragedy—the role of life-giver is so closely associated with potential death and grief. Likewise, Roxana's only power to sabotage the slave system is to destroy the "property" that is also her child. Once she changes the children's identity, her only imaginable alternative to death and murder, her own identity changes as well. Her refusal to commit infanticide is not only a catalyst to the mixup, but also to her own impending schizophrenia.

What about her relationship with the new Chambers, the white child who suddenly becomes her son? Roxy has virtually no relationship with this child at all. The author describes how she practices the appropriate behavior with both children. "She would give her own child a light pat and say humbly, 'Lay still Marse Tom,' then give the real Tom a pat and say with severity, "Lay still, Chambers!—does you want me to take sump's' *to* you?" (35). Twain calls this last comment an example of Roxy's "motherly curtness of speech."

Chambers and Roxy have one sustained conversation in the novel and it is not about their relation to each other but about Tom. In this scene Twain gives us one of the few glimpses into Chambers's life. When Roxy calls him an "imitation nigger," he insists that if he is imitation, then so is she. Roxy is of course making a pun about his true identity, since this Chambers is really white and Chambers is talking about their very fair complexions. My point is that Roxy is *not expected* to have a warm, loving relationship with Chambers, and this works to her advantage. Their interaction is the same as is seen between Aunt Chloe and her children in *Uncle Tom's Cabin;* Roxy chides Chambers brusquely or ignores him completely. Roxy fulfills the expectation that slave mothers have abnormal or nonnurturing relationships with their children. And this is just as important a factor in the success of her plan as the children's physical similarities. She is able to treat Chambers as if he has no real place in her life and to cuddle Tom without raising suspicion. Her behavior results in a mocking tribute to those "standard" fictive mammies who adore their white children and neglect their biological ones. This makes for a most ironic twist on "expected" mammy behavior.

Nevertheless, Roxy's relationship with Tom is disappointing to her because Tom fails to play the expected role in her plan. He thwarts the typical relationship between slave nurse and white charge and treats her only as a slave, instead of a surrogate mother. Roxy's frustration with the way Tom treats her is what gives rise to her threat to expose his real identity. Her anger, then, is inextricable from her expectation that Tom would treat his mammy in a prescribed manner. Alone and ruminating about her frustration, she realizes that her son is ungrateful as well as mean-spirited: "He struck me, en I wasn't no way to blame—struck me in de face . . . en he's always calling' me nigger wench an hussy en all dem mean names when I's doin de very bes' I kin. Oh Lord, I done so much for him—I lift him way up to what he is" (46).

What Roxy is complaining about is Tom's failure to keep his end of the bargain and have the respect and love that a charge usually has for his mammy. This frustration simmers within her until it becomes combustible:

> Sometimes when some outrage of peculiar offensiveness stung her to the heart, she would plan schemes of every vengeance and revel in the fancied spectacle of his exposure to the world as an impostor and a slave; but in the midst of these joys fear would strike her; she had made him too strong; she could prove nothing and—heavens, she might get sold down the river for her pains! So her schemes always went for nothing, and she laid them aside in impotent rage against the fates. (46)

Roxy's "impotent rage" at Tom doesn't remain impotent once she loses her fortune in a bank failure and realizes how dependent she is upon Tom's goodwill. This is when she begins to assert her power over him in a manner that completely contradicts her former behavior.

While Roxy has not been much of a mother to the white Chambers, she knows that she has tried hard to be a good mother to Tom. In her rhetorical question, "Wuz I his mother tell he was fifteen years old or wuzn't I?" Roxy asks the question that she cannot answer herself, because she is both mammy and mother to Tom. Her emotional attachment to Tom is certainly deep enough, but it has been a source of grief for her.

When Roxy does approach Tom after their separation, it is with the "supplicating servilities" of a "born slave" (64), so that her mammy role, her

Figure 1. Andy Warhol, *Mammy,* American Myths series, 1981. (© The Andy Warhol Foundation for the Visual Arts / Artists Rights Society (ARS), New York and Ronald Feldman Fine Arts, New York.)

Figure 2. Andy Warhol, *Aunt Jemima,* American Myths series, 1981. (© The Andy Warhol Foundation for the Visual Arts / Artists Rights Society (ARS), New York and Ronald Feldman Fine Arts, New York.)

Figure 4. Black mammy "nipple dolls," circa 1920s, made from painted rubber nipples with tiny white baby dolls. (Author's collection; photograph by Bernard J. Thoeny, Atlanta.)

An Institution of the "C. S. A."
—COTTON STATES ARISTOCRACY.—

Though now unconscious on Ma Ma's breast,
Glorious destiny awaits the *high born* babe;
A Knight, A Baron, A Duke. A Royal crest
May yet upon his diadem wave.

Figure 5. An enlarged reproduction from a decorative envelope, 1861. (Courtesy of Boston Athenaeum, Boston.)

Figure 3. *Opposite, top:* Italian photographer Olivero Toscani's advertisement for Benetton, late 1980s. The advertisement was met with unbridled criticism from African Americans, yet it won more advertising awards than any other image in Benetton's advertising history.

Figure 6. Postcard from the 1920s: "Madame, could I interest you in a pair of white kids?" (Author's collection.)

Figure 7. Postcard from the 1920s: "Shut yo' mouth and mammy will have you white as snow in a minute." (Author's collection.)

Figure 8. "Mammy's Baby," from *Mammy's Baby* (1890), by Amy Ella Blanchard, illustrations by Ida Waugh

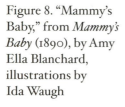

Figure 9. "Care" and "Don't Care" from *Mammy's Baby* (1890), by Amy Ella Blanchard, illustrations by Ida Waugh

Figure 10. Doll tableau from *Godey's Lady's Book,* 1852

Figure 11. Menden trade card: "The Thread that binds the Union North to South." (Courtesy of Mortimer Rare Book Room, Smith College, Northampton, Mass.)

Figure 12. Black doll serving tea to white dolls in photograph of the Cartledge children, 1903 6A.

Figure 13. Cloth topsy-turvy doll with lithographed faces, white child at one end, black nurse at the other, circa 1900. (Courtesy of Strong Museum, Rochester, N.Y.)

Figure 15. *Opposite, bottom:* Three beautiful black cloth dolls made by author Harriet Jacobs. (Courtesy of Elaine Brenenbaum, New York.)

Figure 14. Items reproducing the Beloved Belindy character. *Left to right:* doll by P. F. Volland Co., circa 1926–30 (apron and collar are accurate reproductions of the originals); *Beloved Belindy,* written and illustrated by Johnny Gruelle, published by P. F. Volland Co., 1926; party nut cup by C. A. Reed Co., produced 1941–57; wooden "Rocky Toy" (roly-poly) by Holgate Brothers Co., produced 1941–46; dish towel, unlicensed, maker unknown (circa 1940s–1950s); lithographed tin noisemaker, unlicensed, maker unknown (circa 1920s–1930s). (All items are courtesy of Andrew Tabbat, from his collection.)

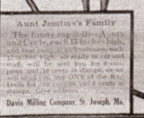

Figure 16. 1890s advertisement by the Davis Milling Company for Aunt Jemima Pancake mix. Depicts the Aunt Jemima rag doll family and another unique doll that was short lived: climbing Jemima, a doll modeled on a popular climbing monkey toy

Pancake Queen tells Mrs. America about her Newest Pancake Success

Aunt Jemima proudly points out to Mrs. Schenk, title-winning homemaker, that her newest pancakes are actually lighter than ever, with even more of that famous Old South goodness.

Mrs. Evelyn Joyce Schenk, talented 1953 "Queen of Homemakers," hears about today's lighter, richer-tasting Aunt Jemima Pancakes

PLACE: Aunt Jemima's kitchen. CAST OF CHARACTERS: Aunt Jemima and lovely Mrs. Schenk, Mrs. America of 1953. PLOT: a demonstration of today's lighter, richer-flavored Aunt Jemimas. "Your newest pancakes *are* even lighter!" enthused Mrs. Schenk, who is just as proud of her cooking ability as of her title. "And that famous Old South flavor is even *more* enticing now," reminded Aunt Jemima proudly. "No *wonder* folks say today's Aunt Jemimas are my *best* success!"

Mrs. America (Evelyn Joyce Schenk) won her crown equally for her beauty *and* her homemaking ability. A good cook, she makes her own clothes, too.

Bob Schenk, salesman, who entered Mrs. Schenk in the contest, gets set to enjoy his *second* golden stack of tempting Aunt Jemimas.

Aunt Jemima's newest pancakes are *her* crowning achievement, too. The batter is creamier and richer; and each light pancake has even *more* of that famous Old South goodness.

Figure 17. "Pancake Queen tells Mrs. America about her Newest Pancake Success," 1953–54. Aunt Jemima magazine advertisement extolling the "famous Old South flavor."

Figure 18. Sargent Johnson, *Forever Free,* 1933. *Forever Free* is one of the best examples of African American artistic response to the long history of tributes honoring the stereotypical southern mammy. (Courtesy of San Francisco Museum of Modern Art, gift of Mrs. E. D. Lederman.)

Figure 19. Illustration bearing the caption "She was never anything but tender with the others," by Genevieve Cowles, from *Social Life in Old Virginia before the War,* by Thomas Nelson Page, 1897

Figure 20. Photograph of an unnamed African American woman with the caption "A Typical 'Mammy,'" from *Social Life in Old Virginia before the War,* by Thomas Nelson Page

" *Go ter sleep, li'l baby,*
Go ter sleep, li'l baby,
Go ter sleep on Mammy's bre's' '"

Figure 21. "Go ter sleep on Mammy's bre's'," from *Old Plantation Days,* by Martha Sawyer Gielow, 1902

Figure 22. Young African American girls in white caps documented only as "unidentified black nurses," 1903. The babies' names are John and Allie Lamon. (Courtesy of Georgia Archives, Vanishing Georgia Collection.)

Figure 23. Bessie Morse holding Earle Sinclair McKey Jr., 1908. (Courtesy of Georgia Archives, Vanishing Georgia Collection.)

Figure 24. Lithograph postcard "Just Arrived," postmarked 1905. (Author's collection.)

Figure 25. "The South that is No More"

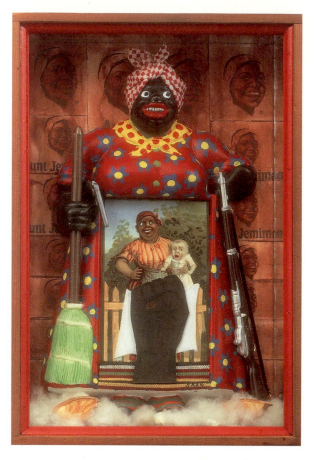

Figure 26. Betye
Saar, *The Liberation
of Aunt Jemima*,
1972. (Courtesy
of University Art
Museum, University
of California at
Berkeley; purchased
with the aid of funds
from the National
Endowment for the
Arts; selected by the
Committee for the
Acquisition of Afro-
American Art.)

Figure 27: Tina Dunkley, "Ain't Cha Mamma Yemanja," 1999

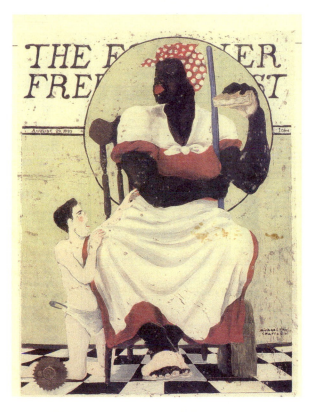

Figure 28. *Untitled* 1993, Michael Ray Charles

Figure 29. "Welcome to Atlanta," 2004, Charles Nelson

Figure 30. "Nanny Now, Nigger Later"

Figure 31. "No Mommy, Me" I

Figure 32. "No Mommy, Me" II

Figure 33. "Nanny Gone Wrong"

Figure 34. "Chainsaw Nanny"

mammy self, and her biological motherly devotion are conflicted. When he does not welcome her affection as his old nurse, she reminds him of her critical role in his life: "Marse Tom, I nussed you when you was a little baby, en I raised you all by myself tell you was 'most a young man" (65).

So her role in his life, as his mammy, mirrors that of a mother; we see a parallel to the position that Mrs. Harper takes in "Her Virginia Mammy," discussed below. In this scene Roxy is clearly Tom's mammy. The moment that immediately follows, when Roxy's mother-rage raises up to replace the begging mammy, is a crucial turning point in her characterization. This is the first time her anger at his behavior becomes empowering for her. Her impotent rage is made quite potent when she is pushed too far. The transition in her character is so dramatic that it is actually visible: "She raised her head slowly till it was well up, and at the same time her great frame unconsciously assumed a erect and masterful attitude, with all the majesty and grace of her vanished youth in it" (65).

This pivotal moment marks Roxy's evolution from the vain and immature "slave girl" of early chapters to the shrewd, calculating free woman of the last half of the novel. Once she decides to tell Tom the truth, and she threatens him with exposure, she is able to stand up to him. This transformation from begging mammy to indignant mother marks a profound distinction in their interaction. Her entrance, before she delivers the threat, is described in this way:

> Tom's mother entered now, closing the door behind her, and approached her son with all the wheedling and supplicating servility that fear and interest can impart to the words and attitudes of the born slave. She stopped a yard from her boy and made two or three admiring exclamations over his manly stature and general handsomeness. (64–65)

Having told him, she exits thus: "Tom humbly held the door for her and she marched out grim and erect as a grenadier" (81). As soon as Tom concedes that she has some secret she can use against him, he sees a new Roxy before him: one who terrifies him. The Roxy who walked into the room bowing and scrapping is suddenly laughing, drinking whiskey, and sauntering about with her hands on her hips. Who is Roxy during this scene, with her flashing eyes and a bravado that makes her laugh when Tom nearly strikes her? She certainly is not a pitiful mammy, pleading for a few crumbs of affection from her charge. She is a mother who is armed with information. This unleashes a fury within her that puts her in complete control of her son's life for the very first time.

Roxy's first move to regain her ground as Tom's mother is to insist that it is inappropriate for him to call her by her first name, demanding that he call her "ma or mammy." But her demeanor breaks down when she remembers what she did for her son and the way he treated her in return. For all Roxy's confidence and shrewdness, it seems she loves her son desperately and craves a "traditional" mother-son relationship with him. But Twain tells us differently, insisting that she "couldn't" love him, because there "warn't anything to him" (81).

Roxy and Tom's relationship is fraught with turmoil and paradoxes; Tom admires her but is repulsed by her need to be affectionate. Roxy finds his behavior reprehensible but wants to protect him. And what are we to make of Roxy's repetitive parroting "it's de nigger in you" whenever Tom does something morally offensive? Since the narrator has already expressed the same sentiment ad nauseam, adding Roxy's voice to that line belabors the theme of nature versus nurture that is impossible to ignore. Roxy's love for Tom fluctuates, and is most often based on pity. Once he has been robbed and is depressed, her love becomes complete: "He was ruined past hope now; his destruction would be immediate and sure, and he would be an outcast and friendless. That was reason enough for a mother to love a child; so she loved him and told him so" (158).

Tom's misery brings out the maternal love in her, which seems to be composed entirely of sympathy. This scene is most crucial to *Pudd'nhead Wilson* because the roles of mother and mammy are intertwined, and Roxy moves from one to the other with astounding fluidity. In the midst of discussing how devoted all mothers are to their children, she makes a gift of herself—of her body to be precise—to save him from destitution. Roxy knows her own worth to be six hundred dollars on an auction block. Her willingness to sell herself for her son is an unprecedented moment deserving of our close attention. Roxy says,

> "Here is de plan, en she'll win, sure. I's a nigger, en nobody ain't gwyne to doubt it hears me talk. I's wurth six hund'd dollahs. Take and en sell me, en pay off dese gamblers."
>
> Tom was dazed. He was not sure he had heard aright.
>
> He was dumb for a moment; then he said:
>
> "Do you mean that you would be sold into slavery to save me?"

"Ain't you my chile? En does you know anything dat a mother won't do for her chile? Dey ain't nothin' a white mother won't do for her chile. Who made 'em so? De Lord done it. En who made niggers? De Lord made 'em. In de inside, mother is all de same. De good Lord he made 'em so. I's gwyne to be sole into slavery, en in a year you's gwyne to buy yo' ole mammy free ag'in. I'll show you how. Dat's de plan." (59)

There is poignant irony in her claim that mothers will do *anything* for their children, when she knows that most slave mothers can do *nothing* for their children. This sacrificial move on her part, giving herself to her nursling, is most certainly the best example of her mammy self in action. Here again we can see that the structure of the text supports my argument. In the scene discussed earlier, Roxy enters as her mammy self and leaves as her mother self. This scene functions to mirror that action since Roxy is feeling maternal when she first sees Tom. By the time she leaves, she is an altruistic mammy that perceives her own body in material terms. The moment she conceives the idea and reveals it to Tom, she has slipped back into her mammy self.

Critics rarely address Roxy's second experience as a slave. But there is a profound incident that occurs during her term of slavery in the Deep South. Roxy fulfills the role of surrogate mother to a sickly and orphaned slave girl. Their attraction and devotion to each other is immediate, which is contrasted with the slower, more evolutionary love Twain tries to convince us develops between her and Tom. Roxy tells her son, "Dey was a little sickly nigger wench 'bout ten years old dat 'uz good to me, en hadn't no mammy, po'thing, en I loved her en she loved me" (171).

Of course, this young slave girl reminds us that if Tom *had* been sold down the river as Roxy once feared, he would be quite similar to this motherless child. The girl also reminds Roxy of her past fear and probably makes her feel less guilty about the switch. Her devotion to this young child leads to the most courageous thing Roxy does in the novel, more courageous than allowing herself to be sold back into slavery. Why have critics tended to ignore her assault on the overseer—*a Yankee overseer*—in defense of this slave child? How often does a black woman, a slave woman, strike a white male in American fiction? Roxy's tale is unusual and perhaps we overlook it because Roxy's actions are so surprising. In a brilliant nod to Harriet Beecher Stowe, Twain makes the Yankee overseer a northerner. This move and the character's cruelty implicitly link him to Simon Legree. Roxy rises up against him to protect a helpless child, but she has also been waiting for the opportunity to vent her frustrations against the patriarchal slave system in some physical manner.

Roxy's tale returns us to the cyclical narrative structure that I alluded to earlier. In Roxy's last conversation with her son, she speaks of killing herself, "You see dis knife. I's toted it aroun' since de day I seed dat man, en bought dese clo'es en it. If he ketch me, I's gwyne to kill myself wid it" (181). She also threatens to kill him as well: "En if you give a sign in dis house, or if anybody comes up to you in de street, I's gwyne to jam it right into you. Chambers, does you b'lieve me when I says dat?" (181). This is a jarring reminder of her desperate state of mind, that she would have to kill herself and her son in order to save them, which led Roxy to exchange the children in the first place.

Roxy's second preoccupation with suicide and murder really signals the end of her story. This Roxy is no longer invested in sacrificing and protecting her son, and she has learned that there is no one she can trust with her own safety but herself. The notion that she will kill her son rather than go back to slavery—when originally she thought she would have to kill him to prevent his sale—lends this circular, or cyclical quality to Roxy's role as well as a sense of finality to the narrative.

The first time Roxy threatens to kill her son, she does so in order to save him; the second time, she needs to save *herself*. We cannot continue to ignore Roxy's second threat to kill her son; her thoughts about infanticide make a more significant parallel between Roxy's threat to drown Tom and the court's decision to sell him down the river.

Roxy mentions suicide twice during this final dramatic scene: first, when she recalls how she would have had to drown herself to keep from being arrested by slave catchers, and second, when she shows Tom the knife she is carrying. This knife-toting, threatening Roxy is simply not the same woman who was sold to pay off Tom's debts. This is partly due to the evolutionary development of her own character, but most notably because she is finished with the mammy role in her son's life. In "Roxana's Plot," Carolyn Porter shows us Roxana's power in her status as mother and explains, "'Mother' is to be understood here not as a 'natural' but as a social, and cultural code that makes the slave mother at once antebellum America's most tragic victim and potentially one of its most powerful subversive agents."[8]

Of course Harriet Beecher Stowe knew the tragedy of the slave mother when she chose Eliza as her heroine for *Uncle Tom's Cabin*. Porter's point that Roxy is both tragic and powerful serves as a foundation for my argument. Ultimately Roxy's power is manifested more clearly in her dual role as a tragic mammy and powerful mother than in her fundamental status as slave mother alone. The mammy Roxy falls prey to cruelty and to her own maternal devotion. The mother Roxy is the powerful subversive agent who changes the fate of two people (and therefore many more) and finally exerts power over her son for her own protection.

Porter also credits Roxy's power with wreaking havoc on Twain's narrative intent, a fact that Twain corroborates in his explanation of the literary caesarean of *Pudd'nhead Wilson* and *Those Extraordinary Twins*. It is surprising that Porter uses Roxy as an example of a definitive slave mother when she points out that "the slave mother's power to negate paternal identity . . . is now unleashed, and aimed not only at Tom, but also through him at the white patriarchy, against which Roxana turns the same threat on which its power lies" (131). What does it mean for a slave mother to have the "power to negate paternal identity?" Here, a critic assigns feminist attributes to what is clearly a *legal* predicament. We know that the system of slavery negated paternal identity by forbidding legal slave marriage.[9] Moreover, Porter points out that in "appealing to such codes to tell the story of a black mother's alienation from a 'white' son become a 'master,' Twain's chapter exacerbates the horror of the slave mother's plight as not only the victim, but also the reproducer of social death" (134). The paradox here is one that Roxy embodies well; that slave mothers give life to their children and simultaneously condemn them to a kind of death sentence through slavery.

The color line functions more like a membrane than a boundary for very light-complexioned African Americans passing for white, as Chambers does. But what are we to make of the African American women who push their children through that membrane by renouncing their own maternity in order to become their children's mammy? They pass as mammies by slipping out of their motherhood like a loose suit of clothes.

We see another example in Charles Chesnutt's short story "Her Virginia Mammy."[10] The story is ostensibly about the reunion between Clara Hohlfelder, a young biracial woman, and her African American mother, Mrs. Harper.

The reunion is thwarted when Mrs. Harper makes a conscious choice to misrepresent herself to Clara. At her daughter's prompting, she identifies herself as Clara's mammy instead of her mother. Clara then embraces a completely fictional heritage and successfully crosses the color line. The act links Mrs. Harper with Roxy of *Pudd'nhead Wilson,* since both voluntarily relinquish their motherhood to become mammies to their own children.

The story begins with Clara's dilemma, which is that she is unable to marry her fiancé until she knows something about her biological family. Clara's craving for a viable personal history is surely symbolic of the freed slave's search for family as a means to establish a post-Emancipation identity. For Clara this is further complicated because her fiancé, John, is from a decidedly highbrow family and she feels that she must find an identity that would make her worthy of him.

In reviewing her own upbringing by adoptive parents, Clara comments about the difference between herself and the kind German family that raised her:

> Mother—poor, dear Mother!—could not have loved me better or cared for me more faithfully had I been her own child. Yet I am ashamed to say it—I always felt that I was not like them, that there was a subtle difference between us. They were contented in prosperity, resigned in misfortune; I was ever restless, and filled with vague ambitions. They were good, but dull. They loved me, but they never said so. I feel that there is a warmer, richer blood coursing in my veins than the placid stream that crept through theirs. (29)

Clara makes herself more exotic by insisting that she is more emotional and ambitious than her German foster parents. But the notion that her *blood* is different from her parents strongly suggests that she believes there is a racial difference. Clara confesses to John, "If I had but to simply turn my hand to learn who I am and whence I came, I should shrink from taking the step for fear that what I might learn would leave me forever unhappy" (31). Here we learn the most important thing we need to know about Clara; that she suspects the birth record she seeks is within her own skin, and it will prove she is not white. And this thought terrifies her enough for her to bury her suspicion so that she can be happier in her denial.

She goes as far as to "test" John to find out his feelings about race when she asks him what he would do if he learned that her origin *"was the worst it could be*—that I not only had no name, but was not entitled to one?" (33; emphasis added). There is no other way for Clara to ask John: "What if it turns out that I'm not who you think I am? What if I am not a white woman, but a black woman *who looks white?"* John assures her that nothing could change his feelings for her and actually has an opportunity to be true to his word at the very end of the story.

Clara's racial consciousness seems incredibly naive because it focuses much more on skin color than racial difference. When she opens her dance studio to blacks she is "surprised, and pleasantly so, when her class came together for the first lesson and at not finding them darker and more uncouth" (36). Yet her admission of feeling "a little shrinking at the thought of personal contact" is related to her secret fear about her identity. John's racial consciousness is summed up in one sentence; he assumes that the fairest blacks are "pathetic" because they are "so near and yet so far," which makes being a white American sound more like an achievement than a genetic factor. Shortly after this point, Chesnutt gives his first description of Clara's biological mother, a very fair-skinned black woman: "The woman was of the indefinite age between forty and fifty. There were lines in her face which, if due to years might have carried her even past the half-century mark, but if caused by trouble or ill health might leave her somewhat below it" (41).

The tension builds as Clara and Mrs. Harper begin to talk and Clara shares her dilemma with her mother. Here Chesnutt might be credited with paying homage to the African American tradition of oral narration, as Clara tells the story of her abandonment and adoption, as it has been told to her. Chesnutt's eloquence is most evident in the conversation between Clara and Mrs. Harper. Clara's poignant plea to her mother—"Who were my father and my mother, and who am I?"—resonates with the African American's search for a viable heritage.

Clara's ancestry is also linked to a few specific details from her childhood. With an odd mirroring of the scene where Roxy exchanges the babies in chapter 3 of *Pudd'nhead Wilson*, the key identifiers are exactly the same: a child's garment and a coral baby necklace. Ironically, here Clara clings to these items in an effort to discern her true identity. For Mrs. Harper, they serve as a code that enables her to interpret her role in Clara's story and life.

There are more similarities between the novel and short story if we compare the language used by Mrs. Harper and Roxy when they proudly reveal the lineage of their children's white fathers. Mrs. Harper tells her daughter, "Your father was a Virginia gentleman, and belonged to one of the first families, the Staffords, of Melton County" (52). Roxy tells her son: "You ain't got no 'casion to be shame o' yo' father, I kin tell you. He wuz the highest quality in dis whole town—ole Virginny stock. Fust famblies he wuz."

Both Twain and Chesnutt exploit an opportunity to connect southern aristocracy with miscegenation. Why are these slave women so proud of these aristocratic Virginia gentlemen who fathered their children? Why would they boast of their sexual liaisons with members of "the first families"? For Roxy this is consistent with the absurd vanity of her early characterization and her bigotry toward other blacks. Because this character is underdeveloped, the implication is that she wants her daughter to know that her mother was "chosen" by a patrician who valued her beauty enough to ignore her race and slave status. Still, the only way her lover could have freed her from slavery was to buy her. Both women end up being vessels that carry the children of noblemen and then sacrifice their motherhood to push these children over the color line. Both of these men are rendered invisible by the authors. They simply sire these children and disappear, leaving the slave mothers to become instruments for the race that enslaves them.

In the pivotal scene in which Mrs. Harper becomes Clara's mammy, she and her daughter enter into an unspoken pact of complicity. Mrs. Harper allows Clara's desperation to overshadow any desire for truthfulness:

> "He went with your mother and you—you were then just a year old—to Cincinnati, to settle up some business connected with his estate. When he had completed his business, he embarked on the Pride of St. Louis with you and your mother and a colored nurse."
>
> "And how did you know about them?" asked Clara.
>
> "I was one of the party. I was—"
>
> "You were the colored nurse?—my 'mammy,' they would have called you in my old Virginia home?"
>
> "Yes child, I was—your mammy. Upon my bosom you have rested; my breasts once gave you nourishment; my hands ministered to you; my arms sheltered you and my heart loved you and mourned you like a mother loves and mourns her firstborn." (54)

Like Roxy, Mrs. Harper denies her motherhood in order to give her child the "gift" of passing from black to white. For Clara, her mother's sacrifice is empowering, as she now has her permission to pass and believe herself to be of purely white aristocratic blood. This passing also enables her to be worthy of John's love and his name. These two women are bound to one another in their agreement to keep Clara's secret.

All of Clara's questions from this point—posed to her "mammy"—are cloaked in double entendre, since they are questions that are equally applicable to her mother. What makes this story stand out in the collection is that Chesnutt insists that the reader decide whether or not to believe that Clara is convinced that Mrs. Harper is her mammy and not her mother. He then draws the reader into this conspiracy of denial and revisionist autobiography.

The final and most striking parallel to *Pudd'nhead Wilson* comes when Mrs. Harper explains her own fate on the crashed steamboat. She is sold down the river because she was unable to prove that she was free; a serious and chilling comment about the vulnerability of free African Americans before Emancipation. Her vulnerability is also gender related: "After floating miles down river, the man who found me kept me prisoner for a time, and there being no inquiry for me, pretended not to believe that I was free and took me down to New Orleans and sold me as a slave" (56).

Mrs. Harper doesn't elaborate on her time spent "as a prisoner," in New Orleans, and Chesnutt probably wanted his readers to associate that city with its well-known reputation, its "fancy trade" in light-skinned African American women. This pattern of enslaved-freed–enslaved again in the two works is surprising. When we consider Roxy voluntarily returning to slavery and Mrs. Harper being kidnapped and enslaved, the implication is that black women must have a negative slave experience as punishment for their former lives of "relative" comfort. This trope may reflect the uneasiness with what Hazel Carby calls the "un-policed black female body."[11]

What do Roxy and Mrs. Harper tell us about the mammy at the end of the nineteenth century? While Aunt Jemima is trapped in the kitchen singing slave songs and serving pancakes, these characters recognize something about the fluidity of race and the ways that the mammy stereotype presents them with unparalleled opportunities. They serve as testimonies to how strongly the mammy type is tied to behavior rather than appearance. They are able to pass as mammies to their own light-skinned black children because, just as Quentin Compson recognizes, the "nigger isn't so much a person but a form of behavior." The late-nineteenth-century mammy is not based upon appearance, as is true of the more standard mammy, but based upon the way that these women behave toward their passing-for-white charges. Our stereotypic mammy has not yet disappeared; Charles Chesnutt is unique in this study as the only author who manages to render both this spin on the stereotype with Mrs. Harper and the stereotypical mammy figure in *The Marrow of Tradition*.

Mammy Meets the New Negro

The following are excerpts from reviews of *The Marrow of Tradition* (1901):

> This novel, like *Uncle Tom's Cabin*, is unfortunately an outburst of pent-up feelings. . . . One becomes tired of seeing black characters that represent only fidelity and honor and white characters that are generally perjurers and murderers.
> —"A New Color Line," *New York Commercial Advertiser*,
>   October 26, 1901

> The book will exert an influence today like *Uncle Tom's Cabin* did in years past.
> —*Springfield* (Massachusetts) *Republican*, November 3, 1901

> This is a novel of character rather than politics. . . . Reminds readers of *Uncle Tom's Cabin*.
> —*Portland* (Maine) *Advertiser*, November 19, 1901

> This is the strongest piece of race fiction since Uncle Tom's Cabin.
> —*New York Age*, December 21, 1901

> The author's aim is to show the oppression of the black man. . . . *Uncle Tom's Cabin* was a book for its times, but those times have passed.
> —*New York Christian Work*, December 5, 1901

> Chesnutt will have a higher place in prose writing than Paul Lawrence Dunbar will have in poetry because Chesnutt writes more as an American, while Dunbar portrays the American black. *In the Marrow of Tradition,* for example, it is not possible to tell from the book that the writer is black. This is also true of the work of Joel Chandler Harris.
> —*New York Age,* July 20, 1905

It may surprise contemporary scholars to see so many reviews of *The Marrow of Tradition* invoking *Uncle Tom's Cabin* (1852), since Chesnutt's subject is the race riots in Wilmington, North Carolina, in 1898 and not slavery.[12] Chesnutt's characters Mammy Jane and Jerry bear remarkable similarities to Stowe's stereotypical characters Aunt Chloe and Sambo.

Chesnutt once sharply critiqued the plantation characters that Stowe made famous: "Their chief virtues have been their dog-like fidelity to their old masters, for whom they have been willing to sacrifice almost life itself. Such characters exist . . . But I can't write about those people, or rather I won't write about them." Yet while Chesnutt rejected those characters in his collections of short fiction, the novel *The Marrow of Tradition* (1901) includes two faithful black retainers that he insisted in 1890 he wouldn't or couldn't write about. What happened in the eleven short years between his comment on Stowe and his creation of Mammy Jane—a quintessential example of the faithful black retainer? Chesnutt apparently chooses to use stereotypical black characters, to symbolize the "Old Negro" mentality best exemplified by disciples of Booker T. Washington. He contrasts these characters with depictions of more educated, politically astute, and socially demanding blacks—representing "New Negroes." Mammy Jane and her grandson Jerry are much more than clones of Stowe's caricatures. They come to symbolize impediments to black progress. By 1925, African Americans were openly critiquing these caricatured images representing a romantic nostalgia about the Old Negro. For example, literary critic and editor of *The New Negro* anthology Alain Locke writes: "The Old Negro had long become more of a myth than a man. The Old Negro, we must remember, was a creature of moral debate and historical controversy. . . . The day of 'aunties,' 'uncles' and 'mammies' is equally gone. Uncle Tom and Sambo have passed on."[13] This theme reappears thirty-five years later during the Civil Rights movement when the pejorative *handkerchief head* was used to describe those African Americans whose political conservatism was interpreted as undermining black progress.

For Chesnutt's purpose, Mammy Jane is a brilliant representation of this conservatism. In her excellent study on regionalism and mammy characters in African American fiction, literary scholar Trudier Harris makes the point that "the social and political climate with which he [Chesnutt] was concerned dictated her presence." Harris also suggests that Mammy Jane is a literary ancestor to Pauline Breedlove, the housekeeper and cook in Toni Morrison's novel *The Bluest Eye* (1970). For Harris both characters, "have difficulty envisioning a world other than one of white masters and black servants, white power and black submissiveness, white expectations and black fulfillment of expectations."[14] Chesnutt orchestrates an Old Negro–New Negro standoff in a scene between Mammy Jane and a younger black nurse, meant to symbolize the Washington-DuBois split. In the hands of an African American author, the mammy figure becomes a powerful platform for exploring key sociopolitical themes within African American culture.

Like the more stereotypical mammies, Mammy Jane positions herself as part of the old guard, when she says, "I's fetch my gran'son Jerry up ter be 'umble, an' keep in 'is place" (90). She believes younger African Americans are taking terrible risks by "crowding" whites, instead of maintaining their loyalty through servitude.

Like Booker T. Washington, Mammy Jane represents an ideology favoring patience and separatism over protest and equality. Unlike Washington, she faults education with ruining younger African Americans who step out of their prescribed place. Later in the novel, she is shocked and offended to see the black character Janet riding in a buggy as if she were a respected lady: "Well, well! Fo'ty yeahs ago who's 'a' ever expected ter see a nigger gal ridin' in her own buggy? My, my! but I don't know, — I don' know! It don' look right, an' it ain' gwine ter las!" (106). Ironically, Mammy Jane's nostalgia for the old slave days and ways is indistinguishable from that of the bigoted character, Major Cateret.

In the aforementioned scene, the young educated nurse is silent; we get her thoughts from the narrator. Mammy Jane tells her that it's a "privilege" for her to be allowed to work for quality white people:

> These old-time negroes, she said to herself, made her sick with their slavering over the white folks, who, she supposed, favored them and made much of them because they had once belonged to them — much the same reason why they fondled their cats and dogs. For her own part, they gave her nothing but her wages, and small wages at that, and she owed them nothing more than equivalent service. It was purely a matter of business; she sold her time for their money. There was no question of love between them.

In this one passage Chesnutt takes on all of the issues and themes raised in the first chapter. Whatever possible genuine affection might have existed between Mammy Jane and the Caterets is acknowledged and summarily dismissed. The last line is most revealing, since it clarifies the New Negro position on intimacy and employment. Invoking the language and sentiment of the most prototypical mammy character, Mammy Jane "loved Mrs. Cateret; towards the Major she entertained a feeling bordering upon awe" (501); the reader can hear the funeral bells tolling for Mammy Jane as the New Negroes emerge on the scene.

Chesnutt is the first African American author to use characters from the plantation school as symbols of an unchanging and unchangeable past. For example, Mammy Jane is both the family historian and family "storyteller," alerting us that not enough attention is paid to the distinction between these roles. Everything about Mammy Jane is stereotypical, including the way she dresses, speaks, behaves toward her white charge, and her folksy superstition.

Mammy Jane's relationship with the baby Dodie is characterized with the same adoration and devotion that we saw from Aunt Judy and Old Chloe in chapter 1. At one point, Mammy Jane is blamed for her mistress's illness. When the family doctor reprimands her, saying, "You ought to have taken better care of your mistress," Jane defends herself by relaying her long-standing loyalty to the Cateret family. She becomes a parody of the stereotypical mammy: "Will I come an' nuss yo' baby? Why, honey, I nussed you, an' nussed yo' mammy. . . . I wouldn' let nobody e'se nuss yo' baby; an' mo' over, I'm gwine ter come an' nuss you too" (469).

In addition to being responsible for her mistress, Mammy Jane behaves as if it is her divine mission to protect the mistress's son Dodie from another character's "evil eye." What role does this kind of superstition play in her mammy stereotype? It contributes to her characterization as being more backward, quirky, and less sophisticated than other characters. Moreover, this is not an example of her respect for traditional African American folk culture, since she uses it to save a white baby from a black woman. Jane's ignorance and lack of sophistication makes her anachronistic in a world moving toward more equitable racial interaction.

Finally, Chesnutt uses Mammy Jane's death as a symbolic gesture with larger ramifications. Jane's death not only signals the demise of Old Negro mentality, it is a call for an end to this caricatured black persona. Chesnutt acknowledges and undercuts the similarities to Stowe that appear in comparisons of his work to hers, when Mammy Jane is shot during a violent race riot and dies at the feet of the "New Negro," Dr. Miller. This is a profound moment in the evolution of the mammy character, because it is the first signal of rebellion against that image by an African American author.

The mammy characters in *Pudd'nhead Wilson* and "Her Virginia Mammy" reflect more complexity and greater depth than the Aunt Jemima of popular culture. Roxy and Mrs. Harper are used as platforms for critical discussion about the most crucial turn-of-the-century-issues. The fact that these women are not stereotypical characters, but multidimensional and interesting, links them indirectly to some of the more heterogeneous characters explored in chapter 1. However, if Chesnutt's Mammy Jane were a more talented and entertaining cook (and perhaps if she were less obsessively superstitious), she could be a smiling Aunt Jemima, serving pancakes to a nation.

Harper's magazine published a volume of essays and editorials on the South at the turn of the century. In one essay the author describes the uniquely innate cooking skills of African Americans: "The Negroes are born cooks as other less favored beings are born poets." Slavery is depicted as a training camp where "the African brute, guided by the superior intelligence of his Caucasian master . . . gradually . . . created an art of cooking for which he should be immortalized."[15] In the late 1890s and early 1900s, there are repeated efforts to immortalize the mammy.

CHAPTER FIVE

Southern Monuments, Southern Memory, and the Subversive Mammy

A traumatized child will sometimes create a fantasy of an idealized family in an imaginary world as a means of emotional respite. As a result of the rapid breakdown of society from the war, the defeated South devised a similar coping mechanism by inverting a mythology about their prewar social order. The traditions and manners ascribed to those halcyon years were expressed in visual and narrative fictions, adding coherence to what came to be known as the "cult of the Lost Cause."

—JO-ANN MORGAN, *Uncle Tom's Cabin as Visual Culture*

Between the 1890s and the 1920s, the mammy image may be seen as a cultural barometer, reflecting ongoing fluctuations in racial attitudes about African American women, about motherhood, and about the American South. The figure's fluidity, to which I alluded in the introduction, is most visible during this period when the mammy's symbolism was updated and reaffirmed for one purpose and then redefined for an opposing purpose. Historian Catherine Clinton contends that "no student of southern history can afford to dismiss the mythology and imagery that have been so tightly entwined with reality throughout the region's experience."[1] The different versions of the black mammy image that emerged during this period were a major coercive force affecting early twentieth-century conceptualizations about the South. In an effort to better capture this complicated moment in American cultural history, this chapter does not adhere to a structured chronology; it relies instead on thematic emphasis.

Using this approach, the chapter seeks to unravel some of the intricately woven propaganda of this period by examining the role that each strand played in perpetuating white supremacy through a blatant reification of the Confederacy and the most romantic revisionist history of slavery. In this way, what has been called "Lost Cause worship" is melded with a post-Reconstruction "mammy worship" invented and disseminated through southern "local color" literature and compounded on a much larger scale through monuments honoring the mammy as a type: the faithful black retainer. The chapter ends with powerful literary responses to these mammy tributes by authors Charlotte Hawkins Brown and Adeline Ries, including one truly memorable mammy who drowns a baby in response to the early death of her own daughter.

Monumental Mammy

The objects used to conjure up the mammy serve as a way to record and concretize a very specific version of the southern past. Records of the American past appear on landscapes across the country and across the South as much as anywhere. As one southern historian comments, "Southerners, no less than others, have displayed great creativity in employing material objects to record their past. Because memories are transitory, people yearn to make them permanent by rendering them into physical form."[2]

There is also a startling urgency in the need to document an acceptable version of domestic interaction between slaves and slaveholders; the southern literature from this period reflects a palpable fear that the Old South was slipping away and that therefore the memories must be anchored in sacred sites: segregated graveyards, Confederate parks, and monuments to faithful African American "servants." In an anonymously authored essay provocatively titled "A Colored Woman, However Respectable, Is Lower than the White Prostitute" (1902), the writer uses this example of the hypocrisy of mammy worship and segregation: "I know of one of the 'black mammies' that the southerner speaks of, in tones low and soft, who is compelled to go to the authorities of a certain southern city for a 'pass' to visit the grave of a man she nursed at her breast, and whose children she afterward reared."[3]

Drawing connections between how race, gender, and southern memory are manifested in the literature and in the sculpture of the Reconstruction and post-Reconstruction periods is less challenging now because of the excellent work already produced in projects like *Monuments to the Lost Cause:*

Women, Art, and the Landscapes of Southern Memory, by Cynthia Mills and Pamela H. Simpson (2003), and *Sites of Southern Memory: The Autobiographies of Katherine Du Pre Lumpkin, Lillian Smith, and Pauli Murray,* by Darlene O'Dell (2001).[4] Both books lay a substantial foundation for this chapter's effort to interweave various genres of literature by white southern women and African American women with statues honoring the mammy's fidelity during slavery and especially after emancipation. O'Dell's book pulls our attention to the haunting power of southern landscapes and rituals surrounding them as "sites where southern identity tactically sought to sustain and preserve itself through Confederate graveyards, ceremonies and monuments."[5]

On Memorial Day 1924, Norman Kittrell, a judge and the author of *Ned, Nigger an' Gent'man* (1907), made this remark in a speech called "Old 'Miss' and 'Mammy.'" "Some day there will be reared somewhere on Southern soil a memorial as worthy of her as is within the power of artistic skill; but no genius . . . will worthily symbolize her patience, and love, and fidelity. Her memory will outlive granite and marble and bronze."[6] Kittrell must not have been aware of the first Faithful Slave Monument erected by the former slaveholder and Confederate veteran Captain Samuel White in Confederate Park in Fort Mill, South Carolina, in 1896. The simple stone obelisk is set on a platform of four stone steps and was built on the town green in close proximity to a monument to Confederate soldiers. White (owner of the local cotton mill) had the following words inscribed on the monument:

> Dedicated to the faithful slaves who, loyal to a sacred trust, toiled for the support of the army, with matchless devotion; and with sterling fidelity guarded our defenseless homes, women and children, during the struggle for the principles of our "Confederated States of America."[7]

The Fort Mill monument was the first representation of the "faithful slave" in a postbellum monument. Comparing two statues dedicated to emancipation in his book, *Standing Soldiers, Kneeling Slaves: Race, War, and Monument in Nineteenth-Century America,*[8] Kirk Savage explains that this "was a monument generated from a former slaveholder's perspective designed not to celebrate slavery's demise but to nostalgically mourn over its passing."[9] There are two representations of slaves on this monument. One is a woman, understood as a mammy with a white child in her arms. The other is an African American male, a field laborer. Astonishing attention to detail was employed to represent the racial differences between the mammy, who stands on the steps of a large plantation home that looms behind her, and the child (obviously not her own biological offspring) that she is holding. In this innocuous symbol of slavery, the mammy reinforces an ideal: her devotion to her owners extends to her nurturance of the next generation of slaveholders despite her status as a free woman. Savage points out that "In both images, work is either suspended or disguised. . . . [B]undles of wheat in the background testify to [the fieldworker's] labor without him having to engage in it. The woman's work is negated more radically: it is transformed into maternal love as she returns the child's embrace and their two heads touch."[10] Here, the mammy's labor—the demands of taking care of someone else's child—becomes synonymous with her love. Author James Loewen comments, "Neither panel quite depicts work, and work was what slavery was all about. Instead, the illustrations invite visitors to think of slavery as a time of relaxation and interracial caring."[11]

We have to ask how these structures that were intended to honor slaves faithful to the Confederacy end up honoring "interracial caring." Setting Loewen's point aside, in the panel that *attempts* to depict fieldwork, the male slave is ostensibly honored for his work; the mammy on the opposite panel is being honored for "love itself." Savage reiterates points made elsewhere in this study, explaining that "the mammy scene received special attention in the local accounts of the monuments precisely because it represented the relationship of the master to slave not as one of domination but of mutual affection." "Love itself," could be read in the features of the mammy's face, according to one account (written before those features were lost to erosion). Captain White told the journalist writing about the statue that he loved his "old Negro Mammy" and that his monument was meant to "to teach generations yet unborn" (Savage 158). In addition to solidifying a tradition of black servility for future generations of southerners, the monument was also intended as an indisputable message, written in stone to northerners, about the southern way of life. For White, the flowery inscriptions and the structures themselves would prove to the nation that slaveholders "respected their [slaves'] good qualities as no one else ever did or will do. . . . The monument would tell future generations that the white men of the South were the negro's best friend then and that the men of the South are the negro's best friend to-day."[12]

African American fidelity after Emancipation remains a disputed matter. Civil War historian Stephen Ash writes that as much as it may surprise twenty-first-century readers, "many whites were profoundly shaken by the revelation that slaves hated slavery and resented their masters . . . the belief that blacks were content in bondage was a cornerstone of proslavery ideology."[13] Some records show that less than 10 percent of emancipated African Americans remained on plantations to work for their former masters after the Civil War. Ash also quotes a mistress who records her disappointment with this idealism: "As to the idea of *faithful servant, it is all a fiction.*" Another planter shares his despair, writing: "There is not *one Negro in all the South, who will remain faithful from attachment to their master and mistress,* not one."[14]

Within a few years various plaques and stone shafts dedicated to the faithful slave began to appear, along with increasing attention to Confederate soldiers and veterans. As a result of this juxtaposition of images (the faithful slave and the Confederate soldier/veteran), an implanted memory—linking African Americans more forcefully with the military Confederacy than before or during the Civil War—began to emerge as part of the larger campaign to justify the plantation system. For example, a tribute to Confederate soldiers that was erected in 1912 in Columbia, South Carolina, bears an inscription stating: "In appreciation of our faithful slaves" (Savage 158). These sculptural renditions of the past were intended to replace the negative image of slavery as an institution of dominance with a nostalgic fictional representation of interracial harmony.

The black mammy played a significant role in this campaign to shift emphasis from slave labor to slave loyalty. One of the best examples of this is the Confederate Monument at Arlington National Cemetery, which was unveiled in 1914 as a gift from the United Daughters of the Confederacy (UDC), whose stated mission was to "correct history." In an excellent essay, "The Confederate Monument at Arlington: A Token of Reconciliation," Karen Cox writes that the monument was "an extraordinary achievement for peace and reconciliation nearly a half century after the close of the Civil War. The federal government had set the stage for this grand gesture by allowing the burial of Confederate soldiers in the cemetery and by giving permission to the UDC to build a tribute there."[15]

Made up of several tableaus, this project has been called a "proslavery textbook illustrated in bronze."[16] The story is a familiar one because by 1914 the UDC had obtained considerable help in "correcting" history from popular authors of romantic plantation tales and sketches of southern life.

I suggest that Faithful Slave Monument in Fort Mill, South Carolina, and the Confederate Monument at Arlington National Cemetery in Virginia are best understood when interpreted together with the literature about the South that was most popular at the time, the genre typically called "local color," which dominated the literary scene largely through widely circulated periodicals.[17] Local color stories emphasized black dialect and the quaintness of African American folk culture as seen and interpreted by white authors who were essentially writing about the domestic bliss of their childhood allies: the African American men and women called uncles and aunties who seemed to exist solely for their entertainment. In Richard Brodhead's scholarship on local color and the literary career of Charles Chesnutt, he argues that the southern authors were nostalgic for "localized identity" in the face of burgeoning national identity, since "the literature of local color emerged as the dominant American literary genre in the same decades as did the transcontinental Railroad and Standard Oil."[18] The best-known and most widely published authors of local color literature were Joel Chandler Harris and Thomas Nelson Page. Page used his writing to contradict what he believed were misrepresentations of southerners as ignorant, violent, and poorly mannered and made a career of writing portraits of African American fidelity in the Reconstruction South, gaining wide popularity for his efforts. Author Grace Elizabeth Hale, discussing Page's work, comments that while "the slave body had been emancipated by the late nineteenth century, representations of slaves had never been more popular or profitable."[19]

It is not difficult to see the connection between southern local color fiction such as that of Thomas Nelson Page and the sculptural representations of an idealized relationship between white southerners and African American slaves. In fact, Page's good friend Moses Ezekiel, a sculptor who longed to have his love of the South recognized in an artistic creation, designed the Arlington Confederate Monument and its engraved representations of slavery.[20] Furthermore, the frieze on the monument depicting an African American "body servant" following his young master to war may have been modeled on the character Sam in Page's short story "Marse Chan," a fictive account that remains the standard for literary treatments of loyal African American slaves and brave Confederate masters.[21]

Looking more closely at a frieze from the Confederate Monument that depicts a plump African American woman wearing an apron, a turban, and earrings, we see a representation of the most stereotypical mammy figure.[22] This mammy molded into bronze is depicted with two white children, a small child clutching her full hips and a baby being handed to her for safekeeping by a Confederate officer. One spokesperson for the Arlington Confederate Memorial Association claimed that this particular frieze accurately illustrated the "kindly relations that existed all over the South between the master and slave." For him the panel relays a truth that cannot be repeated often enough, especially to "generations in which [*sic*] *Uncle Tom's Cabin* survives and is still manufacturing false ideas about the South and slavery" (Cox 158).

I suggest comparing the Confederate Monument with the sculpture *Forever Free* made by the gifted African American artist Sargent Johnson in 1933 (fig. 18). African American art curator Michael Harris elects to contrast this piece with the Aunt Jemima cookie jars that were popular during the 1930s, but I see this piece as presenting a direct contrast to the statues discussed earlier in this chapter. The sculpture has a cylindrical form reminiscent of a small statue. The black woman has erect posture, and the black child stands so close to her that he or she seems to become one with the woman's body. All of these features contribute to the possibility that *Forever Free* is an African American response to black mammies-with-white-children statues at Fort Mill and on the Confederate Memorial. The simplicity of the colors—brown, white, and black—emphasizes what Harris calls "her quiet, defiant, dignity."[23] Harris does not emphasize the significance of the small nude child—surely, the woman's own child under her protective arm—as a symbol of maternal devotion and loyalty.

Returning to Thomas Nelson Page, his book *Social Life in Old Virginia before the War* (1897) was widely read and applauded for its redemptive qualities. In fact, *Social Life* may be one of the best examples of this era's capacity to blur fiction and nostalgic memoir. The text includes both a lushly romantic drawing of a black mammy with a white child accompanied by the caption "She was never anything but tender with the others" (fig. 19) and a photograph of an unnamed African American woman with the caption "A Typical 'Mammy,'" both by illustrator Genevieve Cowles (fig. 20). (Known for her murals and stained-glass windows, Cowles was also a painter. Her illustrations appeared in Hawthorne's *House of Seven Gables* and in *Scribner* and *McClure's* magazines.) Another example appears in Martha Sawyer Gielow's book *Old Plantation Days* (1902). A depiction of a steely looking and unnamed African American woman holding a white baby serves as the frontispiece, offering readers the most nostalgic image of "old plantation days" (fig. 21).[24]

In direct contrast with these romanticized depictions is a photograph from 1903 showing two young African American girls in Georgia with their white charges (fig. 22). The two very young girls wear white ruffled caps and matching pinafores. One girl holds a small change purse on a chain in one hand and a toy in the other hand. The babies are propped on the girls' laps, and both girls peer directly at the camera. The girls' names are not recorded in this portrait that documents the first names and surnames of the siblings, John and Allie Lamon. The young girls are described as "unidentified black nurses." The use of the word *black* instead of *Negro* or *colored* leads me to believe that this phrase was added later, perhaps during the photographs' cataloging at the Georgia Archives. These kinds of portraits were often titled only "baby and colored nurse."

These photographs are important because they provide an opposing view of the happy memories of white southerners: there was nothing jolly about young girls who were employed as baby nurses, many of whom were provided only room and board for their services. As for the very young baby nurses in figure 22, it is difficult for me to imagine that such young girls, barely beyond childhood, had been asked to tend to babies as either part-time or full-time work

Figure 23 is a photograph of an African American baby nurse from Georgia, Bessie Morse, holding Earle McKey Jr. This photograph is unusual because Ms. Morse's name is recorded. Although we cannot be certain of her age, she appears to be about fifteen years old. There is little discernible affection in her facial expression or in her posture as she holds Earle McKey Jr.

In yet another example, a vintage lithograph postcard postmarked 1905 with the title "Just Arrived" depicts a stereotypical mammy with a white apron and red headscarf, smiling as she holds a scale showing the weight of a squalling newborn wrapped in a red blanket. Her delight with the baby is reflected in her expression of personal pride (fig. 24).

Reviving the Plantation Tradition through Local Color Fiction

I am prompted by feminist literary scholar Patricia Yaeger's landmark study *Dirt and Desire: Reconstructing Southern Women's Writing, 1930–1990*

(2000) to consider Sherwood Bonner's work (which will be discussed in detail later in this chapter) as an appropriate example of "southern local color" between 1890 and 1920 instead of relying upon the more well-known male authors from this period. Yaeger argues forcefully that "we need to change the categories we use to think about southern literature, . . . we need to provide a new set of categories for examining southern women's fiction to find new terms for cataloging its arrested systems of knowledge."[25] Yaeger also criticizes what she calls the "huge Faulkner industry" for marginalizing southern women's writing, but clearly southern men were at the center of southern literary studies long before the academically driven Faulkner industry gained momentum.

Literary scholar Kathryn McKee writes that women's southern literature reflects a level of "writing actively engaged in self-representation, actively engaged in preserving region from the homogenizing sway of nation."[26] Yet my look at the mammy character from the 1830s to this Reconstruction moment reveals that while southern white female authors might have been resisting homogenization, they were using the mammy character to sway their Northern peers into rethinking their antislavery beliefs. Plantation fiction dedicated to the Old South and to the memory of characters typically called "old time darkies" was continually being offered to the North as the most appealing image of plantation life, and the offer was being accepted with increasing enthusiasm, particularly through northern periodicals.

McKee goes on to point out that "our traditional understanding of southern local color as a body of fiction nostalgic for paternalism is seriously challenged by the writings of women who . . . may be undermining the conventions of gender and in some cases, race and class relations" (31). It is clear that female authors of local color tales like Sherwood Bonner, Mollie Evelyn Moore Davis (*An Elephant's Track, and Other Stories,* 1897), and Grace Elizabeth King (*Balcony Stories,* 1914) undermined conventions of gender by contending with a male-dominated publishing industry. But it is unfair and unwise to excuse the racist and classist content of their writing in the name of feminist intervention.

Patricia Yaeger calls upon us to pay more attention to "the ways in which an entire culture has taught itself to think about race," (60) and that will mean that we must deal with white women's racist depictions of African American women through their sentimentalized versions of the mammy. What is more frustrating, is that the implication that writing about their mammies, re-telling stories told to the authors, or actually writing their biographies in plantation dialect is an adequate compensation for the African American women who were so important in their lives.

The best example of this genre is Ruby Vaughan Bigger's book about Lady Astor's mammy: *My Miss Nancy* (1924), with its telling (and difficult to decipher) subtitle: *Nancy Astor's Virginia 'Mammy' tells why 'her littl' mistis ain't neber gwine lose her 'sition ober dar in Inglan'.*[27] Astor was the first woman to sit in the British Parliament, and this intimate look at her childhood written through her Aunt Veenie's voice both earned favorable reviews and sold well. Astor's approval of the memoir appears on the first page: "I loved reading your little story and appreciate it very highly. It made me weep, especially the part about my dear Aunt Veenie. You know perfectly well I am just like hundreds of other women in Virginia." In the foreword Biggers writes, "Mammy, dear to the hearts of all Southerners both young and old, belongs to a fast vanishing type . . . the entire Southland is losing something very precious and vital. A little later, they will be considered myths." Unfortunately, the racism of southern white women authors has not yet been fully explored in a way that can deepen our understanding of gender and southern literature.

I want to return to one author mentioned earlier. Katherine Sherwood Bonner McDowell wrote and published under the name Sherwood Bonner. Bonner has the dubious honor of introducing humorous "happy darkie tales," or Negro dialect tales, to northern magazines, which published her work from 1875 until her death in 1884. One critic calls her "the first Southern woman to deal realistically with Negro . . ."[28] Born in Mississippi, she moved to Texas with her husband, Edward McDowell, for a short time before they returned to Mississippi. Bonner eventually dissolved her marriage, charging her husband with "nonsupport," and moved to Boston in a bold effort to try to help financially support her family. (Bonner's experience as a "southern" author was unusual because she spent a significant amount of time in the North.) While living in Boston she experimented with several genres, including poetry, travel letters, and romances set on antebellum plantations. There she met and worked for Henry Wadsworth Longfellow, who eventually became her literary patron.

Writing from her childhood experiences in Mississippi, Bonner in *Dialect Tales* (1883)[29] uses a color illustration of an African American woman wearing a red headscarf and holding a broom (perhaps a new prop replacing a white baby) as the frontispiece. *Dialect Tales* is a collection of eleven stories about the blissful coexistence of African American slaves and white slaveholders. The black characters are used as the primary vehicle for the "humor" driving these stories; their playful antics and their colorful mispronunciations of words in their attempts to mimic whites work together to paint the plantation as a place as benign and joyful as Disneyland. The slave families are all intact, the father enjoys bourbon brought to him by the kind white mistress, and the carefree children have elaborate names like "Hieronymus" and "Tiddlekins."

Bonner's autobiographical *Gran'mammy Tales* and *Suwannee River Tales* (1884)[30] are a formulaic tribute to her childhood mammy Molly Wilson—but importantly, they were published a year before Joel Chandler Harris's well-known Uncle Remus tales. Bonner openly acknowledged that her books were based on her own childhood, yet she does not take the time to represent Molly Wilson as anything even close to a fully developed character. Like Harris's Uncle Remus, Wilson functions as an entertaining storyteller, content in her life and dedicated to her white family. Bonner and Harris record their stories for posterity and prosperity. They claim to honor these African Americans who were significant in their lives, yet they grant them no depth as characters with inner lives and reflections and insights of their own. During their childhoods these authors might not have thought of their family's slaves as adults with thoughts and feelings that did not revolve exclusively around them, but in adulthood neither southern author supplements childhood memories with more mature insights about racism as Lillian Smith, for example, did. Bonner's Gran'mammy represents the same flat, one-dimensional persona throughout, parroting the same lines about her beloved white children and her annoying black neighbors that appear in southern plantation stories from the 1830s. The Confederate Monument brought romanticized southern notions about life on the plantation to northerners. Bonner's stories, after they were published and made popular by northern periodicals like the *Atlantic Monthly,* did the same.

Bonner's work has been appreciated for its "accurate" reflection of regional dialects and its depiction of a southern white woman's struggle for self-identity nearly twenty years before Kate Chopin's famous book *The Awakening.* Anne Razey Gowdy explains, "This new selection of Bonner's work contributes to the ongoing larger project of rediscovering and reappraising the work of American authors who published in periodicals of the nineteenth century."[31] For feminist scholars dedicated to recovering women's writings, Bonner's work presents a challenge. How should we celebrate marginalized women's writing and also critique examples of blatant racism? We might follow Barbara White's lead in her review of Gowdy's edition, *A Sherwood Bonner Sampler*. White makes her point without equivocation: "I'm not fond of most travel writing and I hate seeing African Americans referred to as 'darkies.'"[32] As for Bonner's "Gran'mammy," White describes her as a "stand in for Aunt Jemima, [who] devotes her life to making fried chicken 'fit for white folks to eat.'"[33]

Bonner marks the distinction between "colored mammies" and "black mammies" in this way: "In our Southern home we were very fond of our old colored mammy, who had petted and scolded and nursed . . . us . . . She was not a 'black mammy,' for her complexion was the color of clear coffee."[34] These lines precede the sentiment, noted so often in chapter 1 of this book, that her Gran'mammy (named in this way because she was originally Bonner's mother's mammy) "lov[ed] her foster child, I believe, more than her own, and lov[ed] us for our dear mother's sake" (1). Gran'mammy, who is "worth her weight in gold," according to the narrator, spends her golden years taking care of African American children, whom she refers to as "little trash on the floor," while their parents work in the cotton fields (5). Despite this reality, Gran'mammy's motto is "you know niggers is a shiftless lot" (18), and she dedicates herself to Miss Josephine, her "white and shining angel" (5).

African American women were not silent about the contradictions that were so apparent in efforts to represent the mammy as a perfect example of maternal harmony. Mary Church Terrell, one of the founders of the National Association of Colored Women, boldly invoked the mammy in her scathing criticisms of southern violence directed against both black men and black women in her essay "Lynching, from a Negro's Point of View" (1904). Terrell writes, "The dictionary is searched in vain by Southern gentlemen and gentlewomen for words sufficiently ornate enough to express their admiration for a dear old 'mammy' . . . [yet] southern paternalism insists that the mammy they adore so much can neither read nor write" (quoted in O'Dell 21). This is an eloquent reminder of a sad truth: that many elderly African American women could not read the books that Bonner, Harris, and Page were writing, supposedly as tributes to them.

This does not mean that all African American women were illiterate at this time. Author and political activist Frances Ellen Watkins Harper's novel about an African American woman's decision not to pass for white (*Iola Leroy*, 1892)[35] managed to secure enough of an audience to be considered one of the best selling books by an African American author before the twentieth century. Rather than reiterate the excellent critiques on this novel by exceptional scholars like Frances Smith Foster, Hazel Carby, and Gabrielle Foreman, I remind readers that *Iola Leroy* reflects the nuances and contradictions of race and interracial relations and distinguishes itself as one of the best novels from the "mulatto woman passing for white finds trouble in romance" genre of the 1890s.[36]

In 1912, an anonymous author wrote "More Slavery at the South by a Negro Nurse," an essay published in the *Independent* detailing the grueling schedule of the author's life as a nursemaid in Atlanta.[37] She writes, "Ah, we poor colored women wage-earners in the South are fighting a terrible battle, and because of our weakness, our ignorance, our poverty, and our temptations we deserve the sympathies of mankind." The author seems to be unaware of the Fort Mill monument honoring the mammy:

> In the distant future, it may be, centuries and centuries hence, a monument of brass or stone will be erected to the Old Black Mammies of the South, but what we need is present help, present sympathy, better wages, better hours, more protections, and a chance to breathe for once while alive as free women. If none others will help us, it would seem that the Southern white women themselves might do so in their own defense, because we are rearing their children—we feed them, we bathe them, we teach them to speak the English language. (197)

Between the time of Bonner's stories and Biggers's memoir *My Miss Nancy*, plans for another kind of commemoration for the old southern mammy were brewing. In 1911, the same year that Thomas Nelson Page and Moses Ezekiel sat down to discuss the sketches for the Arlington Confederate Monument, a proposal for a "Black Mammy Memorial Institute" was circulated in Athens, Georgia, that was at once more ingenious and more insidious than the literary tributes. This institute would have combined the Faithful Slave Monument with a domestic training school for young black men and women. The institute's supporters believed that the school would serve multiple purposes. It would honor the African American slave women who served as surrogate mothers and faithful slaves; it would rectify the shortage of domestic servants caused by black migration to the North; and, finally, it could reproduce the mammy's best qualities in the next generation of African Americans. The institute would teach blacks to clean, sew, and cook, thus preparing them for the "practical duties of life." With the mammy image as a symbol of ideal social relations between blacks and whites—one based on blacks' innate ability to serve whites and their implied inferiority—*mammy* becomes a code word for appropriately subordinate black behavior.[38]

Rudimentary architectural plans were drawn up, yet, inexplicably, the school was never built. The plans for this unusual training school have been collected into an extensive pamphlet of supportive letters and sentimental tributes to the old ways, the Old South, and the Old Negro.[39] A homily called "My Old Black Mammy, Martha Ann; A True Sketch of a True Woman" introduces the long list of sentimental accolades to black mammies. The poem begins with a stanza affirming the sublime maternal devotion of the anonymous author's mammy:

> Although I am an aged man
> I love my dear old Mammy yet
> My old black mammy, Martha Ann,
> I know I never can forget
> Forget that friend, the first to fold
> Me in her ebon arms to rest
> My infant form to Mother's breast![40]

After detailing Martha Ann's loyalty to his family before and after the Civil War, the author quotes her instructions to him when he enlisted as a Confederate solider: "My dear, Go kill de Yankees, all you can." Similarly, in a play written in 1915 by Mrs. Bernie Babcock and simply called *Mammy,* the title character actually dresses in her master's Confederate uniform to distract the Union soldiers during a raid on his home. She is then shot to death by the troops who have come to free her from slavery.[41] Thus we see the mammy's heroism as she is catapulted from devoted servant to fierce defender of slavery preferring death to emancipation. When viewed alongside the frieze on the Arlington Confederate Monument depicting a loyal slave going to war with his master and the Faithful Slave Monument's proximity to a monument for Confederate soldiers, we see the cogs within the propaganda machine all working together.

The proposal includes other romantic declarations to Aunt Hannah, Mammy Susan, Mammy Julia Ann, Mammy Frances, and Mammy Dot (whose former master suggested there be a special room named just for her in the Mammy Memorial Institute). All of these tributes illustrate the mammy's loyalty to her white family during the ravages of war—and afterward, when these women voluntarily remained on the plantation.

One tribute uses the mammy's special fidelity to discuss the difference between one group of African Americans and another. The writer declares, "I approve of the . . . Black Mammy Memorial Institute, both as a worthy tribute to the deserving Mammies that made the generation before the civil war [*sic*], as a promising training school for the younger Negroes of this day who *desire to make themselves useful* in our community life" (*Black Mammy Memorial* 6; emphasis added). By proclaiming that the Mammy Memorial Institute will be most beneficial to young African Americans who want to be "useful," the author successfully invokes the difference between those blacks that can be properly trained to appreciate the useful old ways and those seeking other means of educational advancement. He has, in fact, accurately drawn a comparison between the opposing values, behavior, and ideology of the "Old Negro" and those of the "New Negro" of the twentieth century.

Contemporary scholars may be surprised to find a letter by an African American man commending this project. Robert E. Williams first identifies himself as an ardent fan of Joel Chandler Harris and then writes, "If there is anything in the world that the Negro loves it is dear old 'Dixie.'" Williams, who claims to write "in the name of ten million descendants of the 'Old Negro Mammy,'" validates the fantasy of an idealized plantation past and attempts to absolve the memorial of any racist overtones. Unfortunately, when Williams purports to honor those mammies who "set the highest standard of faithfulness," he fails to make any distinction between honoring the lives of African American women and the planned institute that would celebrate the essentialist belief that all African Americans have an innate ability (and desire) to be servants (*Black Mammy Memorial* 6).

I am unwilling to draw a direct line between the plans for the Mammy Memorial Institute and Booker T. Washington's stance on domestic and industrial training, but I want to consider how Washington's words might have been used to justify this kind of school. In Washington's famous speech at the Atlanta Exposition in 1895 (later called the "Atlanta Compromise") and in his autobiography *Up From Slavery* (1901), Washington advocates domestic education for the majority of African Americans. He assures whites that the best relationship (past, present, and future) between blacks and whites was one of service: "As in the past, you and your families will be surrounded by the most patient, faith-ful [*sic*], law-abiding, and unresentful people that the world has seen."[42] Is Washington paying tribute to "typical mammy behavior" when he celebrates the Old Negro and promises that African Americans are still capable of an adoring devotion to whites? Washington may have been savvy enough to use the right language as a kind of code meant to appease whites, but perhaps it was also meant to deflate the stereotypical image of the "black brute." He writes, "As we have proved our loyalty to you in the past, in nursing your children, watching by the sick-bed of your mothers and fathers, and often following them with tear-dimmed eyes to their graves, so in the future, in our humble way, we shall stand by you with a devotion that no foreigner can approach, ready to lay down our lives, if need be, in defense of yours" (DuBois 221).

A year after the institute was proposed, former southern belle Eliza Ripley, in her popular memoir *Social Life in Old New Orleans* (1912),[43] included an entire chapter entitled "A Monument to Mammies" on the ways of the old southern mammy. (Like Kittrell she seems to have been unaware of the monument to the faithful slave in Fort Mill.) Ripley relays an urgency to memorialize the antebellum past when she writes, "let us have a memorial before the last of us who had a black mammy passes away." For Ripley—instead of honoring African American women—a mammy monument would provide a necessary comfort to white southerners who were insulted by the abolitionist movement. "We who still linger would love to see a granite monument to the memory of the dear mammy . . . our grandchildren . . . will never know the kind of mammies their ancestors were blessed with" (Ripley 209).

Ripley's personal contribution to this memorializing is a tribute to the many mammies in her life: her childhood mammy, her husband's Mammy Charlotte, and several unnamed mammies from neighboring plantations. These women raised all of their masters' children and then selflessly elected to remain with "their white folks" after the war. Ripley's words echo the antebellum memoirs and biographies, which are consistent with the plantation mythology of local color literature. This kind of impassioned romanticizing of the slave South is nothing less than pernicious in the wake of Jim Crow laws and a resurgence of lynching and race riots throughout the North and the South at this time. Her memoir and the proposal for a mammy-training school signal a blatant plea for sympathetic interest in the white southerner's version of slavery. Beneath Eliza Ripley's stoic assertion of the need to build a monument "before the last of us who had a black mammy passes away" is her defensive wail, "It wasn't like the Yankee abolitionists said it was; we can prove it; look at our black mammies!"

The notion of the mammy's maternal devotion to whites and ostensibly to her own oppression is appropriated and subverted by W. E. B. DuBois in his editorial response to Ripley, "The Black Mother," which appeared in the *Crisis* the same year Ripley's work was published. DuBois begins with a sarcastic note about the efforts of southern whites like Ripley's to immortalize the black mammy in stone as a display of their "appreciation of the qualities of motherhood in the Negro." He then attacks Thomas Nelson Page and other slavery apologists directly: "Let us hope that the black mammy for whom so many sentimental tears have been shed, has disappeared from American life. She existed under a false social system that deprived her of husband and child. Thomas Nelson Page, after—with wet eyelids—recounting the virtues of his mammy, declares petulantly that she did not care for her own children. Doubtless this was true. How could it have been otherwise? But just so far as it was true it was a perversion of motherhood."[44] DuBois ends with the demand that "present-day mammies" be allowed to "suckle their own children."

DuBois takes his place along with Frederick Douglass and Harriet Jacobs in the tradition of reclaiming black maternity, refocusing black maternal devotion, and returning black mothers to black children. His critique of Page predates poet Sterling Brown's comment on Page in one of Brown's best-known lines from his essay "The Muted South": "Thomas Nelson Page was not lying in his eulogy of the mammy . . . I am sure he loved his mammy *to death*" (emphasis added).[45]

Despite DuBois's criticism of mammy tributes, Eliza Ripley's dream of a national mammy monument almost came to fruition in 1924 when the Daughters of the Confederacy decided that the mammy deserved more than a small statue in South Carolina and the frieze on the Confederate Monument. South Carolina congressman Charles Stedman introduced a bill to the Senate for a "monument in memory of the faithful colored mammies of the South." The bill had strong support, but there was sufficient protest from black newspapers and organizations, and it was never passed as a result.[46]

One of the most eloquent African American responses to these efforts to resurrect the mammy is by DuBois, in the last chapter of his book *The Gift of Black Folk* (1924).[47] In the middle of a discourse on black Christianity, DuBois names the mammy as "one of the most pitiful of the world's Christs" and calls her "an embodied Sorrow." DuBois laments that whatever dignity the mammy possessed was ultimately "surrendered to those who lived to lynch her sons and ravish her daughters. From her great full breast walked forth the governors and judges, ladies of wealth and fashions, merchants and scoundrels who led the South. And the rest gave her memory the reverence of silence. But a few snobs have lately sought to advertise her sacrifice and degradation and (enhance) their own cheap success by building . . . a load of stone miscalled a monument." In this seething commentary aimed at the Daughters of the Confederacy, DuBois shifts his focus from the virtues of black motherhood to southern antiblack violence and deflates the fatuous fantasy of idealized race relations (DuBois 337–38).

Murdering Mammy: Literally

DuBois's portrait of the mammy as martyr figure is a dramatic contrast to another portrait of the mammy that he selected for publication in an issue of the *Crisis* in 1917.[48] In the short story written by Adeline F. Ries, called simply "Mammy, A Story," we see an extreme version of the appropriated and subverted mammy that DuBois had introduced five years earlier. In Ries's rendition, the symbol of racial harmony is distorted until the fantasy and myth dissolve into a tragic nightmare.

The narrative shows that the author was influenced by the romantic language and mystical tone of fables: "Mammy's heart felt heavy indeed when (the time was now two years past) marriage had borne Shiela [*sic*], her white baby, away from the Governor's plantation to the coast."

For an extremely short story—barely three and a half pages long— "Mammy" is a dramatic and memorable piece. The plot and action of the story are simple: the slave woman, "Mammy," raises a "white baby," Shiela, and her own "black baby," Lucy. At first Mammy grieves when Shiela's marriage takes her away from the governor's plantation, but then Lucy is sold away from her ("sold like common household ware!") once Shiela needs a baby nurse. After a year, Mammy's master informs her that her daughter, Lucy, has died suddenly of heart failure—presumably from the stress of caring for Shiela's child. Instead of crying, Mammy repeats, "They took her from me an' she died," over and over again. Mammy travels to the coast for Lucy's funeral, where she comforts Shiela. Claiming that she is too grieved to attend her own daughter's funeral, Mammy stays behind to look after Shiela's baby boy. She then takes the child to the ocean and drowns him. Mammy is discovered on the beach, where she is laughing like a "madwoman" and shouting, "They took her from me an' she died!" (118).

Instead of transferring Mammy's allegiance from a white family to her own family, Ries questions the validity of the mammy's seemingly innocuous presence in the white household. Her character is not innately violent, but she becomes a killer in an Old Testament style of revenge. Historically, the threat of black violence was typically embodied in the "black brute" type appearing, for instance, in the film *Birth of a Nation* (which preceded Ries's story by two years.) In superimposing one type over the other, Ries evokes the unimaginable: a mammy who is a brute. This mammy seems to nurture the oppressor but is also capable of destroying him, exposing an unforgiving and therefore dangerous aspect of black maternity.

In the Ries story, Mammy's progression of loss is matched by her mental and emotional demise: she is saddened when her grown-up white baby moves away, grieved when her own child is sold away, and driven insane when her child is "killed" by overwork by the same white charge. This chronicle of Mammy's emotions prepares the reader for her extreme grief but not for her actions. Ries exploits our expectation that the mammy's grief, and ostensibly any slave mother's grief, is impotent. She then provides a lesson in subversion by reminding her readers that sometimes there are no black children to whom the mammy can return.

At the risk of overemphasizing this story, I want to point out that feminist analyses of slave motherhood fail to provide a context to interpret this killer mammy. Hortense Spillers's landmark article "Mamma's Baby, Papa's Maybe: An American Grammar Book" offers the best framework for understanding the tenuous relationship between slave mothers and their children.[49] Arguing that ownership renders all slaves "kin-less," Spillers concludes that "under conditions of captivity, the offspring of the female does not 'belong' to the mother." In Brown's story her daughter, Lucy, was "her baby," but her status as property superseded her status as daughter. Spillers points out that "we could not say that the enslaved offspring was 'orphaned,'" but the child does become, under the press of a patronymic, patrifocal, patrilineal, and patriarchal order, . . . someone whose human and familial status, by the very nature of the case, had yet to be defined. Spillers concludes that "'kinship' loses meaning, since the property relations can invade it at any given and arbitrary moment" (74).

It is precisely at the arbitrary moment of sale that Mammy begins to comprehend her state of nonkinship to her own daughter and subsequently begins what might be considered a downward spiral toward mad-ness. Significantly, this story complicates the entire paradigm of kin relationships by suggesting that Mammy's relationship with her surrogate daughter, Shiela, also deserved to be honored.

Spillers's argument is reinforced by Angela Davis's earlier work in which she comments that "slave women were not mothers at all."[50] Davis gives the example of a South Carolina court that deemed that slave mothers had no claims on their children that had to be respected by law. Davis concludes with this chilling note: "According to this ruling, children could be sold away from their mothers at any age because 'the young of slaves. . . . stand on the same footing as other animals.'" Both Davis and Spillers recognize the negation of motherhood under slavery as a function of a patriarchal slave system. They do not push their analyses far enough to speculate on how this paradoxical kinless motherhood might have been rationalized by slave women. How did they deal with it? What was the result of their experience as mothers to children owned by someone else? And how does the surrogate relationship of the mammy and white child mimic the mammy's tenuous relationship with her biological child? If this short story can offer us any insight (morbid as it may be) it is in the very first paragraph, when we learn that Mammy loves her white baby yet knows that the baby does not "belong" to her and she loves her black baby, whom she assumes does "belong" to her.

By putting the slave mother's biological and surrogate relationships on equal footing, blood ties and affectionate ties are rendered equally void. Ries makes a profound comment on slave motherhood: when ownership supplants biology, it results in the slave mother having a surrogate relationship to her own child. Ries attacks the mammy as a symbol of sublime love by exposing the fragility of her emotional and biological ties and then explores how that fragility causes emotional distress. Mammy's biological motherhood is repeatedly denied, leaving her powerless to protect her child. Her lament, "They took her from me an' she died," articulates the double offense that proves to be too much for her to endure. Ries gives us the slave mother's heartbreaking pathos and then turns it on its head, whipping the reader from pity to horror within seconds.

In the array of mammies from the nineteenth to the twentieth centuries, this unique depiction of a killer or brute mammy seems to have appeared and disappeared in silence. There is no information available on the author, and there are no clues about the response this story elicited from the readers of *Crisis*.

Dealing the "Mammy Card"

Two years after Ries's story appeared, African American educator Charlotte Hawkins Brown published a remarkable eighteen-page story called "'Mammy': An Appeal to the Heart of the South" (1919) in an effort to raise money for her school for African Americans.[51] The Palmer Memorial Institute, in Sedalia, North Carolina, was in financial peril at the time. "Mammy" is Brown's semiallegorical tale about the failure of white southerners to properly support their devoted black servants (perhaps because so much money was being directed to mammy statues) in spite of what they were writing about these servants in their memoirs and short stories.

Brown's story "Mammy" begins with a short note claiming that the story is based upon the following facts: A wealthy spinster (Polly) died on a farm near Sedalia, and her faithful colored servant, Mammy (Susan), lived a few feet away in a makeshift cabin. Polly left "large and gracious bequests" to "distant relatives and friends." But to "Mammy" she left only twenty-five dollars. The final line reads: "Her best days are gone. Others enjoy the fruits of her many years of labor. She is but one of many who are left destitute in old age by those she has been faithful to unto death" (Brown vii). The destitute condition of Mammy Susan's cabin is symbolic of her failing health. In the story, Mammy Susan has served as wet nurse, cook, and general servant for a white family named Bretherton for many years. When one of her former charges died shortly after childbirth, Mammy's milk saved the baby's life. The narrative focuses on Edith, Mammy Susan's favorite charge, who attends a boarding school where she regales her classmates with tales of "negro fidelity" and "white devotion" and shares with them the famous beaten biscuits that Mammy Susan makes for her. Mammy's fidelity includes lending the family money from her own meager funds when they fall into debt. (This is similar to a theme in *Incidents in the Life of a Slave Girl* reviewed in chap. 2.)

When Edith returns from school, bringing a few of her friends along, she claims that she wants them to see Mammy's quaint cabin and complains, "I know it's spotless, but it looks as if it would tumble down any minute and when I was there last fall, Mammy had a wash tub on top of the bed to catch the large drops of rain" (12). Edith's father insists that the cabin isn't worth repairing because Mammy will be dead soon and the property will be sold. Despite Edith's superficial concern about Mammy and her cabin, her family is too preoccupied to help Mammy. Mammy dies on the same day as Mistress Polly—she actually dies in an effort to get to the big house kitchen to make Edith her special biscuits. Mammy is literally killed by cold whiteness when an avalanche of snow falls on her from a rooftop. Mistress Polly is buried in a well-maintained private cemetery, while Mammy's body is taken to the county burial grounds in a wagon.

In reality, the Palmer Institute shares a few traits with the proposed Black Mammy Memorial Institute. For example, Brown always emphasized the helpful role that trained black women could play in the domestic service of white women. Brown was fond of saying, "Black women educated at Palmer, would learn to become 'fine, clean mothers and good homemakers for themselves and for others.'"[52]

Additionally, Brown met Booker T. Washington while she was still a student. Washington was impressed with her and claimed that Brown was his "only convert from New England."[53] When Brown later invited one of Washington's acquaintances to help her promote her school, she was criticized for using an "impractical curriculum." Apparently Brown never fully embraced Washington's philosophy on vocational education. In *Gender and Jim Crow: Women and the Politics of White Supremacy in North Carolina, 1896–1920* (1996), Glenda E. Gilmore persuasively argues that if Washington believed Brown to be a convert, "she outfoxed the Wizard himself."[54] She accomplished this by portraying the school as being far more industrial than it really was. An unidentified teacher explained the ruse this way: "[Brown] always had a college preparatory class. . . . All the Negroes had to have that in order to get along in the South. . . . you could teach anything you wanted . . . you taught them Latin and French and all the things you knew."[55]

In the seven years since the Palmer Institute's establishment, Brown had relied primarily upon financial support for the school from wealthy white northerners. Brown knew that if she wanted to gain support from white southerners she would have to rely on their consistent nostalgia for the mammy. "Mammies represented the *one consistent point of contact* between southern black and white women, and white women continually bragged about their love for their Mammies" (Gilmore 189; emphasis added). Significantly, "Mammy" is dedicated to a white woman, but Brown's opening paragraph seems to be dedicated to white men as representative "true southerners." Brown writes, "If there is any word that arouses emotion in the heart of a true southerner, it is the word, 'Mammy.' His mind goes back to the tender embraces, the watchful eyes, the crooning melodies, which lulled him to rest, and the sweet old black face. 'What a memory!' he exclaims."[56]

Obviously, Brown considered "Mammy" a tool to promote her educational agenda by stressing interracial cooperation among southern women. But Brown's "Mammy" is not a tale of love rewarded; it is an indictment of white neglect of African Americans. Brown calls upon white women to remember their duty to black women. "It is no longer enough to be fond of old Mammy; white women must act on that affection" (Gilmore 189). Indeed, Brown used the nostalgia surrounding the mammy to appeal not only to the hearts of the South but to southern pockets as well. Interestingly, Gilmore believes that Brown's play on southern sympathies for financial gain was beneath her, saying, "She had spent almost twenty years building her dignity in North Carolina; it was amazing that she would play the Mammy card now." Yet Brown's success could be measured in mortar; by 1922, southern contributions to Palmer increased enough to finance the school's first brick building.

What does Brown's literary "memorial" to the mammy add to the battle over the legacy of the Old South and how the mammy will be remembered?[57] Brown uses "Mammy" to solicit sympathy and financial support from white southerners—this is probably more a case of her playing the guilt card than the "mammy card." Part of the implication is that in supporting the Palmer Institute, whites were supporting or funding African American loyalty.

What does this short story from 1919 by an African American woman add to the puzzle? In many ways Brown's "Mammy" responds to the call for a monument to honor the African American women who worked as mammies with a call for more realistic and pragmatic support. Stone monuments would do little to actually assist those women who were poor, elderly, or ill.

Brown's "appeal" then is one calling for gratitude coupled with financial support; it is an appeal to white southerners to shift their attention from memorializing their mythical mammies in stone to attending to real people and to the education of young African Americans. Brown's response differs dramatically from Ries's, as she shifts the emphasis from the black mammy–white charge relationship to an indictment of white southerners for their failure to provide much-needed assistance to the mammy even as they praised her for her loyalty and devotion. Adeline Ries and Brown use the mammy figure in different ways for different reasons, yet both acknowledge her as the most powerful and most valuable prize in the battle for the Old South.

This struggle to define and redefine the mammy takes a new turn, a more overtly political one, during the New Negro movement. A more holistic picture of New Negro symbols emerges when we look at how essays by New Negro authors W. E. B. DuBois and Elise Johnson McDougald work in tandem with specific examples of art by Winold Reiss and Sargent Johnson. One New Negro symbol of black mother and child is used against another as a means of deflecting the popularization of revisionist history. The Old Negro black mammy memorials and the New Negro movement are significant factors shaping ideas and attitudes during an era of transition in racial identity and racial interaction.

More critical attention should be paid to how visual representations of black motherhood function in our assessment of Harlem Renaissance art. I address this by focusing on two visual interpretations of black maternity in the New Negro movement, the drawing by Winold Reiss just mentioned and the later sculpture *Forever Free* (fig. 18) described earlier in this chapter.

DuBois's 1912 essay "The Black Mother" announces the role of a more idealized version of black maternity as a significant and optimistic emblem of the New Negro movement. This is most apparent in the frontispiece of Alain Locke's seminal work *The New Negro: An Interpretation* (1925), a drawing by Winold Reiss entitled *The Brown Madonna*.[58]

German-born Winold Reiss enjoyed considerable popularity during the Harlem Renaissance. His drawings of African Americans during the 1920s were among the first positive depictions of blacks by a white artist. In 1923, he was selected to paint the major figures of the Harlem Renaissance for a special issue of the social welfare journal *Survey Graphic* entitled "Harlem: Mecca of the New Negro" (March 1, 1925).

Alain Locke was so pleased with Reiss's portrait that he commissioned him to draw the frontispiece for *The New Negro*.[59]

Reiss's drawing *Brown Madonna* shows a slender, dark brown woman wearing a pink sweater holding a young child on her lap. There is a fascinating interplay of light and shade in the drawing, moving from the darkness of the madonna's hair through her face and clothes into the stark white of the baby's gown. The drawing conveys little warmth or human connection between this mother and child; she holds her baby rather carelessly with one hand as the other is draped at her side. Clearly this portrait of black mother with black child was appealing enough for Locke to overlook the lack of emotion in the drawing, perhaps because it was intended to usher in a new era of representations of African American mothers with African American children.

One contributing author to *The New Negro,* author Elise McDougald, admired Reiss's work so much that she took large groups of Harlem school-children on tour to see his portraits. In her essay "The Task of Negro Womanhood," using Aunt Jemima as a trope, McDougald links the insulting caricature of black women and the disrespect accorded them from mainstream America. The author insists that black women are worthy of better treatment and cites their value as good mothers in terms of civic responsibility. "One cannot resist the temptation to pause for a moment and pay tribute to these Negro mothers. And to call attention to the service she is rendering to the nation."[60] She then moves to a covert reference to the National Mammy Monument proposed the previous year, adding, "If the mothers of the race should ever be honored by state or federal legislation, the artist's imagination will not find a more inspiring subject than the modern Negro mother." The modern Negro mother, in case there is any confusion, is progressive and race conscious "but as loyal and tender as the much extolled, yet pitiable black mammy of slavery days" (372). This juxtaposition affirms my argument that New Negro intellectuals appropriated and subverted the mammy image for their own purposes. By identifying and isolating those qualities of the mammy that are easily transferred, they redirected her "loyalty and tenderness" toward her own children to refashion a new model of black maternity as "the modern Negro mother."

The multifaceted mammy prism turns again here, producing a continuous spectrum of views on racial hierarchy. On one side, we see white southerners building a domestic training school in an attempt to reproduce the mammy in the next generation of African Americans; on another side we see a twentieth-century fantasy of a murderous slave mother's vendetta exacted upon her mistress's child. On yet another side of the prism, she is a New Negro emblem of racial progress as a "Brown Madonna," the new standard of racial fidelity, steadfastly nurturing the next generation. The variety of the New Negro movement responses to the black mammy provides an appropriate context for the analyses of the novels *The Sound and the Fury* and *Gone with the Wind* to follow in the next chapter.

CHAPTER SIX

Blown Away: *Gone with the Wind* and *The Sound and the Fury*

> *The household is a school of power. Here within the door,*
> *we learn the tragic-comedy of human life.*
> — RALPH WALDO EMERSON, "EDUCATION"

Within the vast and colorful spectrum of southern households, William Faulkner's Compson family and Margaret Mitchell's O'Hara family are among the most memorable. The families' mammies, Mitchell's Mammy in *Gone with the Wind* (1935)[1] and Faulkner's Dilsey in *The Sound and the Fury* (1929),[2] share enough traits to be isolated in a comparative analysis.

Both authors explore the intricacies of the Lost Cause tradition and the burden of memory. Both authors contend with the overwhelming mythology of the Old South by using the mammy character along with other well-known types: the southern belle and the southern gentleman. Published within the same decade, both novels ask broad, imposing questions about how the Old South and specifically southern aristocracy would be remembered, and about the roles of truth and memory in contemporary explorations of relations between southern African Americans and Anglo Americans. Faulkner and Mitchell engage readers in a discussion about who should and would be responsible for holding the memories of the Old South. Answers may be found in these very different mammy characters and their relationships with the white families with whom they live. Dilsey's and Mammy's roles can be read as symbolic barometers that we check to determine how these southern families will fare in the future. And what about the stormy winds evoked by the titles of these two novels? Dilsey and Mammy are powerful forces that dramatically and permanently alter the emotional landscape of the families to whom they are attached.

This chapter is informed by Foucault's theory of the body as a site of struggle. With that lens in place, these mammy characters serve as the sites where battles surrounding the Lost Cause tradition and the special southern burden of memory are fought within the domestic sphere of family life.[3] If we see Dilsey's and Mammy's bodies in a metonymic relationship to each woman's sense of self, it would force us to recast the mammy, from a vibrant enduring symbol of antebellum loyalty to a more humane and temporal reality. For example, throughout the novels, Mammy's and Dilsey's aging bodies and declining health effectively evoke the demise of the Old South, the old ways and the old relationships between loyal and servile African Americans and white southerners.

Susan Bordo makes an important point that American feminism played a crucial role in developing an understanding of body practice and body theory, but this is rarely acknowledged. Even "feminists who do scholarship on the body claim Foucault as its founding father and guiding light. But Foucault did not invent the idea that the body is the focal point for struggles over the shape of power."[4] Bordo traces this argument from Mary Wollstonecraft to Charlotte Bunch, yet she would agree that Karl Marx makes the most effective argument about how economic class directly affects our experiences and definitions of the body, "because laboring people experience their bodies in different ways than elite people experience their bodies."[5] All of these points come together within and around the body of the mammy laboring in elite southern households; in the novels explored here, the bodies of African American and white women represent labor and elitism, respectively, because of the ways that white female bodies emerge in obvious contrast to their black counterparts: Mammy in relation to Scarlett, and Dilsey in relation to Mrs. Compson.[6]

> "I'm coming just as fast as I can." Dilsey said. "She ought to know by this time I ain't got no wings."
> — The Sound and the Fury, 23

> "Some folks thinks as how Ah kin fly," grumbled Mammy, shuffling up the stairs.
> — Gone with the Wind, 78

Gone with the Wind and *The Sound and the Fury* represent extremes in popularity and obscurity, revealing the irony of the literary business: *Gone with the Wind* continues to sell hundreds of thousands of hardcover copies a year, while *The Sound and the Fury,* though considered a masterpiece of modernistic fiction and widely taught in universities, has not acquired a mainstream readership.[7]

If the obvious value of *The Sound and the Fury* is in its experimental narrative structure, its deeper worth lies in the intricate interracial dynamics of two families, the Gibsons and the Compsons. The African American Gibsons are servants for the white Compson family, who were once solid members of southern aristocracy, but suffer now from abject financial and emotional crisis.[8] Like many blacks and whites in the South in early twentieth century, they share both an immediate daily life and a long, muddled past.

The novel is divided into four dated sections (one in 1910 and three in 1928), each one recording and rerecording some of the same events and milestones for the Compsons and reflecting Faulkner's effort to write the novel four different times, from four different perspectives. By writing the same sequences again and again, Faulkner breaks down and reconstructs the conventions of realistic fiction.[9] The Compsons' servant Dilsey Gibson is most fully developed in the first section (Benjy's perspective) and the last section (the voice of the omniscient narrator). More than fifteen years after the publication of the novel, Faulkner was asked to write a key to the characters, resulting in the "Compson Appendix," which is included in more recent editions. The appendix both emphasizes and clarifies some of the Compson family history and provides a glimpse of what happens to some characters after the last pages of the novel. Dilsey's appendix notation is simply "They endured" (427).

It is easy—and tempting—to place an inordinate emphasis on the appendix in general and in these two provocative words in particular as the best medium for understanding Dilsey. By shifting the focus away from Dilsey's profound endurance to all of the conspicuous warnings that she will not endure, we see how her mortality points to new dimensions of this unique character.

The Compsons' blindness to her declining health and her impending death are signposts revealing their inability to survive in the South of the twentieth century. Diane Roberts notes that "no one laughs at Dilsey the way they might at the mammy in *Gone with the Wind.* . . . But Dilsey performs essentially the same function. She nurtures not just the bodies but also the souls of the unsalvageable Compsons. . . . Dilsey endures, but she does not escape."[10]

> *This thing going to go to pieces under you all some day.*
> — *The Sound and the Fury,* 9

Among the most haunting sounds in the aptly titled novel are Benjy's excruciating cries when his comprehension is challenged and Dilsey's labored thumping up and down the stairs of the ramshackle Compson house. Dilsey's poor health and advancing age are difficult to isolate because of her more obvious strength in carrying on day-to-day activities while the Compsons remain emotionally comatose. Dilsey continues to cook food and serve it, continues to keep the Compson house "warm" both literally and figuratively, and continues to protect the most powerless Compsons: Benjy and Quentin, Caddy's daughter. But it is naive to assume that Dilsey's consistency is synonymous with her endurance.

Dilsey never complains about her health as Mrs. Compson does, but her poor health is apparent to the reader in every way that Caroline Compson's is invisible. Faulkner's emphasis on the *sound* of Dilsey's mobility fully challenges the reader's sensibilities just as his obscure time parameters do. We never see Dilsey limping, but in scene after scene we read about the noise she makes and about the way other characters listen to her move with great difficulty through the house. When Dilsey walks, she "toils painfully" or "heavily"; in one scene Caroline Compson listens to "Dilsey yet descending the stairs with a sort of painful and terrific slowness that would have become maddening." In another scene both she and Jason listen as Dilsey mounts the stairs one at a time: "They heard her a long while on the stairs" (347). Jason refers to her age repeatedly, saying bitterly, "She was so old she couldn't do any more than move hardly." His niece Quentin also calls her an "old fool." Faulkner gives Dilsey's aging tremendous nuance by having us listen to it and feel it before he tells us what Dilsey looks like (333, 347).

When we remember that the mammy's mortality is being debated in this discussion, we see that Faulkner has replaced the fat, eminently healthy mammy of plantation mythology—the one reproduced in Mammy in *Gone with the Wind*—with a decrepit and aging mammy figure.[11] Faulkner establishes Dilsey's humanity by insisting that she is vulnerable to all human weakness, and ultimately a very human death. So much is made of Dilsey's role as the strong black link in a weakening white family structure that it is easy to underestimate the powerful meaning of Dilsey's own decline, her physical disintegration and a breakdown in her ability (and perhaps in her desire) to continue enduring the Compson family crises.

Dilsey's heroic patience with Benjy's mental disability and Mrs. Compson's hypochondriacal complaints are offset by her startling impatience with her own son Luster. Sometimes Luster's impudence deserves retribution; when Dilsey catches him teasing Benjy, she hits him on the head and threatens to tell his father about it. When Dilsey gives Benjy a birthday cake and she thinks Luster is eating more than his share, she warns him: "Reach it again, and I chop it right off with this here butcher knife" (70). These are strong words to a young boy who is just excited about having an out-of-the-ordinary treat. Dilsey strikes Luster again when she worries that he might wake the Compsons early one Sunday morning, and in another exchange she issues a harsh warning to Luster along with a pessimistic prediction about his fate: "En ef you hurts Benjy, Nigger boy, I don't know whut I do! You bound fer de chain gang, but I'll send you dar fo even chain gang ready fer you" (398).

The way Dilsey treats Luster is surprisingly reminiscent of Aunt Chloe knocking her small children around in *Uncle Tom's Cabin,* and it seems that Faulkner has fallen into what I call the "Mammy Trap" that snares Harriet Beecher Stowe and other well-meaning authors. For example, his gesture toward a humane, dignified mammy character is truncated by his inability to transcend the mammy stereotype so ingrained within his imagination and within his own personal life. One of the most consistent traits assigned to the stereotypic mammy character is that these women demonstrate a strong preference for the white children of the families that own or employ them over their own children.

Faulkner succeeds in expressing Dilsey's humanity through her treatment of Luster; clearly it would take superhuman strength to tolerate the Compsons without some kind of displacement. And yet Faulkner is unable to save Dilsey from reminding us of the stereotype, since he has drawn her as a more individualized mammy whose nurturing never extends to her own family. Dilsey's roughness with Luster rounds her out as a character and parrots prototypical mammy behavior simultaneously. In addition to falling into the Mammy Trap, significantly, Faulkner reveals that the mammy is something of a tar baby: it is nearly impossible to strike out against this figure without getting stuck.[12]

It is true that Dilsey cannot completely escape mammy status, but this observation leads us to the question, where else can Dilsey take out her frustrations? When Dilsey is tired and frustrated she hits Luster because she cannot strike out at any of the Compsons. We might prefer that she take out her anger on Jason or his mother, but the author limits her emotional scope in accordance with plausibility; it was unthinkable for a southern black woman in 1928 in the South to display any hostility toward the white people for whom she worked. Dilsey can tolerate the Compsons, she can nurture them and mediate their internal family struggles, but she cannot express her weary frustration with them in any way that reflects her anger or bitterness. In the scene in which Jason burns the carnival tickets instead of giving them to Luster, who begs for them, we see Dilsey at the threshold of her patience, and yet she does restrain herself.

My point is first that Dilsey's ability to tolerate the dysfunctional Compsons is contingent on using Luster as an outlet. Second, since Faulkner has no vision for Dilsey to act out any emotion other than calm endurance for and with the Compsons, what we see instead are the limitations he imposes on the full scope of her behavior.

Ironically, a more innovative analysis of Dilsey calls for de-emphasizing her relationship with the Compsons so that we can more fully appreciate who Dilsey is when she is with her own family and when she is alone. It is her moments of quiet contemplation that truly make Dilsey a radical mammy character.

The final chapter of the novel is often called "Dilsey's chapter" because Faulkner offers the readers more insight into Dilsey's personal life there than in any other chapter. In the first several paragraphs of that chapter Dilsey stands in the doorway to her home, wearing a silk dress and a fur-trimmed cape, and watches the sun rise. Dilsey's solitary moment sets *The Sound and the Fury* apart from every other text in this study. The full passage conveys the serenity of this scene:

> She wore a stiff black straw hat perched upon her turban, and a maroon velvet cape with a border of mangy and anonymous fur above a dress of purple silk, and she stood in the door for a while with her myriad and sunken face lifted to the weather, and one gaunt hand flac-soled [*sic*] as the belly of a fish, then she moved the cape aside and examined the bosom of her gown. (330)

Dilsey's physical appearance is given for the first time and we see the cabin where she lives with her family. It is this moment of Dilsey watching "the weather" before she begins to gather wood that makes Dilsey profoundly unique in this study, even though the reader is not privy to her inner reflection. And it is important that the author himself does not intrude on her moment and try to explain what she is thinking or feeling. By contrast, in *Gone with the Wind,* where Scarlett's interior monologue drives the narrative—sometimes to a cloying extent—there is never a time when Mammy is granted this degree of solitude. Dilsey must have dressed for this private ritual because she changes her clothes before she goes to the Compson house to build a fire and begin cooking for them.

Why is Dilsey wearing her Easter outfit at dawn? Dilsey changes in and out of this dress twice in this chapter; the first time she has it on seems to be a kind of dress rehearsal for going to church later that afternoon. Each time she changes clothes, she returns to her own cabin and "emerges" anew as if she is shedding clothes instead of exchanging them. The significance of the cabin as a haven or sanctuary is easy to overlook in this lengthy sequence where Dilsey changes in and out of clothes almost ritualistically. When she first opens her cabin door, she wears "a stiff black straw hat perched upon her turban, and a maroon velvet cape with a border of mangy and anonymous fur above a dress of purple silk" (330). Later, she is framed by the doorway again, in another more layered outfit, "this time in a man's felt hat and an army overcoat, beneath the frayed skirts of which her blue gingham dress fell in uneven ballooning" (332). The third time Dilsey crosses the threshold, she has retrieved her maroon cape and her purple gown; she has also accentuated her wardrobe with long white gloves and removed her turban (358). For her final appearance in the doorway she wears a faded calico dress (372). Dilsey "emerges" a total of four times, each time dressed anew, to signal either a change of mood or a change of heart.

Once Dilsey goes into the cabin, she becomes invisible to the reader—as she is to the Compsons. Dilsey's exchanging one set of clothes for another may represent her presentation to two very different communities. The old gingham dress is for working in the Compson kitchen; the silk dress is for her "dress rehearsal" for Easter and for church service among her own family and community. It is more important for the cabin to function as a world away from Caroline Compson's demands, Jason's bitterness, Quentin's frustration, and Benjy's incessant and incoherent wailing. For the first time, the reader is aware of the spatial difference between Dilsey's home and the Compsons.

Something truly significant has happened to Dilsey during the Easter sermon preached by Reverend Shegog. Her tears and her cryptic repetition of one line, "I've seed de furst en de last . . . I seed de beginnin, en now I sees de endin" (371, 375), signal a revelation and transformation for Dilsey. When we do not pay proper attention to Dilsey's age, it is easy to assume that her revelation is about the Compson family. Once we attend to Dilsey's decline, it makes sense that the first and the last, the beginning and the end are self-referential, her vision of her own death. Her hobbling about is the death knell for this elderly mammy. Jason and Caroline Compson listen to it, but are unable to fully comprehend it, perhaps because they cannot imagine their lives without the enduring Dilsey.

Most importantly, Faulkner sounds this death knell of the mammy as the most recognizable symbol of the mythic South. Unlike Margaret Mitchell's Mammy, who by the end of the novel remains forever on the plantation waiting for Scarlett, Dilsey has distanced her emotional life from the Compsons by the end of the novel. Dilsey's mortality is Faulkner's ambiguous tribute to the mammy type.

> *Mammy, the last link with the old days.*
> — *Gone with the Wind*, 1024

Gone with the Wind remains a classic because of Margaret Mitchell's ambitious attempt to establish a pinnacle of old southern romanticism. The romance between Scarlett and Rhett is a perennial favorite; the African American actress Audra McDonald included this novel in her list of books that made a profound difference in her life, along with *Sister Carrie* and *One Hundred Years of Solitude*.

Mitchell's domineering Mammy is a composite character with almost all of the stereotypical mammy qualities,[13] with each trait exaggerated until Mammy is reduced to a comical caricature. She is not just fat, she is grossly obese, and she is not just subservient to her master's family, she has adopted their entire belief system, which insists on her inferiority.

Mammy is not a biological mother; her familial ties have been sacrificed so that she may belong more fully to the O'Haras. We learn early in the novel that Mammy was raised "in the bedroom of Solange Robillard, Ellen

O'Hara's mother," removing her so completely from contact with her own race that we understand that her behavior, her attitudes, and her values are the result of her completely isolated existence as a black servant for three generations of O'Hara women. In this one line, Mitchell carefully detaches Mammy from the historic black community and the mythic slave quarters of Joel Chandler Harris's Uncle Remus stories. Like Topsy's, Mammy's parentage is erased so that she comes to her white owners as a tabula rasa, making her the perfect mammy—the product of such specialized upbringing that her loyalty, indeed her heart and soul, belongs to the O'Haras—because she has never belonged to her own race or to herself in any way.

When Mitchell formally introduces Mammy, she creates an improbable sense of mutuality, insisting, "Mammy felt that she owned the O'Haras, body and soul," and that Mammy was "devoted to her last drop of blood to the O'Haras" (24–25). Mammy "owns" the O'Hara's only in her obsessive need to run their lives and to hold Scarlett to ridiculous codes of southern propriety. The length to which she has internalized white southern values and codes of behavior is so extreme that Mammy's world consists only of "quality" (wealthy) white folks, white trash, and "wuthless nigguhs"—her general category for nearly all blacks. Mammy has no concept of any positive black qualities because she exists in a vacuum; she does not even have a name for herself other than "Mammy." Mammy affirms Trudier Harris's argument that the "true southern maid is the mammy whose ineffective compromise in the home of the white mistresses causes her to identify completely with the status quo[;] she believes within her heart in the rightness of the established order of which she is a part. She has lost her black cultural identity (if she ever had one) and all sense of spiritual identification with black people" (24–25).

Mitchell affirms the mythology that mammies were a "special breed" of slave women by constructing a slave who supports the slave system through her maternity. Instead of displaying the kind of ignorant fidelity that the slave butler Pork does, Mammy nearly nurtures Scarlett to death. She chases her with a shawl so she doesn't catch a cold, orders her to stay out of the sun to protect her fragile white skin, and forces her to eat privately so that she can keep up the public appearance of being dainty. She embodies the old southern manifesto in her efforts to imitate her oppressors. Mitchell tells us that "Mammy was black, but her code of conduct and her sense of pride were as high as or higher than those of her owners" (79). Not only is the mammy completely satisfied with her role as slave, but she also upholds all of the most fundamental properties of southern aristocracy.

The metaphorical breast-feeding in *Gone with the Wind* is Mammy's perpetual force-feeding of Scarlett and her mother, Ellen. Southern idealism runs through her body like mother's milk for Scarlett, whose "natural impulses were unladylike" (79). Mammy's trumped-up indignity is at once comical and pathetic: a slave woman convinced that she is part of a good southern family is teaching her mistress to be a good southern belle. When Mammy constrains Scarlett's antibelle impulses by insisting that she knows the standard of "white ladyhood" in the South, Mitchell mocks the racist exclusivity of the cult of true womanhood.

Whatever Mitchell's intention might have been, there is something monstrous about Mammy. Her enormous size, her towering strength and endurance, her nonstop nagging often make her seem more monstrous than compassionate. These extraordinary qualities actually detract from her humanity instead of affirming it.

The mammy's role as surrogate mother is usually hinged on the white mother and slave mistress being sickly (like Caroline Compson or Marie St. Clare in *Uncle Tom's Cabin*), but Mitchell establishes another mode and makes Ellen O'Hara too ethereal and holy to withstand mundane maternal responsibilities. Mitchell asserts that

> Ellen O'Hara was different, and Scarlett regarded her as something holy and apart from all the rest of humankind. When Scarlett was a child, she had confused her mother with the Virgin Mary, and now that she was older she saw no reason for changing her opinion. To her, Ellen represented the utter security that only Heaven or a mother can give. She knew that her mother was the embodiment of justice, truth, loving tenderness and profound wisdom—a great lady. (63)

By endowing her with the purist qualities of white womanhood—beauty, truth, wisdom, love, and justice—Mitchell implies that Ellen can be admired and worshipped as a Madonna, but not as the kind of practical mother that Mammy is for Scarlett. Mammy is the one who worries about Scarlett getting sick or forgetting her manners, who calls Scarlett her "lamb" and always, always admonishes her to be a lady. Mitchell tries to have it both ways, saying that both Ellen and Mammy are Scarlett's mentors, but she also makes it clear that Mammy is the one who can best "handle" Scarlett since "Mammy's eyes were sharper than Ellen's" (60). Mammy is so much more active in Scarlett's parenting than either Ellen or Gerald, her father, that we easily forget they exist.

If Ellen O'Hara were rendered with greater depth or complexity, we could read *Gone with the Wind* as a classic study of the mammy/Madonna/ Child triptych. Had little Eva lived, she might have grown up to be Ellen O'Hara. Like Eva, Ellen's death is the moment of her fullest characterization. Ellen retains her purity because she passes through the novel on wings, an angelic presence blessing Tara with the ethereal quality it needs to be a proper southern mansion.

Mammy force-feeds her senior mistress, showing herself to be as much Ellen's surrogate mother as she is Scarlett's. This is one major similarity between Mammy and Dilsey: they infantilize white women and white children in exactly the same manner. Dilsey repeatedly sends Mrs. Compson back to her bedroom whenever there is any excitement or stress in the house. In one scene Mrs. Compson actually asks Dilsey's permission to have a hot water-bottle for her aches and pains. Similarly, Mammy feeds and fusses after Ellen and Scarlett in exactly the same way that she tends to Scarlett's children.

Mammy may be able to serve as nursemaid for Scarlett's children, but she cannot pass on her maternal instincts to Scarlett. As part of her inability to be a good southern belle, Scarlett finds pregnancy and motherhood a nuisance instead of an honor. One scholar finds that Mitchell's characterization supports the theory that Scarlett has identifiable masculine qualities that are evident in her business sense and general aggressiveness. "The novel confirms the appropriateness of Scarlett's gender reversal through emphasizing a repugnance towards her own sexuality and child-bearing and her inadequacy as a mother to the three children she unwillingly bears and rears."[14]

But Scarlett does not rear those children: she hands them over to Mammy as soon as they are born, and goes on with her life. The children are completely inconsequential to her, floating around her only as reminders of the men she married for the wrong reasons. We are aware of Scarlett's horror with pregnancy through her obsession with her eighteen-inch waist, which is ruined anew with each birth. When she hears that one of her slaves has given birth, she thinks: "Babies, babies, babies. Why did God make so many babies? But no, God didn't make them. Stupid people made them" (402). Scarlett seems doomed to become a composite of

Stowe's Marie St. Clare and Faulkner's Caroline Compson: the southern belle turned cranky hypochondriac, whose children cause her endless grief.

Mammy cannot *give* Scarlett the *desire* to nurture; Scarlett is fated to remain infantilized by her need for Mammy and her inability to nurture anyone in return. But Mammy does pass on *her* maternal torch to Dilcey and Prissy, who eventually replace her, while Mammy is deified within the highest standard of what one could call the "Cult of True Mammyhood." Like Charles Chesnutt's Mammy Jane, Mammy's disdain for the new help is palpable, as she "viewed with displeasure the nurses that came and went, for she was jealous of any strange negro and saw no reason why she could not care for the baby and Wade and Ella, too" (880). And like Dilsey, Mammy's mortality shifts to center stage since "age and rheumatism was slowing her lumbering tread" (880).

There seems to be an endless string of mammies at Tara, since along with the indomitable Mammy, there are two other mammies, Dilcey, brought in solely as a wet nurse for Melanie's baby, and her daughter Prissy, the mammy in training (359).

Dilcey's body and even her ethnicity are compared favorably with Mammy's body:

> Dilcey was tall and bore herself erectly. She might have been any age from thirty to sixty, so unlined was her immobile bronze face. Indian blood was plain in her feature, overbalancing the Negroid characteristics. She was self-possessed and walked with a dignity that surpassed even Mammy's, for Mammy had acquired her dignity and Dilcey's was in her blood. (65)

Why does Mitchell introduce another mammy-type character? Clearly, Dilcey's maternity and the fact that she is lactating enable her to serve as the requisite wet-nurse for the O'Hara plantation, the one role that Mammy cannot fulfill because of her age. This moment reminds us that while Mammy's maternal impulses help her to keep Scarlett in line, she has never had any children of her own.

When Scarlett returns to the decimated Tara with Melanie, she is too weak to nurse her newborn baby. Pork's assuring Scarlett that Dilcey can feed Melanie's baby, in addition to her own, is reminiscent of the days before the war when Tara was a symbol of abundance: "Ma Dilcey got a new chile herseff an' she got mo'n nuff fer both" (402). We are reminded of the overweight Mammy carrying huge trays laden with food—imploring Scarlett to eat when she wasn't hungry (81). While the elderly Mammy can only hug Scarlett and dry her tears, Dilcey actually uses her body to save the life of Melanie's daughter. Mitchell imbues the scene with heavy aesthetic overtones seen in early depictions of the wet-nursing mammy when she describes "a still bronze image with the sleeping pink morsel against her dark breast" (413).[15] This nurturing embrace is echoed on the very last page of the novel, when Scarlett longs to be in Mammy's arms: "Suddenly she wanted Mammy desperately, as she had wanted her when she was a little girl, wanted the broad bosom on which to lay her head" (1024).

Mammy fusses her way through this epic novel, complaining about Scarlett's high spirits or about Ellen's misplaced kindnesses in the first section; disappearing until Scarlett returns to Tara; reappearing then as the newly emancipated Mammy who helps Scarlett rebuild the O'Hara fortune by exploiting one wealthy husband after another. In over a thousand pages, Mammy never has an extended conversation with any other blacks and never once considers what her life might be like away from Tara. Significantly, Mammy never has the kind of quiet reflection that Faulkner grants to Dilsey.

Literary critic Leslie Fielder suggests a connection between these two novels. He compares Faulkner to James Joyce, noting that *The Sound and the Fury* was modeled on *Ulysses.*[16] Fielder reminds us that Faulkner's only comment on *Gone with the Wind* and its popularity was that "no story should take a thousand pages to tell." Then Fiedler invokes Aunt Jemima, and subsequently links Faulkner, Mitchell, and Stowe in his discussion of Dilsey in a fascinating and troubling move that I call "mammy blurring":

> Dilsey seems to me a dismayingly stock character, an Aunt Jemima Type, scarcely distinguishable from the Black mammy in whose arms Scarlett O'Hara seeks refuge at the end of *Gone with the Wind;* or for that matter, from Harriet Beecher Stowe's equally pious and faithful Uncle Tom (the gender difference is irrelevant, since both are essentially sexless). But of course, almost all of Faulkner's females are stereotypes, though few of them are as benign as Dilsey. Besides Black Mammies like her, the only women in Faulkner rendered sympathetically are certain safely post-menopausal white old maids and widows. (79–80)

It is almost as if there are Aunt Jemimas everywhere an overweight black woman appears, thus knocking all of the mammy dominos down with one glance. Dilsey does share some fundamental similarities with the older Mammy we see at the end of *Gone with the Wind,* particularly as a refuge for troubled southern belles like Scarlett and Quentin. At the same time, Dilsey, Mammy, and Uncle Tom may be stereotypical, but they are by no means indistinguishable even for the least discriminating reader. Neither Mammy nor Dilsey is as pious as even a female version of Uncle Tom; Dilsey's attendance at church for Easter service is the sole indication of her religious belief. Mitchell's Mammy never goes to church, not in a thousand pages; her Christianity may be implied by her strong moral sense, but it is never indicated by religious practice. Uncle Tom is truly rendered sexless by his pious femininity, but Mammy, after all, wears the red petticoat that Rhett Butler gave her and flirts shamelessly with him by lifting up her dress for him to admire it. Dilsey is sexless only because of her age and infirmity and because she cannot compete with Quentin's sexuality. Nevertheless, Fiedler invites us to speculate on the possible kinship between these two mammies and Uncle Tom.

Ultimately, the mammy stereotype that blurs our vision is an exceptional example of the fluidity of social memory as well as a testimony to the dynamic power of cultural manipulation. As a symbol affirming the slave system hierarchy, the mammy is celebrated again and again as all that was ideal between the races before the destruction of the Civil War. Nowhere is the tribute to the mammy more ambiguous than in Faulkner's novel, and nowhere is it more ambitious than in Margaret Mitchell's epic romance. When we ask, "Which is the real mammy?" we miss the opportunity to see and to comprehend American culture through the vast complexity of my notion of a "mammy prism."[17]

Mammy is part of the Tara plantation landscape, like the magnolia trees and the cotton fields. Scarlett underscores this when, on the last page of the novel, she lists Mammy along with the rest of her family's property, "the avenue of dark cedars leading to Tara, the banks of cape jessamine bushes, . . . the fluttering white curtains. And Mammy would be there . . . Mammy, the last link with the old days" (1024). For Scarlett, the mammy stands like a statue on the horizon, fixed and permanent.

Like the Compsons, Scarlett, too, is trapped in the fossilizing amber of her Old South memories while the New South emerges, like an inevitable storm on the horizon. *Gone with the Wind* and *The Sound and the Fury* reflect a fear that the sacred southern relationship between black women and white families will be demolished. This relationship is deeply invested in preserving a particular narrative about race relations. In his work on southern history and memory, historian Fitzhugh Brundage reminds us that the "identity of any group goes hand in hand with the continuous creation of its sense of the past. *No enduring social memory can be entirely static.*"[18] The complicated relationship that African Americans and white Americans have with the mammy symbol as an enduring memory that is social, cultural, regional, and on many levels national, reveals the mammy's role in the remembered southern past as one that is as dynamic and forceful as a hurricane. Figure 25 is a color postcard of an African American woman posing with a younger white woman, her arms thrown around the older woman's neck. The postcard has the title "The South that is No More," is dated 1910, and is an example of a nostalgic version of the old South.

CONCLUSION

Mammy on My Mind

My goal with this book was to experiment with a synthesized approach to the mammy stereotype by asking questions about how separate cultural forces like a best-selling novel, or a popular rag doll, or a statue, or a collection of poems for children work together to magnify the influence each might have on its own. The mammy's role in American culture has been magnified by the variety of forces that joined together at specific moments to resist the changes that affected other stereotypes. I hoped to use this book to devise a critical framework for future evaluations of stereotypes as powerful forces that reveal and reflect vital information about who we are as Americans and how we might deal with one another more honestly in our interactions.

This book began with several premises. One was that the well-known mammy figure is much more intriguing and revealing than we usually assume. My aim was to argue that the fragmenting of the mammy figure into a literary stereotype, or a historic reality, or an advertising trademark, or a visual subject, reduces the complexity of this figure's powerful presence in American consciousness. This study has promoted a synthesis of approaches in order to restore coherence to the mammy figure, as a precursor to understanding how these various representations reflect and influence cultural memory. This study also suggests that one figure of a black woman served as a cultural metaphor revealing specific themes in American racial history. We know that African American women tended white children during slavery, but how do we assess the marginal appearance of this relationship in slave narratives and former slave biographies when compared with the numbers of white authors who emphasize this relationship?

By reconceptualizing the mammy as a quintessential interdisciplinary topic we will develop more progressive theories about this pervasive image as one of the best examples of how our ideas and ideals about race and about gender are continually shaped by the force of memory.

Throughout this book I have made the argument that this particular figure looms over the American imagination as a commanding cultural influence and that only a comprehensive and integrated approach will do her justice. This conclusion offers a final look at the mammy's transformational nature that both shapes and is shaped by a uniquely American and uniquely southern consciousness where race and gender are branches of the mammy tree, and selective memory is the decorative clinging vine that actually threatens the life of the tree itself.

Southern historian Fitzhugh Brundage writes that "because memories are transitory, people yearn to make them permanent by rendering them in physical form."[1] He reminds us that the mammy stereotype is a manifestation of this long-standing need to defy memory's transitory nature. This book has explored the question of whose memory is made permanent by considering how mammy has been used to reflect specific historic moments in the United States. The most memorable examples may well be Hattie McDaniel's rendering of Mammy in the film version of *Gone with the Wind* and the Aunt Jemima pancake mix trademark. When these personas are presumed to be an unaltered standard, then we make the mistake of assuming that the mammy's shape, speech and behavior have remained unchanged over the years.

Yet the mammy characters from chapter 1, for example, bear little physical resemblance to either Hattie McDaniel or the women portraying Aunt Jemima (there have been several). In antebellum plantation fiction, the characters varied from light-skinned mulatto women to darker-skinned African women; in these portraits the women also reflected a range in body type from very slender to very large. This book's analyses of antebellum fiction and plantation memoir reveal genuine efforts to capture and convey a range of individual differences in African American women's appearances. The first chapter sought to recast and redefine the mammy's significance in American culture by emphasizing and fully exploring her maternity and by comparing the complexion, dialect, and size of six mammy characters. In those early characterizations, the mammy's appearance is truly secondary to her role as an "other mother" to white children. Over the years, the mammy became part of the antebellum literary vocabulary and a significant prop granting authenticity to the southern household.

My discussion of representations of African American slave motherhood takes a dual look at the books by Harriet Beecher Stowe, Frederick Douglass, and Harriet Jacobs and nineteenth-century dolls depicting the southern mammy with white children. These texts and the dolls provided a more complete picture of southern African Americans and southern white Americans as intrinsically bound together in a society that was both racially segregated and racially interactive. Stowe, Douglass, and Jacobs offer us disparate portraits of African American motherhood, yet Stowe's portrait became a fixture in popular culture through the success of *Uncle Tom's Cabin* as a best-selling novel and a well-attended traveling minstrel show. Blackface minstrelsy provided a platform for other "auntie" acts, including one about a slave cook named Aunt Jemima.

Chapter 3 addressed the Aunt Jemima trademark, beginning with its introduction in the late nineteenth century when the mammy figure became a prototype of successful American commercialism. The image of a heavyset black woman serving food to white families became an updated symbol of the alleged racial harmony first represented by a mammy with a white child. As family cook, Aunt Jemima came to serve as the mammy for a national household, transcending regional tensions.

The same year that Aunt Jemima made her debut at the World's Columbian Exhibition, the novel *Pudd'nhead Wilson* by Mark Twain appeared, and six years later the short story "Her Virginia Mammy" by Charles Chesnutt was published; both feature slave mothers who choose to act as mammies in order to allow their light-skinned children to pass as white. Concurrently Chesnutt's novel *The Marrow of Tradition* uses a typical mammy image to explore the emerging social tensions between "Old Negroes" and "New Negroes" ideology. This exploration showed readers how the mammy caricature became a symbol of voluntary peonage and therefore how the word and the character became a pariah among African Americans. Chesnutt's character Mammy Jane probably points to the moment at which calling an African American woman a mammy, an auntie, or an Aunt Jemima became a pejorative. Chesnutt and Twain also introduced us to African American women characters, Roxy and Mrs. Harper, who recognize and then use the mammy stereotype as a cloak donned to achieve racial privileges for their children.

In chapter 4 my emphasis shifted from the mammy's original symbolism to its revision as a Neo-Confederate symbol used to honor "loyal" African American slave women with statues or monuments, just as the New Negro movement gained momentum. African American artists then responded by appropriating and subverting this image into a black Madonna with a black child. Finally, the last chapter uses the readings of *The Sound and the Fury* and *Gone with the Wind* to show how Faulkner and Mitchell affirm and challenge long-standing assumptions about this figure's enduring appeal, with a special focus on mammy's mortality. Both novels revisit the southern plantation a decade after the New Negro movement.

Blown Away—Again: A Few Words about The Wind Done Gone

Alice Randall's recent novel falls well outside of the chronological parameters that frame this book. Given the final chapter's look at *Gone with the Wind,* it may be useful to consider what this author's direct response to Mitchell's novel might add to this book's discussion about mammy characters. Because I am hesitant to privilege this novel over others, particularly those mentioned below, this commentary focuses on how one African American female author has rewritten Mammy from *Gone with the Wind* in her own words.

In an interview about her response to *Gone with the Wind,* called *The Wind Done Gone* (2001), author Randall says: "I think *Gone With the Wind* represents a point of view. I think *Gone With the Wind* in fact is more significantly understood as propaganda for the perpetuation of Jim Crow segregation that existed in the 1930s. It's more about that than it is about the Civil War. It's as much about what the future should be, than what the past is. And that is why it's so important to take the novel on."[2]

The controversy surrounding Randall's book and the legal battle with the Margaret Mitchell Trust Foundation is well documented elsewhere.[3] Among the papers filed in support of its publication are letters from award-winning authors Toni Morrison, Harper Lee, Charles Johnson, and the late historian Shelby Foote. Those letters make the authors' position clear: "Because of the prominence of *Gone With the Wind* in American culture, we believe that prohibiting the publication of Alice Randall's book would not be in the public interest." Morrison writes, "Considering the First Amendment rights properly accorded *Gone With the Wind,* in spite of the pain, humiliation, and outrage its historical representation has caused African Americans, it seems particularly odd for the Mitchell estate to deny this clever but gentle effort to assuage the damage *Gone With the Wind* has caused."[4]

Most reviews of the *The Wind Done Gone* consult the author's own words as to why she was compelled to write a parody of *Gone with the Wind.* Randall wanted to know, "Where are the mulattos on Tara? Where is Scarlett's half-sister? . . . I knew I had to tell her story, tell the story that hadn't been told."[5] Yet there are so many stories that are not told in *Gone with the Wind,* so many points of view that are not explored, that it would be unrealistic to insist that one novel right all of the wrongs that Mitchell put into motion.[6]

The Wind Done Gone takes its place along a formidable line of African American authors and artists intent upon putting their own spin on the moonlight-and-magnolia mythology of slavery upon which *Gone with the Wind* is based: *Iola Leroy: or, Shadows Uplifted* (1892) by Frances Harper, *Jubilee* (1967) by Margaret Walker, *Dessa Rose* (1986) by Shirley Anne Williams, *Beloved: A Novel* (1986) by Toni Morrison, Kara Walker's *Gone: An Historical Romance of a Civil War as it Occurred between the Dusky Thighs of One Young Negress and Her Heart* (1996), and others. Within this context, the contributions of this book are limited simply because parody is a literary genre restricted by limitations. When asked about the best-known African American response to Mitchell, *Jubilee,* Randall admitted that she had not read Walker's novel and that her book is not about slavery, but about the way slavery was represented in *Gone with the Wind.*[7]

One can only wonder how *The Wind Done Gone* might have developed if Randall had explored the tension between the story of the biracial slave daughter Cynara and a mammy's story—a long-awaited narrative from her point of view. Mammy's role as a revered slave, is truncated by page 9, when Randall begins Mammy's very slow death and we know without a doubt that this will not be the novel that allows her the kind of centrality and depth that is missing from *Gone with the Wind.* Randall gives us one more book that leaves Mammy without a name, since each one of her characters is based upon the original Mitchell characters and renamed—except for Mammy. Even the plantation Tara is renamed Tata. The characters are Planter (Gerald O'Hara), Lady (Ellen O'Hara), Other (Scarlett), Garlic

(Pork), Mrs. Garlic (Dilcey), Miss Priss (Prissy), Dreamy Gentleman (Ashley), Mealy Mouth (Melanie), and R. (Rhett). And Cynara's name is taken from the same Ernest Dawson poem that inspired Mitchell's title.

Randall evokes Mitchell's Mammy right away: "They called her Mammy . . . I heard tell down the years, they compared her to an elephant. They shouted down to their ancestors: she was big as an elephant with tiny dark round eyes. But she wasn't big enough to own a name. To me she was as big as a house. Big as two houses. I'd be scared to be that."[8] Randall's choice to portray Mammy as a large African American woman does little to offset the original stereotype, but there are ways that her Mammy stands in strong contrast to her namesake.

Randall's writing is more eloquent in the following passage about Cynara's jealousy over Mammy and the attention paid to her half-sister Other:

> She walked right past me, past Lady, she walked right past Lady and me, over to Mammy, reached up for Mammy, and my Mammy reached down to pull Other up onto her hip. Other reached into the top of Mammy's dress and pulled out my mother's breast. . . . I ached in some place I didn't know I had, where my heart should have been but wasn't. I've come to believe that was the very first time I ever felt my soul, and it was having a spasm. . . . pulling the air out of me in a hiccup. I flushed in a rage of possession as those little white hands drew the nipple toward the little pink mouth, then clasped on. (13)

Lady staggers and faints as she responds to "the rosebud mouth attached to the black moon in the brown breast," not necessarily because this is a shocking sight to her, but because fainting is what Lady does best. Cynara says that Planter "didn't see me hiding behind Lady's skirts or see the look Mammy gave me over Other's head. Planter only saw his daughter taking pleasure where he himself had done" (14). In this scene Mammy's body is shared between Planter and his daughter, and we don't know what kind of look Mammy has given Cynara; was it one of resignation or rage?

The turning point of Cynara's narrative comes when she finally learns that Other was never the serious threat to her relationship with her mother that she suspected. "Maybe Mammy loved her [Other]] and maybe Mammy didn't. Slavery made it impossible for Other to know. . . . Other could never be sure of Mammy's love." Mammy's love is disputed, but as a character Mammy is not nearly as effective as it might have been had Randall been more invested in giving this character her due. Mammy's sexual relationship with Planter is Randall's boldest move, yet even there we don't learn anything about what this relationship means to Mammy, whether it is based on coercion, consent, or something in between. The reader learns that Lady drinks too much on her wedding night and passes out in Mammy's arms. After tending to Lady, Mammy goes to Planter's bedroom and "gave him what he wanted in his bed. She gave it so good, he never complained" (61). Planter never complains; nor does Mammy. By making Mammy and Planter sexual partners, Randall challenges the presupposition of this figure's role as a benign presence in the antebellum household in addition to challenging the stereotype of Mammy as an asexual figure. Yet Randall stops short of granting Mammy full sexual agency; and her loyalty to Lady (whom she washes and lays out on clean sheets before giving her body to Planter) and to Planter do more to affirm the stereotype than contradict it.

Are Lady and Mammy sharing Planter? And if so why are they doing so? Why does Mammy enter into this relationship and why does she stay in it after Cynara is born into slavery on the Tata plantation? And what are we to make of Mammy's using her own body to satisfy Planter on his wedding night? Her sexual relations with Planter don't require her loyalty; after Mammy's death, Garlic tells Cynara that Mammy killed a set of newborn twin boys born to Planter and Lady. When Cynara expresses shock, Miss Priss asks her this cryptic question: "What would we have done with a sober white man on this place?" (63). The reader might ask what they did with a drunken white man at Tata since nothing stopped him from fathering Cynara with Mammy.

Cynara begins to construct her own version of life and work at Tata: "Garlic pulled the string, and Planter danced like a bandy-legged Irish marionette" (63). For Garlic, the death and removal of the boys means that his authority will not be questioned, but what is Mammy's motivation? Ostensibly, she might not have been able to protect her daughter Cynara from her half brothers who might have chosen to prey on her as a sexual target, but again, Randall does not make this clear enough.

Mammy's death in Randall's novel might be read as a positive, progressive narrative strategy when compared with the way that Mitchell's character stays on at Tara after Emancipation, waiting for Scarlet. It is also true that Mammy's memory is significant for the other slaves, long after her funeral is over. The African American characters come to terms with her death by revealing bits of her life to Cynara. On the day of Mammy's funeral, Garlic explains to Cynara: "I built this place with my hands. . . . Every column fluted was a monument to the slaves and the whips our bodies had received. . . . Right this morning we're burying the real mistress of the house." What good is it that Mammy is the real mistress if we don't understand why she offers her body to Planter on his wedding night and then kills his sons? When he stands to give Mammy's eulogy, Garlic evokes the kind of blurring of religion and Old southern values seen in *Gone with the Wind*: "You might could say we was the whole Trinity around this place, me, Mammy, and Miss Priss" (50). Mrs. Garlic isn't happy about her omission from her husband's remarks. Cynara tells us that while Garlic's wife was beautiful, "she had changed nothing of significance in any of our lives" (50).

Randall has this to say about the African American characters in her book: "Mammy and other house servants have complex minds and complex motivations in my novel. As I've said, this is an antidote to the poisonous portrayal of blacks in the first novel, as one-dimensional, childlike or animal-like stereotypes." The author says also, "In my book, *The Wind Done Gone*, Cynara's very words argue that blacks can be brilliant and insightful, and intellectually competent. I think all too unfortunately, the myth of black intellectual inferiority haunts us to this day. That is the myth perpetuated by *Gone With the Wind*."[9]

I agree with the critic who pointed out that while Randall bemoans the absence of credible black characters with believable lives in *Gone with the Wind*, "Randall falls short of creating fully realized characters herself, instead simply eliminating the blatant stereotypes as if that were all that character development required. Cynara writes that Miss Priss (Prissy) 'possessed a keen and labyrinthine intelligence,' but Randall produces no rival to challenge the dim-witted Prissy of page and screen."[10] Another scholar asks the crucial question about parody: "How do you exaggerate a stereotype, something that is already an exaggeration? At what point does the caricature become an agent working against itself?"[11]

As for Mammy's actions: having sex with Planter, killing his sons, wet-nursing his daughter, dictating a letter to Cynara professing her love are all intriguing in their own way, but her character is not developed enough to sustain the intrigue. Randall deserves credit for pursuing some of Mammy's more enigmatic qualities, even if they are unresolved. *Gone with the Wind* is still the central story of *The Wind Done Gone*, and while Mammy's love may be a central part of Randall's story, Mammy's life story is not central enough to significantly free her by the end of the novel.

The New Local Color

Images do their work silently and persistently. Images are unruly. They resist containment and rational controls, often doing unintended things despite the intention of their owners.

— MICHAEL HARRIS, *Colored Pictures*

One scholar writes that the popularity and influence of the plantation genre made it virtually impossible for African Americans to locate a "noble, meaningful past."[12] Throughout this book, particularly in the early chapters, I found that the real problem with the plantation genre was its enormous popularity among white southerners and northerners who seemed oblivious to its revisionist history. I suspect that the proponents of plantation literature became entranced by the romantic stories of charming plantation life that supplied a version preferable to the ragged, tragic truth of that life: one group of human beings owning another group. The southern past represented in the plantation genre is a past that was created and produced exclusively by white southerners.

But this referent leads us to the question: Where might African Americans look for a "suitable past"? The past that would be significant to African Americans would come from their own hands and hearts and memories. It might be located in slave narratives, and autobiographies of former slaves, in the letters and memories of free, literate African Americans, in autobiographical fiction, music, poetry, and craftwork. This African American past might be more hidden than exposed, more subtle than overt, and might prove to be more liberating than most scholars would expect.

What if African Americans were to locate a noble, meaningful past through the retelling of painful stories, perhaps because they represent an accessible medium—a common language? What if nobility were to be found in the recasting of the loyal aunties and mammies, as inherently noble, as inherently significant? What if the key to the kind of past described above could in fact only be found in the very derogatory and shameful figures that were so wounding in the first place because they displaced or replaced a legacy of resistance and struggle? What if one figure could be transformed sufficiently by latter generations into a new figure representing resistance instead of subservience? Is it more difficult to learn a new language or to learn new meanings within a known language?

Michael Harris's excellent book *Colored Pictures* (2003) supplies a comprehensive look at both Aunt Jemima and the mammy as the stereotypes used more than any other during the Black Arts movement of the 1960s and 1970s.[13] For curator and artist Harris, these examples indicate how terribly the stereotype affected African Americans: "If we accept black caricatures to be projections of white imagination, . . . a fictional character embodying the inverted concept of a mammy, then she is not a black woman" (230). The Black Arts movement recognized that, instead of reflecting the realities of African American women's lives, the mammy was "a white fantasy in black face, an embodiment of certain white needs and projections that have more to do with white identity construction than African American personalities" (233).

In his analysis, Harris credits Jon Lockard and Murray DePillars with genuine attempts to give "voice and perhaps humanity and ethnicity to the black women working as domestic and cooks for whites as a way of exploding the mammy fantasy / myth" (121). Why did so many artists choose the Aunt Jemima figure over stereotypes like Uncle Remus from the Disney film *Song of the South,* or other trademarks that played upon antebellum nostalgia like Uncle Ben, Rastus the Cream of Wheat Man, or the Gold Dust Twins? Each one revealed something about the way that African Americans were perceived, and each one might have been refashioned into a tool for a progressive civil rights agenda.

For these artists, the Aunt Jemima image signaled a particular kind of insult for African Americans during the 1960s, one that inspired artists to juxtapose the trademark from the 1890s with the new attitudes and agenda of the 1960s.[14] By using Aunt Jemima—the most recognizable mammy for mainstream culture—they were able to subvert this innocuous household item into something much more threatening. It was as if artists such as Lockard, DePillars, Overstreet, Donaldson, and Saar were warning white Americans that even the safety of their favorite breakfast foods could not be trusted; the revolution would explode out of their kitchen cabinets and confront them while they were innocently eating pancakes. By pairing the happy cook with weapons like a rifle, as Betye Saar does in *The Liberation of Aunt Jemima* (1972), or a machine gun, as Joe Overstreet does in *New Jemima* (1964), the artists transfer their own frustration and simmering rage onto a beloved African American woman. Essentially they were challenging people to reconsider what might be behind or beneath Aunt Jemima's smile. The use of weapons is compounded by titles like *No More*

(Lockard) and *New Jemima* (Overstreet). For example, DePillars's 1968 highly sexualized pen and ink drawing of Aunt Jemima shows her literally bursting both out of the pancake box and out of her clothes—her large breasts and her nude buttocks look like they have escaped from captivity. By blending both anger and overt sexuality in this drawing, DePillars suggests that his updated Aunt Jemima will not be content with singing and making pancakes in the 1960s.

As significant and provocative as this artwork is, only Betye Saar's *The Liberation of Aunt Jemima* includes a child as part of the image (fig. 26). In a twist on the original tableau, Saar says that the baby on *her* Aunt Jemima's lap is not white at all, but a "mulatto child who serves as a testimony about how black women were sexually abused or misused" by predatory white men in domestic settings. In her later revision of that piece called *Dubl' Duty: I's back wid a Vengeance,* Saar replaces the child altogether with a message pad bearing text that reads in part: "They broke us like limbs from trees and carved Europe upon our African masks" (Harris 117). Perhaps Saar's best-known work, *The Liberation of Aunt Jemima* uses three different renditions of the mammy/Aunt Jemima stereotype. The middle figure holds both a rifle and a pistol along with her broom as a way to indicate that her "liberation" will come by force if necessary and it will require her to put down the old tools of her trade as a domestic servant and take up the tools for revolutionary transformation. The glass display box mimics the pancake box and also works as a kind of self-contained museum piece, making the mammy/Aunt Jemima of the past a relic under glass. Saar is an avid collector of black Americana, and her use of these objects in her work is a tradition that has been followed by many other contemporary African American artists, including Fred Wilson and Michael Ray Charles.

Atlanta artist and curator Tina Dunkley's work, *Ain't Cha Mama Yemanja?* (fig. 27) uses a more international and multilayered approach combining representations of African, Caribbean, and African American women wearing elaborately tied headscarves. The intricate wrapping of beautiful fabrics as turbans, gelees, and bandannas by women of African descent around the globe connects these women in a powerful way. Dunkley says she was moved to do this piece as a result of traveling throughout the African Diaspora and seeing black women in African gelees and then considering a possible connection with Aunt Jemima. She says, "I realized that this is who Aunt Jemima *might* have become had she been left in Nigeria." Here she is also playing on the phonetic similarities between *Jemima* and *Yemanja,* the Yoruba deity representing motherhood in the Santeria pantheon of goddesses.

The prevalence of the mammy motif in African American art is surprising even to me. I continue to be both impressed and startled when I see Michael Ray Charles using a thinner, meaner-looking mammy who refuses to give up her piece of "American pie" to a distraught adult white male in diapers in his piece *Untitled* (1993), from his "Forever Free Post" series (fig. 28). Charles says this about his choice of the Aunt Jemima over other stereotypes of African Americans: "Initially I started out trying to deal with the Sambo image. I worked and researched [and] as I discovered more, I began to use the Aunt Jemima image. . . . .The Aunt Jemima image was about power, about that domineering figure. . . . She had the ability to take care of two households. . . . She was a *powerful* figure, but also a *stereotype.*"[15]

Artist Charles Nelson's mock billboard *Welcome to Atlanta* ("Sweet Flypaper of Life" series, 2004) shows us his understanding of the racial divide in Atlanta through an African American woman (fig. 29). His black Madonna is a beautiful African American woman nursing a rather mature-looking white child through her red and blue robe. Like Charles, Nelson wants the viewer to consider how African American women have served, and how they continue to serve, as caretakers for white Americans, regardless of age.[16] Nelson's use of the Madonna icon here provides a critical link between Winold Reiss's *Brown Madonna* from chapter 4 and Joyce Scott's black Madonna figure discussed below.

Black feminist historian Darlene Clark Hine writes, "Creating and disseminating a visual history is perhaps more important with Black women than with any other single segment of the American population. We know all too well what this society believes Black women look like. . . . What we have not seen nearly enough is the simple truth of our complex and multidimensional lives."[17] With these words in mind as I was completing this book, I felt compelled to end it with the work of an African American woman. I've chosen multimedia artist Joyce Scott because she integrates some of the unspoken aspects of mammy into her work without relying on Aunt Jemima.

Scott was born in Baltimore in 1948 and still resides in Baltimore, where she shares a home with her mother, textile artist Elizabeth Talford Scott. Joyce Scott specializes in weaving, quilting, beadwork, and glass. Her soft-sculptured figures are each about eighteen inches tall and are made of leather and beadwork. Scott's decision to make her figures three-dimensional reflects her understanding of mammy as multidimensional, not flat. Additionally, they resemble large dolls, providing an echo of the mammy dolls covered in chapter 2. Joyce's "Race Break" series and the "Mammy/ Nanny" series both depict African American women who served as caretakers of white children, yet she provides us with completely innovative scenes between the mammy and two children, one black and one white. Her "Mammy/Nanny" series is unique in both form and content (figs. 30–34).

Through the black nanny Scott gives a voice to the often-invisible children of the mammy. Scott says of these sculptures that she was interested in investigating the notion of the mammy image as "black monolith . . . a big, black mask." Feminist art critic Terry Gips writes that "Scott confronts the viewer with the contradictions and hypocrisies embedded in the historical and continuing culture surrounding the Black women who served as nannies for white America . . . ."[18]

In an interview I conducted with Scott in June 2004, she spoke at length about the art she produced during the 1980s and 1990s and about how her childhood experiences inspired her art. I learned that Scott's mother told her about her own experiences working as childcare provider for white families, a job she took at an early age in South Carolina.[19] Born in 1916, Elizabeth Scott picked cotton before moving to Baltimore in 1940. She worked in factories, cleaned houses, and served as a nanny, somehow always managing to continue the sewing and craftwork, she had learned as a child. Scott says: "My mother told me how offended she was when the white children she took care of began to call her by pejorative names." In more than one instance her mother recalls the parents teaching their children that she was a "nigger." The last time this happened to her, she was so hurt that she left to live with another family, with whom she stayed extremely close. This incident inspired Scott to create the seventeen-inch piece called *Nanny Now, Nigger Later* (fig. 30), with her black leather nanny holding a white beaded baby against her front while the child sucks its thumb.

When asked if she thought her mother loved the children she took care of, Scott said, "Yes, and sometimes I was jealous of them. I was friends with those children. We played together but sometimes I felt like asking her to stay home with me; that's what the piece *No Mommy, Me* was about." This two-part creation includes a black female figure made of black leather and iridescent black beads resembling a large mammy doll complete with turban and apron (fig. 31). This figure holds a white baby made of pink beads up to her face as if she is cooing to her, while a black child figure made of black beads clutches the mammy/nanny's long skirt, howling in jealousy. In *No Mommy, Me I,* Scott shows that the caretaker often must comfort one child while her own may feel abandoned. In the second piece, *No Mommy Me II* (fig. 32), the same kind of black figure holds a white child figure out at arm's length while a small black girl sits crying on the floor, her arms wide open and empty. In this piece the mammy/nanny's mouth is twisted in a grimace—in the mask that Scott describes in the quote above and instead of being enclosed in a tidy turban, her hair is loose, perhaps in braids or dreadlocks. In a piece called *Nanny Gone Wrong* (fig. 33), the leather nanny wears her headscarf tied in a knot at the front of her head, and she dangles a beaded white baby by the hair while a tiny black baby sits at her feet. The piece that I find most evocative is *Chainsaw Nanny* (fig. 34). In this piece, Scott shows us a topless mammy/nanny with a beaded white baby chained to her waist. For me, this piece speaks of the unrelenting quality of mammy's day and of being chained to a baby of another race. Or perhaps the chainsaw is cutting the Nanny in half so there will be enough of her to go around. As Terry Gips explains: "These sculptures also remind us that the Black children of nannies often seem to take a back seat to the white children their mothers care for. Perhaps there aren't enough arms or hours to go around. . . . While the days of the wet nurse's need to short her own child to feed her master's are behind us, the tug-of-war over her body still exists."[20]

A true understanding of African American identity, both self-imposed and externally constructed, requires us to pay greater attention to this kind of creative work because it provides us with more than new words about an old image; indeed, it provides a new language altogether. This new language is crucial if we are to begin to express and process the difficult emotions related to this country's past. This study challenges us to read again what we believe we know well and to search with renewed enthusiasm for what we have missed.

NOTES

Preface

1. Howell Raines, "Grady's Gift," *New York Times Magazine,* December 1, 1991, 90.

Introduction

David Blight, public lecture, Emory University, Atlanta, April 5, 2001.

1. Excerpted from "A Brief Warhol Biography," www.childrensmuseum.org. This short biography states: "With his Myths Series, he portrayed nothing less than the universal view of America's once enchanted and powerful past."

2. Deborah Willis and Carla Williams, eds., *The Black Female Body: A Photographic History* (Philadelphia: Temple University Press, 2002), 128–34.

3. See http://owsleyhouse.8m.com/ow.htm. Mammy benches currently sell for about twenty-five hundred dollars.

4. Wendy Lavitt, *Dolls,* Knopf Collectors' Guides to American Antiques (New York: Knopf, 1983), 13; Lavitt, *American Folk Dolls* (New York: Knopf, 1982), 40–42. Lavitt notes that "rubber nipple dolls were popular in the 1920s and 1930s and were always Black. Many hold white babies." See also Evelyn Coleman, *The Collector's Encyclopedia of Dolls* (New York: Crown, 1971), 237 and 469–70.

5. In *Toms, Coons, Mulattoes, Mammies and Bucks: An Interpretive History of Black in American Films* (New York: Continuum, 1973), Donald Bogle credits actress Louise Beavers with setting the physical standard for the mammy character in film: "Even before she appeared in *Imitation of Life,* she had played an assortment of maid roles in Hollywood pictures and she had been carefully groomed by herself and the studios to fit into the mammy-aunt Jemima category. Before her there had been no distinctive mammy figure" (62–63). Bogle also reminds his readers that we have been greatly influenced by illusions created by Hollywood directors as well as costume and makeup artists. Apparently in the late 1920s, Beavers was considered for a mammy role in *Uncle Tom's Cabin* but studio executives decided Beavers "was heavy and hearty but not heavy and hearty enough. There-

after she went on force-feed diets, compelling herself to eat beyond her normal appetite." And later in her career, Beavers learned to speak what Bogle calls the "the slow and easy backwoods accent [that was] compulsory for every black servant" (62–63). Also see Bogle's landmark study, *Blacks in American Films and Television: An Illustrated Encyclopedia* (New York: Fireside Books, Simon and Schuster, 1989), 93–95.

6. *Dictionary of American Regional English* (Cambridge: Belknap Press of Harvard University Press, 1985), s.v. "Mammy."

7. Kimberly Wallace-Sanders, "Dishing up Dixie," in *Burning Down the House: Recycling Domesticity,* ed. Rosemary Marangoly George (Boulder, Colo.: Westview Press, 1998), 215–32.

8. M. M. Manring, *Slave in a Box: The Strange Career of Aunt Jemima* (Charlottesville: University Press of Virginia, 1998).

9. JoAnn Morgan, "Mammy the Huckster," *American Art,* Spring 1995, 87–107.

10. Ralph Ellison, *Invisible Man* (1947; reprint, New York: Random House, 1980), 196–202.

11. Isabel Drysdale, *Scenes in Georgia* (Philadelphia: American Sunday School Union, 1827), 4.

12. Readers may be familiar with Harris's character Aunt Minervy Ann from *The Chronicles of Aunt Minervy Ann* (New York: Scribner, 1899).

13. Jesse Parkhurst, "The Role of the Black Mammy in the Plantation Household," *Journal of Negro History* 23 (1938): 25.

14. Deborah Gray White, *Aren't I a Woman?* (New York: Norton, 1985).

15. Barbara Christian, *Black Women Novelists: The Development of a Tradition, 1892–1976* (Westport, Conn.: Greenwood Press, 1980), 11.

16. See Bonnie Thornton Dill, "Across the Boundaries of Race and Class: An Exploration of the Relationship Between Work and Family among Black Female Domestic Servants," Ph.D. diss., New York University, 1979; Judith Rollins, *Between Women* (Philadelphia: Temple University Press, 1985); Trudier Harris, *From Mammies to Militants: Domestics in Black American Literature* (Philadelphia: Temple University Press, 1982); Patricia Morton, *Distorted Images: The Historical Assault on Afro-American Women* (Westport, Conn.: Praeger, 1991); and Patricia Turner, *Ceramic Uncles and Celluloid Mammies* (New York: Anchor Books, 1994).

17. Francis P. Gaines, *The Southern Plantation: A Study in the Development and the Accuracy of a Tradition* (New York: Columbia University Press, 1924).

18. I make an effort to remedy these oversights. Mammy's legendary and mythical devotion to the master's children is a fundamental aspect of her role as proslavery propaganda. My work builds upon the emphasis on black maternal power found in Stephanie Smith's *Conceived by Liberty: Maternal Figures and Nineteenth-Century American Literature* (Ithaca, N.Y.: Cornell University Press, 1994); Jennifer Fleischer's *Mastering Slavery: Memory, Family, and Identity in Women's*

Slave Narratives (New York: New York University Press, 1996); and Susan Tracy's *In the Master's Eye: Representations of Women, Blacks, and Poor Whites in Antebellum Southern Literature* (Amherst: University of Massachusetts Press, 1995). Their analyses provide the appropriate platform for this book's premise that fictional narratives and autobiographical narratives are best understood in dialogue with each other and are further enriched by an emphasis on visual and material culture.

19. Jean Fagin Yellin, *Harriet Jacobs: A Life* (New York: Basic Civitas Books, 2004), 129 and illustrations.

20. Lavitt, *Dolls* (Knopf Collectors' Guides), 31.

21. Cheryl Thurber, "Development of the Mammy Image and Mythology," in *Southern Women: Histories and Identities,* ed. Virginia Berhard et al. (Columbia: University of Missouri Press, 1992), 96.

22. Robert Crease, *The Prism and the Pendulum* (New York: Random House, 2003), 64.

Chapter One

1. P. J. Gibbs, *Black Collectibles Sold in America* (Paducah, Ky.: Collector Books, 1987), 22.

2. Parkhurst, "Role of Black Mammy."

3. Eugene Genovese, *Roll Jordan Roll* (New York: Vintage, 1974), 355.

4. White, *Aren't I a Woman?*

5. Genovese, *Roll Jordan Roll,* 353.

6. Gaines, *The Southern Plantation,* 2–5.

7. Harris, *From Mammies to Militants,* 23–26.

8. George Tucker, *The Valley of Shenandoah; or, Memoirs of the Graysons* (1824; reprint Chapel Hill: University of North Carolina Press, 1970).

9. Mark Twain, *Pudd'nhead Wilson* (New York: Harper Brothers, 1894).

10. Charles Chesnutt, "Her Virginia Mammy," in *The Wife of His Youth* (Ridgewood, N.J.: Gregg Press, 1899).

11. Caroline Hentz, *Linda, or the Young Pilot of the Belle Creole* (Philadelphia: A. Hart, 1852), 15. Hentz is perhaps best known for her novel *The Planter's Northern Bride* (1854).

12. Hentz's agenda is not pursued; Harriet Beecher Stowe describes Eva's Mammy very clearly as a "middle aged mulatto woman of very respectable appearance" (109). And in Mary Eastman's proslavery response to Stowe, *Aunt Phillis's Cabin* (Philadelphia: Lippincott, Grambo, 1852), the main character is "a tall, dignified, bright mulatto woman" (102). Both authors used mixed-heritage slaves to draw broad lines between the way that these characters speak, think, and behave and the way other slaves, usually field hands, do.

13. Lillian Eugenia Smith, *Killers of the Dream,* rev. ed. (New York: Norton, 1961).

14. Joseph Cobb, *Mississippi Scenes* (Philadelphia: A. Hart, 1851).

15. I am grateful to a reader for the University of Michigan Press who made this observation.

16. Thomas Gossett, *Uncle Tom's Cabin and American Culture* (Dallas: Southern Methodist University Press, 1985), 260.

17. Stephen Vincent Benet, *John Brown's Body* (New York: Rinehart, 1927), 152.

18. Unsigned, *Southern Literary Messenger Review* (1852).

19. Martha Haines Butt, *Antifanaticism* (Philadelphia: Lippincott, Grambo, 1853), 25.

20. James Mellon, *Bull Whip Days: The Slaves Remember* (New York: Weidenfeld and Nicolson, 1988), 39.

21. Amy Ella Blanchard, *Mammy's Baby* (Worthington, N.Y.: Worthington, 1890), n.p.

22. For more information on the lives of African American slave children see Wilma King, *Stolen Childhood: Slave Youth in Nineteenth Century America* (Bloomington: Indiana University Press, 1995); and Marie Jenkins Schwartz, *Born in Bondage: Growing up Enslaved in the Antebellum South* (Cambridge: Harvard University Press, 2000).

23. Eastman, *Aunt Phillis's Cabin*, 57–58.

24. Anonymous, "Grace Merry," *Godey's Lady's Magazine,* April 1839, 178–88.

25. Description of steel fashion plate; doll no. 3187, *Godey's Lady's Book* (Philadelphia), October 1852, 398.

26. Douglas Congdon-Martin, *Images in Black: 150 Years of Black Collectibles* (Atglen, Pa.: Schiffer, 1999), 14. One of the earliest mechanical toys was a weight-driven cradle with a white baby and a black mammy doll, manufactured by the New York Toy Company in the 1860s and distributed by Ives.

27. "Grace Merry," 178–88.

28. Raines, "Grady's Gift," 90.

Chapter Two

1. Mildred Jailer, "Non-Traditional Dolls," *Antiques and Collecting* 96 (1991): 28–30. Since Jailer makes no reference citation, there is no way to explore the basis of her claim that Pennsylvania Dutch–style dolls influenced the design of topsy-turvy dolls. Jailer considers the dolls rare examples of Americana and therefore tends to assign monetary value to the dolls rather than consider their significant historical value.

2. Jan Thalberg, "Topsy-Turvy; The Upside-Down Girl, a State of Confusion," *Black Ethnic Collectibles* 5, no. 5 (1993): 16.

3. "Teaching history through dolls," January 13, 2004, www.iun.edu/-ne.wsnw/pg/2004/040113_dolls.shtml.

4. Karen Calvert, *Children in the House: The Material Culture of Early Childhood*

(Boston: Northeastern University Press, 1992), 4. See also Miriam Formanek-Brunell, *Made to Play House: Dolls and the Commercialization of American Girlhood: 1830–1930* (New Haven: Yale University Press, 1993); Doris Wilkinson, "The Doll's Exhibit: A Psycho-Cultural Analysis of Black Female Role Stereotypes," *Journal of Popular Culture* 21 (Fall 1987): 19–29.

5. Coleman, *Collector's Encyclopedia of Dolls*, 237 and 469–70; Congdon-Martin, *Images in Black*, 14. Black-collectible expert Congdon-Martin writes, "With the growth of the industrial age manufactured dolls entered the marketplace. They included the topsy-turvy dolls, which had a black face and a white face and could be turned either way. Usually, but not always, the black side of the dolls would be dressed as a servant and the white side dressed as a mistress" (13).

6. Valerie Borey, "Topics in Anthropology—Two Headed American Story-telling." February 29, 2004, www.suite101.com.

7. Determining the pragmatics of making the dolls is relatively simple. It is quite likely that house slaves who had access to sewing materials could make these dolls. Since we know that slave mothers often took care of both white and black children, it is plausible that both black and white children played with topsy-turvy dolls.

8. Alyssa Zelkowitz, "Raggedy Ancestors Dolls and Didacticism, 1783–1861," master's thesis, Department of History, Emory University, May 2005.

9. John Gruelle, *Beloved Belindy* (New York: Volland, 1926). See also the illustration on the songsheet "Raggedy Ann's Sunny Songs," published in 1930 by Miller Music.

10. George Rawick, ed., *The American Slave: A Composite Autobiography*, Georgia Narratives, vol. 13 (Westport, Conn.: Greenwood, 1972), 96–97.

11. Harriet Jacobs, *Incidents in the Life of a Slave Girl, Written by Herself*, ed. Jean Fagin Yellin (Cambridge: Harvard University Press, 1987), 34.

12. Jacobs, *Incidents*, 7.

13. Smith, *Conceived by Liberty*, 352.

14. Joan D. Hedrick, *Harriet Beecher Stowe: A Life* (New York: Oxford University Press, 1994), 193.

15. Gary Saul Morson and Caryl Emerson, *Mikhail Bakhtin: Creation of Prosaics* (Stanford: Stanford University Press, 1990), 448–49.

16. Douglass, *Narrative* (New York: Signet, 1968).

17. Smith, *Conceived by Liberty*, 352.

18. Douglass, *Narrative*.

19. Hazel Carby, *Reconstructing Womanhood* (New York: Oxford University Press, 1987), 47.

20. William Wells Brown, *Clotel; or the President's Daughter: A Narrative of Slave Life in the United States* (London: Partridge and Oakey, 1853), 218–19. The novel's frontispiece shows Clotel jumping off a bridge to her death in the Potomac River;

it is one of the most important images from the nineteenth century because it so graphically depicts an African American heroine choosing death over slavery.

21. See Clarence Darrow, "The Problem of the Negro," http://www.law.umkc.edu/faculty/projects/ftrials/sweet/darrowessay.html. Also see Clarence Darrow, "The Negro in the North," in *The Story of My Life* (New York: Scribner and Sons, 1932).

Chapter Three

A different version of this chapter appears as "Dishin' up Dixie," in *Burning Down the House, Recycling Domesticity,* ed. Rosemary Marangoly George (Boulder, Colo.: Westview Press, 1998), 215–31.

1. *Emerge Magazine,* December–January 1995, 67.

2. Joleen Robison, *Advertising Dolls: Identification and Value Guide* (Paducah, Ky.: Collector Books, 1980), 40–41.

3. Excerpts from advertisements appearing in the *Saturday Evening Post* and the *Ladies Home Journal* circa 1920–25.

4. M. M. Manring compiled this chronology from the *Slave in a Box* website for Aunt Jemima.

5. Hortense Spillers, "National Brands/National Body," in *Comparative American Identities: Race, Sex and Nationality in the Modern Text,* ed. Lauren Berlant (New York: Routledge, 1991), 122.

6. Elizabeth O'Leary, *At Beck and Call* (Washington, D.C.: Smithsonian Institution Press, 1996), 5.

7. According to a historian for the Quaker Oats Company, the real triumph of Aunt Jemima as an advertising symbol was its ability to obliterate boundaries between legend and history, or fiction and autobiography. When he describes Green's performance at the fair, he writes: "The crowds loved the fantasy and many took it for gospel." Arthur Marquette, *Brands, Trademarks and Goodwill* (New York: McGraw-Hill, 1967), 155.

8. Chris Rutt, one of the original owners of the Pearl Milling Company, adapted the trademark of a plump and smiling black woman from a New Orleans blackface minstrel song-and-dance routine called "Old Aunt Jemima." See Marilyn Kern-Foxworth, "Aunt Jemima," *Black Ethnic Collectibles* 2, no. 5 (1989): 8–19; and Phil Patton, "Mammy: Her Life and Times," *American Heritage,* September 1993, 78.

9. Jeanne Weidman, *The Fair Women* (Chicago: Academy, 1981), 104.

10. Ann Massa, "Black Women in the White City," *American Studies* 7 (1989): 319.

11. Beverly Guy-Sheftall, *Daughters of Sorrow* (New York: Carlson, 1990), 172; and Massa, "Black Women," 319.

12. Anna Julia Cooper, *A Voice from the South* (New York: Oxford University Press, 1988), 100.

13. Cooper, *Voice from the South,* 101.

14. While Wells was insulted by the patronizing implications of "Negro Day," her coauthor, Frederick Douglass, insisted that it was a triumph for them since all of the gains made by the race began with small concessions. Douglass was also the scheduled keynote speaker.

15. Mier and Rudwick, "Black Man in the White City," *Phylon* 26 (1965): 360.

16. Marilyn Kern-Foxworth, *Aunt Jemima, Uncle Ben and Rastus: Blacks in Advertising, Yesterday, Today, and Tomorrow* (Westport, CT: Greenwood Press, 1994), 71. The advertisements use several strategies to evoke the southern aristocracy; one lists the "names" of the families who were privy to Aunt Jemima's breakfasts at Rosewood: "From New Orleans, the Southwoods, the Carters and the Marshalls came frequently, for it wasn't so far up the river to Colonel Higbee's mansion. But folks came too from all over the South, even from far Virginia."

17. Marquette, *Brands, Trademarks and Goodwill,* 155.

18. "Do you know this secret of making lighter, fluffier pancakes?" *Good Housekeeping,* November 1927, 124.

19. *Ladies Home Journal,* June 1925 and January 1927: "Throughout the old South, the Maxwell House was celebrated for its hospitality and for its delicious food."

20. *Good Housekeeping,* March 1931, 185. In addition to this advertisement, slavery was a familiar reference point for cleaning products as well. Premier electric vacuum cleaner used this theme in a 1928 promotion: "My Premier Duplex freed me from the slavery of cleaning. I would rather let my Premier do my cleaning in an hour or so and then go out and enjoy myself than work like a slave all day and then go to be all tired out like I used to." *Good Housekeeping,* May 1928, 183.

21. T. J. Jackson Lears, "From Salvation to Self-Realization: Advertising and the Therapeutic Roots of the Consumer Culture, 1880–1930," in *The Culture of Consumption: Critical Essays in American History, 1880–1980,* ed. Richard Wightman Fox and T. J. Jackson Lears (New York: Pantheon, 1983), 18.

22. Lears, "From Salvation to Self-Realization," 18.

23. *Ladies Home Journal,* 1896.

24. *Ladies Home Journal,* March 1924, 145.

25. Marquette, *Brands, Trademarks and Goodwill,* 155.

26. "The Night the Emily Dunston Burned."

27. *Ladies Home Journal,* March 1924, 145.

28. *Good Housekeeping,* September 1927, 35.

29. My copy of the advertisement is missing publication information; the date is clear from the text of the advertisement.

30. *Good Housekeeping,* February 1929, 99; and Ellen McCracken, "The Codes of Overt Advertisements," in *Decoding Women's Magazines* (New York: St. Martin's Press, 1993), 97–105.

31. Paule Marshall, "The Negro Woman in Literature," *Freedomways* 6 (1966): 21.

Chapter Four

1. Smith, *Conceived by Liberty,* 18.

2. Twain, *Pudd'nhead Wilson,* 15; emphasis added.

3. Chesnutt, "Her Virginia Mammy," 30.

4. See: Stephan Talty, *Mulatto America at the Crossroads of Black and White Culture: A Special History* (New York: HarperCollins, 2003); Kathleen Pfeiffer, *Race Passing and American Individualism* (Amherst: University of Massachusetts Press, 2003); Maria Giulia Fabi, *Passing and the Rise of the African American Novel* (Urbana: University of Illinois Press, 2001); Gayle Wald, *Crossing the Line: Racial Passing in Twentieth-Century U.S. Literature and Culture* (Durham, N.C.: Duke University Press, 2000); Juda Bennett, *The Passing Figure: Racial Confusion in Modern American Literature* (New York: Peter Lang, 1996).

5. Harriet Beecher Stowe describes Eva's Mammy as "middle aged mulatto woman of very respectable appearance" (109). Mary Eastman's Aunt Phillis is "a tall, dignified bright mulatto woman" (102).

6. Carolyn Porter, "Roxanna's Plot," in *Mark Twain's Pudd'nhead Wilson: Race, Conflict, and Culture,* ed. Susan Gillman (Durham, N.C.: Duke University Press, 1990), 124.

7. Toni Morrison, *Beloved* (New York: Knopf, 1987).

8. Porter, "Roxanna's Plot," 124.

9. This point has been made by several black feminists; two excellent examples of their work are Hortense Spillers, "Mama's Baby, Papa's Maybe: An American Primer," *Diacritics* (1987); and Angela Davis, *Women, Race, and Class* (New York: Vintage, 1981).

10. Chesnutt, "Her Virginia Mammy," in *The Wife of His Youth and Other Stories* (Ann Arbor: University of Michigan Press, 1968), 30.

11. Hazel Carby, "Policing the Black Woman's Body," *Critical Inquiry* 18 (Summer 1992): 738–55.

12. Curtis Ellison, *Charles Chesnutt: A Reference Guide* (Boston: G. K. Hall, 1977), 46–50.

13. Robert Bone, *Down Home: Origins of the Afro-American Short Story* (New York: Columbia University Press, 1988), 74.

14. Harris, *From Mammies to Militants,* 37.

15. "Plantation Life," in *The South: A Collection from Harpers Magazine* (New York: Gallery Books, 1990), 93.

Chapter Five

1. Catherine Clinton, "Women and Southern History: Images and Reflections," in *Perspectives on the American South,* ed. James C. Cobb and Charles R Wilson (New York: Gordon and Breach, 1977), 45.

2. W. Fitzhugh Brundage, *Where Memories Grow: History, Memory, and Southern Identity* (Chapel Hill: University of North Carolina Press, 2000), 8.

3. Quoted in Gerda Lerner, *Black Women in White America: A Documentary* (New York: Pantheon, 1972), 186.

4. Cynthia Mills and Pamela H. Simpson, *Monuments to the Lost Cause: Women, Art, and the Landscapes of Southern Memory* (Knoxville: University of Tennessee Press, 2003); and Darlene O'Dell, *Sites of Southern Memory: The Autobiographies of Katharine Du Pre Lumpkin, Lillian Smith, and Pauli Murray* (Charlottesville: University Press of Virginia, 2001).

5. Dawn Trouard, "Southern Women Writers, Racism, and Racists," *Southern Literary Journal* 37, no. 1 (2004): 176–79.

6. Norman Kittrell, "Old 'Miss' and 'Mammy.'" Address delivered on Memorial Day, April 26, 1924, First Presbyterian Church, Houston, Texas, 1924. Printed pamphlet, 11.

7. Text on monument, photo from author's collection.

8. Kirk Savage, *Standing Soldiers, Kneeling Slaves: Race, War, and Monument in Nineteenth-Century America* (Princeton, NJ: Princeton University Press, 1997).

9. Savage, *Standing Soldiers,* 157–58.

10. Ibid.

11. James Loewen, *Lies across America* (New York: Simon and Schuster, 1999). Loewen writes that "Markers and monuments like the Fort Mill obelisk must swim upstream against a torrent of facts . . . these neo-Confederate markers and monuments overlook African American service to the Union," 276–78.

12. Paul A. Shackel, *Memory in Black and White: Race, Commemoration, and the Post-Bellum Landscape* (Walnut Creek, CA: AltaMira Press, 2003), 86.

13. Stephan Ash, quoted in Loewen, *Lies across America,* 278.

14. Ibid.

15. Karen Cox, "The Confederate Monument in Arlington: A Token of Reconciliation," in *Monuments to the Lost Cause: Women, Art, and the Landscapes of Southern Memory,* ed. Cynthia Mills and Pamela H. Simpson (Knoxville: University of Tennessee Press, 2003), 150–86.

16. Richard Brodhead, introduction to *The Conjure Woman and Other Conjure Tales* (Durham: Duke University Press, 1993), 3.

17. Ibid.

18. Lucinda MacKethan, "Plantation Fiction," in *The History of Southern Literature,* ed. Louis Rubin et al. (Baton Rouge: Louisiana University Press, 1985), 209–18.

19. Grace Elizabeth Hale, quoted in Cox, "The Confederate Monument in Arlington," 153.

20. See Donald Bogle, *Toms, Coons, Mulattoes, Mammies, and Bucks: An Interpretive History of Black in American Films* (Continuum: New York, 1973); and *Blacks in American Films and Television: An Illustrated Encyclopedia* (New York: Fireside Books, Simon and Schuster, 1989), 93–95, for an analysis of this film and the role of mammy.

21. Thomas Nelson Page, "Marse Chan," in *Ole Virginia: Or, Marse Chan and Other Stories* (New York: Scribner's, 1887).

22. Details of this frieze appear in *Monuments to the Lost Cause: Women, Art, and the Landscapes of Southern Memory,* ed. Cynthia Mills and Pamela H. Simpson (Knoxville: University of Tennessee Press, 2003), 159. Photographs by Sean McCormally. See also the Web site for the Confederate Monument at Arlington National Cemetery with detailed photographs by Michael Robert Patterson (http://www.arlingtoncemetery.net).

23. Michael Harris, 209.

24. Gielow was both the founder of the National Historical Society and the author of fifteen books, including *Marse George an' de Hachet: Being the True Story of George Washington as Told to Martha S. Gielow by Her Old Colored "Mammy"* (1928) and *Mammy's Reminiscences, and Other Sketches* (1898). The figure appears on page 137 of *Old Plantation Days.*

25. Patricia Yaeger, *Dirt and Desire: Reconstructing Southern Women's Writing, 1930–1990* (Chicago: University of Chicago Press, 2000).

26. Sherwood Bonner, *Dialect Tales* (New York: Harper, 1883).

27. Ruby Vaughan Bigger, *My Miss Nancy: Nancy Astor's Virginia 'Mammy' tells why 'her littl' mistis ain't neber gwine lose her 'sition ober dar in Inglan'* (Macon: J. W. Burke, 1924).

28. Sherwood Bonner, *Suwannee River Tales* (Boston: Roberts, 1884).

29. Katharine Sherwood Bonner McDowell, *A Sherwood Bonner Sampler, 1869–1884: What a Bright, Educated, Witty, Lively, Snappy Young Woman Can Say on a Variety of Topics,* ed. Anne Razey Gowdy (Knoxville: University of Tennessee Press, 2000).

30. Barbara A. White, review of *A Sherwood Bonner Sampler, 1869–1884: What a Bright, Educated, Witty, Lively, Snappy Young Woman Can Say on a Variety of Topics,* by Katharine Sherwood Bonner McDowell, *NWSA Journal* 15, no. 1 (2003): 142.

31. *Black Mammy Memorial or Peace Monument* (Athens: Banner Printery, 1910), 1–3.

32. Barbara A. White, review of *A Sherwood Bonner Sampler, 1869–1884: What a Bright, Educated, Witty, Lively, Snappy Young Woman Can Say on a Variety of Topics,* by Katharine Sherwood Bonner McDowell, *NWSA Journal* 15, no. 1 (2003): 142.

33. Ibid., 3.

34. Bonner, *Suwannee River Tales,* 1.

35. Frances Ellen Watkins Harper, *Iola Leroy; or, Shadows Uplifted,* (Philadelphia: Garrigues Brothers, 1892).

36. Gabrielle Foreman, "'Reading Aright': White Slavery, Black Referents, and the Strategy of Histotextuality in *Iola Leroy,*" *Yale Journal of Criticism* 10, no. 2 (1997): 327–54. In her endnotes to this wonderful essay, Forman writes, "Many of the critics who have paid more than passing attention to Harper's novel have been African American women. Most prominent among them are Melba Joyce Boyd, Hazel Carby, Barbara Christian, Deborah McDowell, Frances Smith Foster and Claudia Tate. On *Iola Leroy* see especially: Hazel Carby, *Reconstructing Womanhood: The Emergence of the Afro-American Woman Novelist* (New York: Oxford University Press, 1987), chapter 4; Frances Smith Foster, *Written by Herself: Literary Production by African American Women, 1746–1892* (Bloomington: Indiana University Press, 1993); Claudia Tate, *Domestic Allegories of Political Desire: The Black Heroine's Text at the Turn of the Century* (New York: Oxford University Press, 1992)."

37. "More Slavery at the South by a Negro Nurse," *Independent,* January 25, 1912, 196–200. Reprinted as "I Live a Treadmill Life," in *Black Women in White America: A Documentary,* ed Gerda Lerner (New York: Pantheon, 1972), 227–29.

38. Mrs. Bernie Babcock, *Mammy: A Drama* (New York: Neale Publishing, 1915).

39. *Black Mammy Memorial or Peace Monument* (Athens: Banner Printery, 1910).

40. Ibid., 3.

41. Mrs. Bernie Babcock, *Mammy: A Drama* (New York: Neale Publishing, 1915).

42. W. E. B. DuBois, *The Gift of Black Folk* (Boston: Stratford, 1924), 337–38.

43. Eliza Ripley, *Social Life in Old New Orleans* (New York: D. Appleton, 1912).

44. W. E. B. DuBois, *The Gift of Black Folk* (Boston: Stratford, 1924), 337–38.

45. Sterling Brown, "The Muted South" *Phylon* 6 Winter (1945): 22–34.

46. Joseph Boskin, "Mammy," *Helicon Nine* 17/18 (1987): 37. For arguments in favor of the monument that are similar to the example discussed in the text, see Reverend I. E. Lowery's biography, *Life on the Old Plantation in Antebellum Days, or, A Story Based on Facts* (Columbia, SC: State Company Printers, 1911). Lowery writes that "An appeal to erect a monument to the former slaves of the South was issued in New Orleans a few days ago from the headquarters of the United Confederate Veterans by Gen. George W. Gordon, commander-in-chief of the veterans. The appeal is in the form of a general order, which quotes the resolutions favoring such a monument adopted at the Birmingham reunion in 1908, and adds:

'Only those familiar with the beautiful patriarchial [*sic*] life on the Southern plantations previous to 1865 know of the devotions of the slaves to their owners and the children of the family. They were raised more like members of a large household.'"

47. Du Bois, *The Gift of Black Folk,* 337.

48. Adeline F. Ries, "Mammy, a Story," *Crisis,* January 13, 1917, 117–18. Reprinted in *Short Fiction by Black Women: 1900–1920,* collected with an introduction by Elizabeth Ammons, Schomburg Library of Nineteenth-Century Black Women Writers, ed. Henry Louis Gates, Jr. (New York: Oxford University Press, 1991), 520–23.

49. Hortense Spillers, "Mama's Baby, Papa's Maybe: An American Grammar Book," *Diacritics* 17 (1987): 64–81.

50. Angela Davis, *Women, Race, and Class* (New York: Vintage Books, 1983).

51. Ries's and Brown's short stories have been virtually ignored until recently; they are reprinted in the multivolume series the Schomburg Library of Nineteenth-Century Black Women Writers published by Oxford University Press and edited by Henry Louis Gates, Jr. In the series volume *Short Fiction by Black Women, 1900–1920* (New York: Oxford University Press, 1991), Elizabeth Ammons omits Adeline Ries completely from her introduction but includes this comment in the endnotes: "I welcome information about authors in the volume, most of whom do not show up in the usual sources." She also writes that "simply because a person's work appeared in either the *Colored American Magazine* or the *Crisis* does not automatically mean than she was African American. As [Penelope] Bullock points out, 'Contributions by white persons became a significant part of the *Colored American Magazine* in the latter period of its publication,' and the *Crisis* regularly, if not often, published white writers — Mary White Ovington, Jane Addams, Jacob Riss, Dorothy Canfield. These white writers, however, were usually well-known, the likelihood of lesser known authors in this volume not being African American is very small" (8).

52. Carolyn Denard, introduction to Charlotte Hawkins Brown, *Mammy: An Appeal to the Heart of the South; and, The Correct Thing to Do—to Say—to Wear* (New York: G. K. Hall, 1995), xx.

53. Ibid.

54. See Glenda E. Gilmore, *Gender and Jim Crow: Women and the Politics of White Supremacy in North Carolina, 1896–1920* (Chapel Hill: University of North Carolina Press, 1996), 184. Gilmore mistakenly writes, "Ultimately, they stand by as Mammy goes to the county home," 189. The text actually describes her death: "A new board marked the last resting place of 'mammy,' to which she journeyed in the county wagon . . . Only the kind honeysuckle creeps over the grave of the body in ebony whose soul was whiter than snow," 17–18.

55. Brown, *Mammy,* 1.

56. Brown, *Mammy,* 1.

57. In her introduction to *Mammy: An Appeal to the Heart of the South,* Carolyn Denard writes, "Mammy garnered little if any interest from the black press. Distribution seems to have been limited to the New England areas and to southern readers in North Carolina. There were no reviews in the major black social and literary magazines" (xxv).

58. Alain Locke, *The New Negro: An Interpretation* (1925; reprint, New York: Athenaeum, 1968).

59. Jeffrey C. Stewart, *Winold Reiss: An Illustrated Checklist of His Portraits* (Washington City: Smithsonian Institution Press for the National Portrait Gallery, 1990), 8.

60. Elise Johnson McDougald, "The Task of Negro Womanhood," in *The New Negro: An Interpretation,* ed. Alain Locke (1925; reprint, New York: Athenaeum, 1968), 371–72.

Chapter Six

1. Margaret Mitchell, *Gone with the Wind* (1935; reprint, New York: Avon, 1973).

2. William Faulkner, *The Sound and the Fury* (New York: Vintage, 1929).

3. The South of *Gone with the Wind* and the South of *The Sound and the Fury* are represented in different times: Faulkner sets his novel at the beginning of the twentieth century, while Mitchell's cyclical narrative takes the reader from pre-war rural Georgian aristocracy to reconstructed Atlanta and back again. Nonetheless, the novels are bound by their preoccupation with, and investigation of, southern representation and each author's need to construct a South that will test the limits of our imagination.

4. Susan Bordo, "The Body, Which One, Whose?" in *Unbearable Weight: Feminism, Western Culture, and the Body* (Berkeley and Los Angeles: University of California Press, 1993). I agree with Bordo and think that her argument would be more complete if she did the same kind of historical charting with the Black Power movement that she does with feminism—women like Angela Davis and Kathleen Cleaver and Elaine Brown contributed important questions about the role of the black female body in the Black Power movement, and I suspect that we might find similar arguments dating from slave narratives through contemporary African American literature and scholarship.

5. Bordo, *Unbearable Weight.* See also Yaeger, *Dirt and Desire;* and Carolyn Porter, *Seeing and Being: The Plight of The Participant Observer in Emerson, James, Adams, and Faulkner* (Middletown, Conn.: Wesleyan University Press; Irvington, N.Y.: distributed by Columbia University Press, 1981). Yaeger and Porter have made significant contributions to my thinking on this subject.

6. Bordo is also critical of scholars like Don Hanlon Johnson who chart a direct lineage between Karl Marx and Michel Foucault, completely ignoring the role so-

cial movements of the sixties like black power and women's liberation played in awakening us to the body as an instrument of power. Surely visual representations of the mammy body, popularized by Aunt Jemima iconography, and taken up during the Black Arts movement, as seen in *The Liberation of Aunt Jemima* (Betye Saar, 1972), *Aunt Jemima and the Pillsbury Doughboy* (Jeff Donaldson, 1964), and *New Jemima* (Joe Overstreet, 1964) reaffirm the significance of the mammy's body in this discourse.

7. John Matthews, *The Sound and the Fury: Faulkner and the Lost Cause* (Boston: Twayne, 1991), 13. Matthews suggests that by the time the novel was published, Faulkner knew that his work would never "reach a popular audience, and that his art would have to create its own readership."

8. Between the Compson house and the Gibson cabin there are over a dozen characters; the principals being Dilsey and Roskus Gibson, their children T.P., Versh, and Frony, and Frony's son, Luster; Caroline and Jason Compson Sr., their children Benjy (who is mute and disabled), Jason, Quentin, and Caddy, and Caddy's daughter Quentin.

9. Matthews, *Sound and Fury,* 115.

10. Diane Roberts, *Faulkner and Southern Womanhood* (Athens: University of Georgia Press, 1994), 68.

11. Southern literature scholar Thadious Davis finds that it is Dilsey's physical appearance and dress that "connects Dilsey to a long line of actual and fictional portraits of 'mammy,' the loving black servant praised for her service to a white family but often ridiculed because of her appearance." Thadious Davis, *Faulkner's Negro* (Baton Rouge: Louisiana State University Press. 1983), 104–5. By contrast, Sandra Milloy offers a reading typical of the kind that *The Sound and the Fury* received in the post–Civil Rights era. Milloy builds her argument by comparing Dilsey's neglect of her own family with her catering to the Compsons. Sandra Milloy, "Dilsey: Faulkner's Black Mammy in *The Sound and the Fury,*" *Negro History Bulletin* 46, no. 3 (1983): 70. See also Margaret Walker Alexander, "Faulkner and Race," in *The Maker and the Myth: Faulkner and Yopknapatwpha,* ed. Evans Harrington (Jackson: University Press of Mississippi, 1978), 113.

12. In *Faulkner and Southern Womanhood,* Diane Roberts describes this kind of tar baby effect: "Nonetheless, in celebrating the self-sacrificial all-mother, the exemplary Mammy of the old southern model partially, but significantly, reasserts herself. No one laughs at Dilsey the way they might at the mammy in *Gone with the Wind. . . .* But Dilsey performs essentially the same function. She nurtures not just the bodies but also the souls of the unsalvageable Compsons. *The Sound and the Fury's* shifting narratives subvert the reductive stereotyping of the black mother as laughing, fleshy feeder, while at the same time reinforcing the discourses that deny her liberty. Dilsey endures, but she does not escape" (68).

13. See Kimberly Wallace-Sanders, "A Peculiar Motherhood: The Black

Mammy Figure in American Literature and Popular Iconography," Ph.D. diss., Boston University, 1995.

14. Helen Taylor, *Circling Dixie: Contemporary Southern Culture Through a Transatlantic Lens* (New Brunswick: Rutgers University Press, 2001).

15. This scene is reversed in *Dessa Rose,* when Rufel nurses Dessa Rose's baby when Dessa cannot. See Shirley Anne Williams, *Dessa Rose* (New York: W. Morrow, 1986), 90.

16. Doreen Fowler and Ann Abadie, *Faulkner and Popular Culture* (Jackson: University Press of Mississippi, 1990), 79.

17. See the introduction.

18. Brundage, *Where These Memories Grow,* 7.

Conclusion

1. Brundage, *Where These Memories Grow,* 9.

2. Alice Randall, interview, CNN.com chat room, June 22, 2001, posted 2:44 PM EDT.

3. Patti Embry-Tautenhan, "Toni Morrison and Major Literary Associations Join Leading Authors and Scholars in Opposition to Mitchell Trusts' Efforts to Prevent Book Publication," April 16, 2001, www.houghtonmifflinbooks.com/features/randall.

4. Embry-Tautenhan, "Morrison and Literary Associations."

5. "'The Wind Done Gone' a Mild Breeze," CNN.com, June 29, 2001, posted 11:51 AM EDT.

6. Randall, interview.

7. Ibid.

8. Alice Randall, *The Wind Done Gone* (Boston: Houghton Mifflin, 2001), 6.

9. J. M. Lucas, "Exposed Roots," *Arts Feature,* February 27, 2002.

10. Harris, *Colored Pictures,* 117.

11. Harris, *Colored Pictures,* 217.

12. Blight, *Race and Reunion: The Civil War in American Memory* (Cambridge: Belknap Press of Harvard University Press, 2001), 231–32.

13. Harris, *Colored Pictures,* 118.

14. In chronological order the Black Arts Movement artists whose work subverted the Aunt Jemima stereotype are: Jeff Donaldson: "Aunt Jemima and the Pillsbury Dough Boy" (1963), Joe Overstreet: "New Jemima" (1964), Murray DePillars "Aunt Jemima" (1968), Jon Lockard: "No More" (1972), Betye Saar: "The Liberation of Aunt Jemima" (1972).

15. Harris, *Colored Pictures,* 217.

16. Felicia Feaster, "Look to the Future," *Creative Loafing,* November 10, 2004, 11.

17. Darlene Clark Hine, "Introduction," *The Face of Our Past,* ed. Kathleen

Thompson and Hilary Mac Austin (Bloomington: University of Indiana Press, 1999), xi.

18. Terry Gips, "Joyce Scott's Mammy/Nanny Series," *Feminist Studies* 22, no 2. (1996): 312.

19. Joyce Scott, interview by the author, June 15, 2004, Atlanta. See also Joyce J. Scott, *Fearless Beadwork: Handwriting and Drawings from Hell* (Rochester, N.Y.: Visual Studies Workshop, 1994).

20. Gips, "Scott's Mammy/Nanny Series," 311.

PRIMARY SOURCES

Anonymous. "Grace Merry." Written for *Godey's Lady's Book* 18 (1839), 178–83.

Babcock, Bernie. *Mammy—A Drama*. New York: Neale Publishing, 1915.

Bigger, Ruby Vaughan. *My Miss Nancy*. Macon, GA: J.W. Burke, 1924.

Chesnutt, Charles. "Her Virginia Mammy." *The Wife of His Youth*. Ridgewood, NJ: Gregg Press, 1899.

Chesnutt, Charles. *The Marrow of Tradition*. 1901. Ann Arbor: University of Michigan Press, 1970.

Cobb, Joseph. *Mississippi Scenes*. Philadelphia: A Hart, 1851.

Douglass, Frederick. *My Bondage and My Freedom*. Ed. William Andrews. Urbana: University of Illinois Press, 1988.

Douglass, Frederick. *Narrative of the Life of Frederick Douglass, an American Slave, Written by Himself*. New York: Signet, 1968.

Drysdale, Isabel. *Scenes in Georgia*. Philadelphia: American Sunday School Union, 1827.

Eastman, Mary. *Aunt Phillis's Cabin*. Philadelphia: Lippincott, Grambo & Co., 1852.

Faulkner, William. *The Sound and the Fury*. New York: Vintage Books, 1929.

Harper, Frances Ellen Watkins. *Iola Leroy: Or Shadows Uplifted*. Boston: James H. Earle, 1892.

Harris, Joel Chandler. *Uncle Remus*. 1899. New York: D. Appleton & Co., 1929.

Harris, Joel Chandler. *On the Plantation*. New York: D. Appleton & Co., 1892.

Hawkins-Brown, Charlotte. *Mammy: An Appeal to the Heart of the South; and The Correct Thing to Do—To Say—To Wear*. Introduction by Carloyn Denard. New York: G. K. Hall & Co., 1995.

Hentz, Caroline. *Linda; or the Pilot of the Belle Creole*. Philadelphia: T. B. Petersen, 1850.

Hentz, Caroline. *The Planter's Northern Bride*. Philadelphia: A. Hart, 1854.

Jackson, Helen. *Mammy and Her Family*. Boston: Robert Brothers, 1881.

Kearney, Belle. *A Slaveholder's Daughter*. New York: The Abbey Press, 1900.

Kennedy, Thomas Pendleton. *Swallow Barn, or, A Sojourn in the Old Dominion.* 1832. York: Hafner Publishing, 1962.

Kittrell, Norman. "'Old Miss' and "Mammy.'" Address delivered on Memorial Day, April 26, 1924, First Presbyterian Church, Houston, TX. 1924 (pamphlet published by the church).

Langhorne, Gertrude. *Mammy's Letter's.* Macon, GA: J.W. Burke Company, 1922.

Mitchell, Margaret. *Gone with the Wind.* New York: McMillan, 1936.

Page, John. *Uncle Robin in His Cabin in Virginia, and Tom without One in Boston.* Richmond: J.W. Randolph, 1853.

Page, Thomas Nelson. *Befo' the War: Echoes in Negro Dialogue.* New York: Charles Scribner, 1888.

Page, Thomas Nelson. *The Old South.* New York: Charles Scribner, 1892.

Page, Thomas Nelson. *In Ole Virginia.* 1887. Ridgewood, NJ: Gregg Press, 1968.

Page, Thomas Nelson. *Red Rock; A Chronicle of Reconstruction.* 1887. Ridgewood, NJ: Gregg Press, 1967.

Page, Thomas Nelson. *Social Life in Old Virginia Before the War.* New York: Charles Scribner, 1897.

Pollard, Edman. *Black Diamonds Gathered in the Darkey Homes of the South.* New York: Rodney Russell Publishing, 1859.

Roe, Elizabeth. *Aunt Leanna or Early Scenes in Kentucky.* Chicago: Published for the author, 1855.

Sampson, Emma. *Mammy's White Folks.* Chicago: Reilly & Lee Co., 1919.

Sims, William Woodcraft. *A Story of the South at the Close of the Revolution.* New York: J. S. Redfield, 1854.

Smedes, Susan Dabney. *Memorial of a Southern Planter.* New York: Knopf, 1887.

Stowe, Harriet Beecher. *Men of Our Times.* Hartford, CT: Hartford Publishing Co., 1868.

Stowe, Harriet Beecher. *Uncle Tom's Cabin.* 1854. New York: The Heritage Press, 1938.

Stuart, Ruth. *Plantation Songs.* New York: D. Appleton and Company, 1916.

Terrell, Mary Chuch. "Lynching From a Negro's Point of View." *North American Review* 178 (1904): 853–68.

Thorpe, Thomas. *The Master's House.* New York: J. C. Derby, 1855.

Tourgee, Albion. *Toinette.* New York: Henry Churton, 1884.

Tucker, George Beverly. *Valley of the Shenandoah.* 1824. Chapel Hill: University of North Carolina Press, 1970.

Twain, Mark. *Pudd'nhead Wilson.* 1894. San Francisco: Chandler Publishing Company, 1968.

BIBLIOGRAPHY

Adams, Richard P. "Work: The Sound and the Fury." *Faulkner: Myth and Motion.* Princeton, NJ: Princeton University Press, 1968.

Ammons, Elizabeth. "Heroines in Uncle Tom's Cabin." *American Literature* 49 (1977): 16–179.

Ammons, Elizabeth, ed. *Critical Essays on Harriet Beecher Stowe.* Boston: G. K. Hall, 1980.

Anderson, Lisa M. *Mammies No More: The Changing Image of Black Wwomen on Stage and Screen.* Lanham, MD: Rowman & Littlefield, 1997.

Bailey, Hugh C., and William P. Dale. "Missus Alone in de Big House." *Alabama Review* 8 (1955): 43–54.

Bakhtin, Mikhail. *The Dialogic Imagination: Four Essays by M. M. Bakhtin.* Trans. Caryl Emerson and Michael Holquist. Austin: Texas UP, 1981.

Barlett, Irving, and C. Glenn Cambor. "The History and Psychodynamics of Southern Womanhood." *Women's Studies* 2 (1974): 9–24.

Bassin, Donna Margaret Honey, and Meryle Mahrer Kaplan. Ed. *Representations of Motherhood.* New Haven: Yale University Press, 1994.

Bauer, Raymond and Alice Bauer. "Day to Day Resistance to Slavery." *Journal of Negro History* (1942): 388–19.

Bell, Roseanne. *Sturdy Black Bridges: Vision of Black Women in Literature.* Garden City, NY: Anchor Books, 1979.

Bell-Scott, Patricia. *Double Stitch: Black Women Write about Mothers and Daughters.* Boston: Beacon Press, 1991.

Benét, Stephen Vincent. *John Brown's Body.* New York: Rhinehart and Company, 1927.

Berg, Allison. *Mothering The Race: Women's Narratives on Reproduction, 1890–1930.* Urbana: Illinois University Press, 2002.

Bigger, Ruby Vaughan. *My Miss Nancy.* Macon, GA: Press of J. W. Burke & Co., 1924.

Blassingame, John. *The Slave Community: Plantation Life in the Antebellum South.* New York: Oxford University Press, 1972.

Bleikasten, Andre. *The Ink of Melancholy: Faulkner's Novels, from* The Sound and the Fury *to* Light in August. Bloomington: Indiana University Press, 1990.

Bleikasten, Andre. *William Faulkner's* The Sound and the Fury: *A Critical Casebook*. New York: Garland Publishers, 1982.

Bleikasten, Andre. *The Most Splendid Failure: Faulkner's* The Sound and the Fury. Bloomington: Indiana University Press, 1976.

Blight, David. *Race and Reunion: The Civil War in American Memory*. Cambridge, MA: Belknap Press, 2001.

Blight, David. Public lecture. Emory University, Atlanta, GA, April 5, 2001.

Bloch, Ruth. "American Feminine Ideals in Transition: The Rise of the Moral Mother, 1785–1815." *Feminist Studies* 4 (June 1978): 101–26.

Bogle, David. *Toms, Coons, Mulattoes, Mammies, and Bucks*. New York: Continuum, 1990.

Boime, Albert. *The Art of Exclusion: Representing Blacks in the Nineteenth Century*. Washington: Smithsonian Institution Press, 1990.

Boles, John. *Black Southerners, 1619–1869*. Lexington: University Press of Kentucky, 1983.

Bonner, Sherwood. *Like Unto Like*. New York: Harper, 1878; republished as *Blythe Herndon*. London: Ward, Locke, 1882.

Bonner, Sherwood. *Dialect Tales*. New York: Harper, 1883.

Bonner, Sherwood. *Suwannee River Tales*. Boston: Roberts, 1884.

Boskin, Joseph. "Mammy." *Helicon Nine* 17/18 (1987): 37.

Boskin, Joseph. *Sambo: The Rise and Demise of an American Jester*. New York: Oxford University Press, 1986.

Broadhead, Richard. *Faulkner: New Perspectives*. Englewood Cliffs, NJ: Prentice-Hall, 1983.

Brooks, Cleanth. *On the Prejudices, Predilections, and Firm Beliefs of William Faulkner: Essays*. Baton Rouge: Louisiana State University Press, 1987.

Brown, Sterling. "The Muted South." *Phylon* 6 (Winter 1945): 22–34.

Brown, Sterling. *The Negro in American Fiction*. Washington, DC: Associates in Negro Folk Education, 1938.

Brundage, Fitzhugh, ed. *Where These Memories Grow*. Chapel Hill: University of North Carolina Press, 2000.

Burnham, Dorothy. "Black Women as Producers and Reproducers for Profit." In *Woman's Nature: Rationalizations for Inequality*. Ed. Marion Lowe and Ruth Hubbard. New York: Pergamon, 1983.

Burnham, Margaret. "An Impossible Marriage: Slave Law and Family Law." *Law and Inequality* 5 (1987): 187–25.

Butterfield, Stephan. *Black Autobiography in America*. Amherst: University of Massachusetts Press, 1974.

Calhoun, Arthur W. *A Social History of the American Family from Colonial Times to the Present.* 3 vols. Cleveland: Arthur Clarke & Co., 1918.

Calvert, Karen. *Children in the House: The Material Culture of Early Childhood, 1600–1900.* Boston: Northeastern University Press, 1992.

Caraway, Nancie. *Segregated Sisterhood: Racism and the Politics of American Feminism.* Knoxville: University of Tennessee Press, 1991.

Cardwell, Guy. *The Man Who Was Mark Twain: Images and Ideologies.* New Haven, CT: Yale University Press, 1991.

Carson, Jane. *Plantation Housekeeping in Colonial Virginia.* Williamsburg, VA: Panton, 1982.

Cassidy, Frederic G., ed. *Dictionary of American Regional English,* Cambridge, MA.: Belknap Press, 1985.

Chodorow, Nancy. *Feminism and Psychoanalytic Theory.* New Haven, CT: Yale University Press, 1989.

Christian, Barbara. *Black Women Novelists: The Development of a Tradition, 1892–1976.* Westport, CT: Greenwood Press, 1980.

Christian, Barbara. *Black Feminist Criticism: Perspectives on Black Women Writers.* New York: Pergamon, 1985.

Clinton, Catherine. *The Plantation Mistress: Woman's World in the Old South.* New York: Pantheon, 1982.

Cobb, Joseph. *Mississippi Scenes.* Philadelphia: A. Hart, 1851.

Cody, Cheryll. "Slave Demography and Family Formation: A Community Study of the Ball Family Plantations, 1786–1833." *William and Mary Quarterly* (1982): 192–11.

Congdon-Martin, Douglas. *Images in Black: 150 Years of Black Collectibles.* Westchester, PA: Schiffer Publishing, 1990.

Cowan, Michael H., ed., *Twentieth Century Interpretations of* The Sound and the Fury: *A Collection of Critical Essays.* Englewood Cliffs, NJ: Prentice-Hall, 1968.

Cox, Karen, "The Confederate Monument in Arlington: A Token of Reconciliation." *Monuments to the Lost Cause: Women, Art and the Landscapes of Southern Memory.* Ed. Cynthia Mills and Pamela H. Simpson. Knoxville: University of Tennessee Press.

Crozier, Alice. *The Novels of Harriet Beecher Stowe.* New York: Oxford University Press, 1969.

David, Beverly. *Mark Twain and His Illustrators.* Troy, NY: Whitston, 1986.

Davis, Angela. "Reflections on the Black Woman's Role in the Community of Slaves." *Black Scholar* (1971): 3–15.

Davis, Angela. *Women, Race, and Class.* New York: Vintage Books, 1981.

Davis, Thadious. *Faulkner's "Negro": Art and the Southern Context.* Baton Rouge: Louisiana State University Press, 1983.

Douglas, Ann. *The Feminization of American Culture.* New York: Knopf, 1977.

Drysdale, Isabel. *Scenes in Georgia*. Philadelphia: American Sunday School Union, 1827.

Du Cille, Ann. *Skin Trade*. Cambridge, MA: Harvard University Press, 1996.

Dundes, Alan. *Cracking Jokes: Studies of Humor and Stereotypes*. Berkeley: Ten Speed Press, 1987.

Dunkley, Tina. Public lecture. Women Studies Colloquium. Emory University, Atlanta, GA. March 2004.

Ferguson, Ann. *Sexual Democracy; Women, Oppression and Revolution*. Boulder, CO: Westview Press, 1991.

Fiedler, Leslie. *The Inadvertent Epic: From Uncle Tom's Cabin to Roots*. New York: Simon and Schuster, 1980.

Fields, Annie, ed. *Life and Letters of Harriet Beecher Stowe*. Boston: Houghton Mifflin and Company, 1897.

Fildes, Valerie. *Wet Nursing: A History from Antiquity to the Present*. Oxford: Basil Blackwell, 1988.

Fildes, Valerie. *Breasts, Bottles, and Babies*. Edinburgh: Edinburgh University Press, 1986.

Fishburn, Katherine. *Women in Popular Culture: A Reference Guide*. Westport, CT: Greenwood Press, 1982.

Fleischer, Jennifer. *Mastering Slavery: Memory, Family, and Identity in Women's Slave Narratives*. New York: New York University Press, 1996.

Formanek-Brunell, Miriam. *Made to Play House: Dolls and the Commercialization of American Girlhood: 1830–1930*. New Haven, CT: Yale University Press, 1993.

Foster, Frances. *Witnessing Slavery: The Development of Antebellum Slave Narrative*. Westport, CT: Greenwood Press, 1979.

Fox-Kernworth, Marilyn. *Aunt Jemima, Uncle Ben and Rastus*. Westport, CT: Greenwood Press, 1994.

Frederickson, George. *The Black Image in the White Mind: The Debate on Afro-American Character and Destiny, 1817–1914*. New York: Harper & Row, 1971.

Gaines, Francis P. *The Southern Plantation: A Study in the Development and the Accuracy of a Tradition*. New York: Columbia University Press, 1925.

Gale, Robert. *Plots and Characters in the Works of Mark Twain*. Hamden, CT: Archon Books, 1973.

Gallop, Jane. *Criticizing Feminist Criticism*. New York: Routledge, 1990.

Gardner, Richard. "Stereotypes and Sentimentality: The Coarser Sieve." *Midwest Quarterly: A Journal of Contemporary Thought* 29 (1988): 232–48.

Gates, Henry Louis. *Figures in Black*. New York: Oxford University Press, 1987.

Gates, Henry Louis. *Six Women's Slave Narratives*. New York, Oxford University Press, 1988.

Gerould, Daniel. *American Melodrama*. New York: Performing Arts Journal Publications, 1983.

Gibbs, Patikii. *Black Collectibles Sold in America*. Paducah, KY: Collector Books, 1987.

Gillman, Susan. *Dark Twins: Imposture and Identity in Mark Twain's America*. Chicago: University of Chicago Press, 1989.

Gillman, Susan, ed. Pudd'nhead Wilson: *Race, Conflict, and Culture*. Durham, NC: Duke University Press, 1990.

Gilman, Sander L. "Black Bodies, White Bodies: Toward An Iconography Of Female Sexuality in Late Nineteenth Century Art, Medicine, and Literature." *Critical Inquiry* 12 (Autumn 1985): 213–19.

Gilmore, Glenda E.. *Gender and Jim Crow: Women and the Politics of White Supremacy in North Carolina, 1896–1920*. Chapel Hill: University of North Carolina, 1996.

Goings, Ken. *Mammy and Uncle Mose: Black Collectibles and American Stereotyping*. Bloomington: Indiana University Press, 1994.

Gonzalez, Nancie. "Toward a Definition of Matrifociality." In *Afro-American Anthropology*. Ed. Norman Whitten, Jr. and John Szwed. New York: Free Press, 1970.

Greer, Dorothy D. "Dilsey and Lucas: Faulkner's Use of the Negro as a Gauge of Moral Character." *Emporia State Research Studies* 11 (September 1962): 43–61.

Gross, Seymour. *Images of the Negro in American Literature*. Chicago: University of Chicago Press, 1966.

Gutman, Herbert. *The Black Family in Slavery and Freedom, 1750–1925*. New York: Pantheon Books, 1976.

Gwin, Minrose. *Black and White Women of the Old South: The Peculiar Sisterhood in American Literature*. Knoxville: University of Tennessee Press, 1989.

Hall, Wade. *The Smiling Phoenix: Southern Humor from 1865–1914*. Gainesville: University of Florida Press, 1968.

Harris, Joel Chandler. *The Chronicles of Aunt Minervy Ann*. New York: Scribner, 1899.

Harris, Michael D. *Colored Pictures: Race and Visual Representations*. Chapel Hill: University of North Carolina Press, 2003.

Harris, Trudier. "Moms Mabley: A Study in Humor, Role-Playing, and the Violation of Taboo." *The Southern Review* 24 (1988): 765–76.

Harris, Trudier. *From Mammies to Militants*. Philadelphia: Temple University Press, 1982.

Hawkesworth, M. E. *Beyond Oppression: Feminist Theory and Political Strategy*. New York: Continuum, 1990.

Hawks, Joanne. *Sex, Race, and the Role of Women in the South*. Jackson: University Press of Mississippi, 1983.

Hentz, Caroline. *Linda; or, the Young Pilot of the Belle Creole*. Philadelphia: A. Hart, 1852.

Hill, Herbert. *Anger and Beyond: The Negro Writer in the United States.* New York: Harper & Row, 1966.

Hill-Collins, Patricia. *Black Feminist Thought.* London: Hammersmith, 1990.

Hill-Collins, Patricia. "The Meaning of Motherhood in Black Culture and Black Mother/Daughter Relationships." *Sage: A Scholarly Journal on Black Women* 4 (1987): 4–11.

Hoffman, Andrew. *Twain's Heroes, Twain's Worlds: Mark Twains'* Adventures of Huckleberry Finn, A Connecticut Yankee in King Arthur's Court *and* Pudd'nhead Wilson. Philadelphia: University of Pennsylvania Press, 1988.

Holliday, Cal. *Woman's Life in Colonial Days.* Williamstown, MA: Corner House, 1968.

Honour, Hugh. *The Image of the Black in Western Art: From the American Revolution to World War I.* Vol. 4. Cambridge, MA: Harvard University Press, 1989.

Honour, Hugh. *The Visual Arts: A History.* Englewood Cliffs, NJ: Prentice-Hall, 1982.

Hooton, Bruce. *Mother and Child in Modern Art.* New York: Duell, Sloan and Pearce, 1964.

Howell, Elmo. "A Note on Faulkner's Negro Characters." *Mississippi Quarterly* 11 (Fall 1958): 201–3.

Jackson, Edward. *American Slavery and the American Novel, 1852–1977.* Bristol, IN: Wyndham Hall Press, 1987.

Jackson, Margaret Young. "An Investigation of Biographies and Autobiographies of American Slaves Published between 1840 and 1860." Diss. Cornell University, 1954.

Jehlen, Myra. "The Family Militant: Domesticity versus Slavery in Uncle Tom's Cabin." *Criticism* 31 (1989): 383–400.

Jewell, K. Sue. *From Mammy to Miss America: Cultural Images and the Shaping of U.S. Social Policy.* New York: Routledge, 1993.

Johnson, Michael P. "Smothered Infants: Were Slave Mothers at Fault?" *Journal of Southern History* (1981): 493–520.

Johnson, Paul. "'Good-bye to Sambo': The Contribution of Black Slave Narratives to the Abolition Movement." *Negro American Literature Forum* 6 (1972): 79–84.

Jones, Jacqueline. "'My Mother Was Much of a Woman': Black Women and the Family Under Slavery." *Feminist Studies* (1982): 235–67.

Jordan, Winthrop. *White Over Black.* Chapel Hill: University of North Carolina Press, 1968.

Kennedy, John Pendleton. *Swallow Barn, or, A Soujourn in the Old Dominion.* Philadelphia: Carey & Lea, 1832.

Kennedy, Theodore. *"You Gotta Deal with It": Black Family Relations in a Southern Community.* New York: Oxford University Press, 1980.

King, Marian. *A Gallery of Mothers and Their Children*. Philadelphia: Lippincott, 1958.

King, Wilma. *Stolen Childhood: Slave Youth in Nineteenth-Century America*. Bloomington: Indiana University Press, 1995.

Kittrell, Norman. "'Old Miss' and 'Mammy.'" Address, 26 April 1924, first Presbyterian Church, Houston, TX. Pamphlet published by the church.

Kulikoff, Allan. "The Beginnings of the Afro-American Family in Maryland." *The American Family in Social Historical Perspective*. Ed. Michael Gordon. New York: St. Martins, 1978.

Lavitt, Wendy. *Dolls*. New York: Knopf, 1983.

Lerner, Gerda. *Black Women in White America: A Documentary History*. New York: Random House, 1972.

Levinson, Melanie. Review of *Conjure Woman and Other Conjure Tales*. MELUS 24.2 (1993): 201–3.

Levy, David M. "Racial Stereotypes in Anti-Slavery Fiction." *Phylon* 31 (Fall 1970): 265–79.

Loewen, James W. *Lies across America*. New York: Simon and Schuster, 2007.

Loggins, Vernon. *The Negro Author: His Development in America to 1900*. 1931. Kennikat: Port Washington, NY, 1964.

MacKethan, Lucinda. "Plantation Fiction." *The History of Southern Literature*. Ed. Louis Rubin Blyden Jackson et al. Baton Rouge: Louisiana University Press, 1985.

Manning, M. M. *Slave in a Box: The Strange Career of Aunt Jemima*. Charlottesville: University Press of Virginia, 1998.

Marquette, Arthur. *Brands, Trademarks and Good Will; The Story of the Quaker Oats Company*. New York: McGraw-Hill, 1967.

Matthews, John. The Sound and the Fury: *Faulkner and the Lost Cause*. Boston: Twayne, 1991.

McDowell, Tremaine. "The Negro in the Southern Novel Prior to 1850." *Journal of English and Germanic Philology* 25 (1926): 455–73.

McDowell, Deborah. *Slavery and the Literary Imagination*. Baltimore: Johns Hopkins University Press, 1989.

McElroy, Guy. *Facing History: The Black Image in American Art 1710–1940*. Corcoran Gallery of Art, Washington, DC, 13 January–25 March, 1990.

McElya, Miki. "Commemorating the Color Line: The National Mammy Monument Controversy of the 1920s." *Monuments to the Lost Cause; Women, Art and the Landscapes of Southern Memory*. Ed. Cynthia Mills and Pamela H. Simpson. Knoxville: University of Tennessee Press.

McKee, Karen. "'Honey, yer ain't harf as smart as yer think yer is': Race and Humor in Sherwood Bonner's Short Fiction." *Southern Literary Journal* 35.1 (2002): 28–47.

McMillien, Sally. *Motherhood in the Old South: Pregnancy, Childbirth, and Infant Rearing*. Baton Rouge: Louisiana State University Press, 1990.

Milloy, Sandra. "Dilsey: Faulkner's Black Mammy in *The Sound and the Fury*." *Negro History Bulletin* 46.3 (1983): 70–82.

Mills, Cynthia, and Pamela H. Simpson, eds. *Monuments to the Lost Cause: Women, Art and the Landscapes of Southern Memory*. Knoxville: University of Tennessee Press, 2003.

Minogue, Sally. *Problems for Feminist Criticism*. London: Routledge, 1990.

Moers, Ellen. *Harriet Beecher Stowe and American Literature*. Hartford, CT: Stowe-Day Foundation, 1978.

Morgan, Jo-Ann. "Mammy the Huckster." *American Art* 9.1 (1995): 86–109.

Morgan, Jo-Ann. "African American Women in Nineteenth-Century Visual Culture." *American Art* (Fall 1999).

Morgan, Jo-Ann. *Uncle Tom's Cabin as Visual Culture*. Columbia: University of Missouri Press, 2007.

Morrison Toni. *Beloved: A Novel*. New York: Plume, 1988.

Morson, Gary Saul, and Caryl Emerson. *Mikhail Bakhtin: Creation of Prosaics*. Stanford, CA: Stanford University Press, 1990, 448–49.

Nelson, John H. *The Negro Character in American Literature*. College Park, MD: McGrath, 1926.

O'Leary, Elizabeth. *At Beck and Call: Representations of Domestic Servants in Nineteenth Century American Painting*. Washington, DC: Smithsonian Institution Press, 1996.

Page, Sally. "The Ideal of Motherhood: *The Sound and the Fury*." In *Faulkner's Women: Characterization and Meaning*. De Land, FL: Everett/Edwards, 1972.

Payne, Ladell. *Black Novelists and the Southern Literary Tradition*. Athens: University of Georgia Press, 1960.

Peters, Erskine. *William Faulkner, the Yopknapatwpha World and Black Being*. Darby, PA: Norwood Editions, 1983.

Phillips, U. B. *Life and Labor in the Old South*. Boston: Little, Brown, 1929.

Preston, Dickson. *Young Frederick Douglass*. Baltimore: Johns Hopkins University Press, 1980.

Rawick, George. *From Sundown to Sunup*. Westport, CT: Greenwood Publishing Co., 1972.

Reddy, Maureen. *Narrating Mothers: Theorizing Maternal Subjectivities*. Knoxville: University of Tennessee Press, 1991.

Reno, Dawn. *Collecting Black Americana*. New York: Crown, 1986.

Reynolds, Miora. *Uncle Tom's Cabin and Mid-Nineteenth Century United States: Pen and Conscience*. Jefferson, NC: McFarland, 1985.

Ricks, Beatrice. *William Faulkner: A Bibliography of Secondary Works*. Metuchen, NJ: Scarecrow Press, 1981.

Roark, James. *Masters without Slaves*. New York: Norton, 1977.

Roberts, Diane. *The Myth of Aunt Jemima*. New York: Routledge, 1994.

Ruoff, John C. "Frivolity to Consumption: Or, Southern Womanhood in Antebellum Literature." *Civil War History* 18 (1972): 213–29.

Schwartz, Marie Jenkins. *Born in Bondage: Growing up Enslaved in the Antebellum South*. Cambridge, MA: Harvard University Press, 2000.

Scott, Anne. *The Southern Lady: From Pedestal to Politics, 1830–1930*. Chicago: University of Chicago Press, 1970.

Scott, Joyce J. *Fearless Beadwork: Handwriting and Drawings from Hell*. Rochester, NY: Visual Studies Workshop, 1994.

Sculle, Keith. "Narrating the Emergence of Mammy's Cupboard as a Roadside Icon." *Pioneer American Society Transactions* 21 (1998): 47–56.

Sekora, John. *The Art of Slave Narrative: Original Essays in Criticism and Theory*. Macomb: Western Illinois University, 1982.

Sellers, Susan. *Feminist Criticism: Theory and Practice*. Toronto: University of Toronto Press, 1991.

Scott, Joyce. Personal interview. Atlanta, GA. 15 June 2004.

Sides, Sadie. "Southern Women and Slavery." *History Today* 20 (1970): 124–30.

Smedes, Susan Dabney. *Memorials of a Southern Planter*. Jackson: University Press of Mississippi, 1981.

Smith, Daniel. "Family Limitation, Sexual Control and Domestic Feminism in Victorian American." *Clio's Consciousness Raised, New Perspectives on the History of Women*. Ed. Mary Hartman and Lois Banner. New York: Harper and Row, 1974.

Smith, Darrell. *Black Americana: A Personal Collection*. Minneapolis: Star Press, 1978.

Smith, Raymond. "The Nuclear Family in Afro-American Kinship." *Journal of Comparative Family Studies* 1 (1970): 57–70.

Smith, Stephanie. *Conceived by Liberty: Maternal Figures and Nineteenth-Century American Literature*. Ithaca, NY: Cornell University Press, 1994.

Snead, James. *Figures of Division: William Faulkner's Major Novels*. New York: Methuen, 1986.

Sollors, Werner. *Neither Black Nor White Yet Both: Thematic Explorations of Interracial Literature*. New York: Oxford University Press, 1997.

Spillers, Hortense. *Comparative American Identities: Race, Sex, and Nationality in the Modern Text*. New York: Routledge, 1991.

Spruill, Julia Cherry. *Women's Life and Work in the Southern Colonies*. Chapel Hill: University of North Carolina Press, 1938.

St. John, Maria. "'It Ain't Fittin': Cinematic Contours of Mammy in *Gone with the Wind* and Beyond." *Qui Parle: Literature, Philosophy, Visual Arts, History* 11.2 (1999):127–36.

Stampp, Kenneth. *The Peculiar Institution: Slavery in the Antebellum South.* New York: Knopf, 1956.

Stark, Catharine. *Black Portraiture in American Fiction: Stock Characters, Archetypes, and Individuals.* New York: Basic Books, 1971.

Sundquist, Eric, ed. *New Essays on Uncle Tom's Cabin.* New York: Cambridge University Press.

Takai, Ron. *Iron Cages: Race and Culture in Nineteenth-Century America.* New York: Knopf, 1979.

Taylor, Helen. *Circling Dixie: Culture through a Transatlantic Lens.* New Brunswick, NJ: Rutgers University Press, 2001.

Taylor, Rosser. *Antebellum South Carolina: A Social and Cultural History.* Chapel Hill: University of North Carolina Press, 1926.

Terrell, Mary Church. "Lynching from A Negro's Point of View." *North American Review* 178 (1904): 853–68.

Thurber, Cheryl. "Development of the Mammy Image and Mythology." *Southern Women: Histories and Identities.* Ed. Virginia Berhard et al. Columbia: University of Missouri Press, 1992.

Toll, Robert. *Blacking Up: The Minstrel Show in Nineteenth-Century America.* New York: Oxford University Press, 1974.

Tracy, Susan. *In the Master's Eye: Representations of Women, Blacks, and Poor Whites in Antebellum Southern Literature.* Amherst: University of Massachusetts Press, 1995.

Tronto, Joan C. "The 'Nanny' Question in Feminism," *Hypatia* 17.2 (Spring 2002): 34–51.

Trouard, Dawn. "Southern Women Writers, Racism and Racists." *Southern Literary Journal* 37.1 (Fall 2004): 176–79.

Turner, Patricia A. *Ceramic Uncles and Celluloid Mammies.* New York: Anchor Books, 1994.

Tyre, Peg. "Shocking the Jocks." *Newsweek* 8 March 2004 <http://findarticles.com/p/articles/mi_kmnew/is_200403/ai_kepm388321>.

Van Buren, Jane. *The Modernist Madonna: Semiotics of the Maternal Metaphor.* Bloomington: Indiana University Press, 1989.

Van Deburg, William. *Slavery and Race in American Popular Culture.* Madison: University of Wisconsin Press, 1984.

Wade-Gayle, Gloria. "She Who Is Black and Mother: In Sociology and Fiction, 1940–1970." In *The Black Woman.* Ed. La Frances Rodgers-Rose. Beverly Hills, CA: Sage, 1980.

Walker, Margaret. *Jubilee.* New York: Bantam, 1966.

Walker, Peter. *Moral Choices.* Baton Rouge: Louisiana State University Press, 1978.

Ward, Hazel. "The Black Woman as Character: Images in the American Novel, 1852–1953." Diss. University of Texas at Austin, 1977.

Webb, Dorothy Ann. "Particular Places: Local Color Writing in the United States 1870–1910" Diss. University of Michigan, 2000.

West, Carolyn. "Mammy, Sapphire, and Jezebel: Historical Images of Black Women and Their Implications for Psychotherapy." *Psychotherapy* 32.3 (1995): 458–66.

White, Deborah Gray. *Aren't I a Woman?* New York: Norton.

White, Barbara A. Review of *A Sherwood Bonner Sampler, 1869–1884: What a Bright, Educated, Witty, Lively, Snappy Young Woman Can Say on a Variety of Topics. NWSA Journal* 15.1 (2003).

Williams, Crystal. "Jemima in the Mirror" *Ms.* 11.1 (December/January 2001): 40–43.

Williams, Sherley Ann. *Dessa Rose.* New York: William Morrow, 1986.

Willis, Deborah. *The Black Female Body: A Photographic History.* Philadelphia: Temple University Press, 2002.

Winter, Kari. *Subjects of Slavery, Agents of Change: Women and Power in Gothic Novels and Slave Narratives, 1790–1865.* Athens: University of Georgia Press, 1992.

Yeager, Patricia. *Dirt and Desire: Reconstructing Southern Women's Writing 1930–1990.* Chicago: University of Chicago Press, 2001.

Yellin, Jean Fagan. *The Pen Is Ours: A Listing of Writings by and about African-American Women before 1910 with a Secondary Bibliography to the Present.* New York: Oxford University Press, 1991.

Yellin, Jean Fagan. *The Intricate Knot: Black Figures in American Literature.* New York: New York University Press, 1972.

Yellin, Jean Fagan. *A Life.* Ed. Harriet Jacobs. New York: Basic Civitas Books, 2004.

Yetman, Norman. *Voices from Slavery.* New York: Holt, Rhinehart and Winston, 1970.

INDEX

TEXT DESIGN BY PAULA NEWCOMB

TYPESETTING BY DELMASTYPE, ANN ARBOR, MICHIGAN

TEXT FONT: HOEFLER TEXT

The Hoefler Text family of typefaces, designed by Jonathan Hoefler, was designed to celebrate some favorite aspects of two beloved Old Style typefaces: Janson Text 55 and Garamond No. 3. Unwittingly, the names "Janson" and "Garamond" both honor men unconnected with these designs: Janson is named for Dutch printer Anton Janson but based on types cut by Hungarian punch cutter Nicholas Kis; Garamond is a revival of types thought to have originated with Claude Garamond in the sixteenth century, but in fact made a century later by Swiss typefounder Jean Jannon. Hoefler Text is published by Hoefler & Frere-Jones at www.typography.com.